# EARLY LIBYAN
# CHRISTIANITY

## UNCOVERING A
## NORTH AFRICAN TRADITION

■■■

# THOMAS C. ODEN

IVP Academic
An imprint of InterVarsity Press
Downers Grove, Illinois

*InterVarsity Press*
*P.O. Box 1400, Downers Grove, IL 60515-1426*
*World Wide Web: www.ivpress.com*
*E-mail: email@ivpress.com*

*InterVarsity Press® is the book-publishing division of InterVarsity Christian Fellowship/USA®, a movement of students and faculty active on campus at hundreds of universities, colleges and schools of nursing in the United States of America, and a member movement of the International Fellowship of Evangelical Students. For information about local and regional activities, write Public Relations Dept., InterVarsity Christian Fellowship/USA, 6400 Schroeder Rd., P.O. Box 7895, Madison, WI 53707-7895, or visit the IVCF website at <www.intervarsity.org>.*

*Scripture quotations, unless otherwise noted, are from the New Revised Standard Version of the Bible, copyright 1989 by the Division of Christian Education of the National Council of the Churches of Christ in the USA. Used by permission. All rights reserved.*

*See page 334 for image credits.*

*Cover design: Cindy Kiple*
*Interior design: Beth Hagenberg*
*Images: Ruins of the Severian Basilica at Leptis Magna, Lyba. © Gilles Mermet/Art Resource, NY*

*ISBN 978-0-8308-3943-8*

*Printed in the United States of America* ∞

**Library of Congress Cataloging-in-Publication Data**

Oden, Thomas C.
  Early Libyan Christianity: uncovering a North African tradition/
Thomas C. Oden
    p. cm.
  Includes bibliographical references (p.  ) and indexes.
  ISBN 978-0-8308-3943-8 (pbk.: alk. paper)
  1. Libya—Church history. I. Title.
  BR190.O36 2911
  276.12'01—dc23

2011023113

| P | 20 | 19 | 18 | 17 | 16 | 15 | 14 | 13 | 12 | 11 | 10 | 9 | 8 | 7 | 6 | 5 | 4 | 3 | 2 | 1 |
|---|----|----|----|----|----|----|----|----|----|----|----|---|---|---|---|---|---|---|---|---|
| Y | 29 | 28 | 27 | 26 | 25 | 24 | 23 | 22 | 21 | 20 | 19 | 18 | 17 | 16 | 15 | 14 | 13 | 12 | 11 |

# CONTENTS

# ACKNOWLEDGMENTS

I am grateful to Da'wa Islamic University in Libya for their invitation to offer the core of these lectures to Muslim university students in Tripoli, Libya, in 2008. My thanks also to Dallas Theological Seminary for offering the occasion for me to further develop these reflections in the W. H. Griffith Thomas Lectures of 2009, and for publishing them in their early form in *Bibliotheca Sacra* as four articles. In this book, those lectures have been refined and extended for publication. I am here offering a broader and more fully referenced argument than was possible in the lectures either in Tripoli or Dallas.

Sources from antiquity are identified by standard section and subsection numbers. Modern sources are identified by page, unless otherwise noted.

*Thomas C. Oden*

# ABBREVIATIONS

| | |
|---|---|
| ACCS | Ancient Christian Commentary on Scripture. Edited by Thomas C. Oden. 29 vols. Downers Grove, Ill.: InterVarsity Press, 1998-2010. |
| *Ag. Her.* | Irenaeus. *Against Heresies* [*Adversus Haereses*] |
| *Ag. Prax.* | Tertullian. *Against Praxeas* [*Adversus Praxean*] |
| A.H. | *anno Hegirae* (after Hegira of A.D. 622) |
| ANF | Ante-Nicene Fathers. Edited by Alexander Roberts, James Donaldson, and A. Cleveland Coxe. Buffalo, N.Y.: Christian Literature Publishing, 1885–1896. |
| *Arius* | Rowan Williams. *Arius: Heresy and Tradition.* 2nd ed. London: SCM, 2001. |
| *B&P* | Alan Cameron, Jacqueline Long and Lee Sherry. *Barbarians and Politics at the Court of Arcadius.* Berkeley: University of California Press, 1993. |
| Barrington Atlas | Richard J. A. Talbert et al., eds. *Barrington Atlas of the Greek and Roman World.* Princeton, N.J.: Princeton University Press, 2000. |
| Bregman | Jay Bregman. *Synesius of Cyrene: Philosopher-Bishop.* Berkeley: University of California Press, 1982. |
| CCSL | Corpus Christanorum Series Latina |
| CEV | Contemporary English Version |
| *CH* | *Church History* [*Historia ecclesiastica*]. Identified by author: Eusebius, Socrates Scholasticus, Sozomen or Theodoret of Cyr. |
| *Chron.* | Jerome. *Chronicon.* A Latin translation of Eusebius's |

|  | *Chronicon* with additions from Jerome. |
| *Chronicon* | Eusebius. *Chronicon bipartitum*. Classical Armenian text translated into English by Robert Bedrosian. Available online at <http://rbedrosian.com/euseb.html>. Armenian and Latin parallel version, edited by Baptistae Aucher Ancyrani. |
| *Comm. on Matt.* | Origen. *Commentary on Matthew* |
| *De insomn.* | Synesius. *De Insomniis* [*On Dreams*] |
| *De prov.* | Synesius. *De providentia* [*On Providence* or *The Egyptian Tale*] |
| *De reg.* | Synesius. *De regno* [*On Imperial Rule* or *On Kingly Rule*] |
| De Rossi | Giovanni Battista De Rossi. *Inscriptiones christianae urbis Romae*. Rome, 1861. |
| Dio, *RH* | Cassius Dio (Dio Cassius). *Roman History*. Translated by Earnest Cary. 9 vols. LCL 32, 37, 53, 66, 82, 83, 175, 176, 177. Cambridge, Mass.: Harvard University Press, 1914–1927. |
| *Haer. fab. comp.* | Theodoret of Cyr. *Haereticarum fabularum compendium* [*History of Heresies*] |
| *HCC* | Philip Schaff. *History of the Christian Church*. 8 vols. 3rd ed. Peabody, Mass.: Hendrickson, 1996. |
| *HEO* | Giorgio Fedalto. *Hierarchia ecclesiastica orientalis*. Series Episcoporum Ecclesiarum Christianarum Orientalium. 2 vols. Padua: Messaggero, 1988. |
| *Heresies* | Epiphanius. *Against Heresies* [*Adversus Haereses*] or *Refutation of All Heresies* or *Panarion*. See *The Panarion of St. Epiphanius, Bishop of Salamis: Selected Passages*, ed. Philip R. Amidon (New York: Oxford University Press, 1990). |
| Herodian, *HE* | Herodian. *History of the Empire*. LCL 454, 455. Cambridge, Mass.: Harvard University Press, 1969–1970. |
| *HOA* | Maria Dzielska. *Hypatia of Alexandria*. Translated by F. Lyra. Cambridge, Mass.: Harvard University Press, 1995. |
| *ISBE* | *International Standard Bible Encyclopedia*. 4 vols. Edited by Geoffrey W. Bromiley. Grand Rapids: Eerdmans, 1979–1988. |
| LCL | Loeb Classical Library |

| | |
|---|---|
| LCM | Mohamed Talbi. "Le Christianisme maghrébin de la co- quête musulmane à sa disparition d'une tentative explica- tion." In *Conversion and Continuity: Indigenous Christian Communities in Islamic Lands: Eighth to Eighteenth Centu- ries.* Edited by Michael Gervers and Ramzi Jibran Bik- hazi. Toronto: Pontifical Institute of Mediaeval Studies, 1990. |
| *LLC* | *Libya: The Lost Cities of the Roman Empire.* Text by Anto- nio Di Vita, Ginette Di Vita-Evrard and Lidiano Bac- chielli. Photos by Robert Polidori. Cologne, Germany: Könemann, 1999. |
| Mansi | Giovanni Domenico Mansi. *Sacrorum conciliorum nova et amplissima collectio.* 53 vols. 1927. Reprint, Graz, Austria: Akademische Druck- und Verlangsanstalt, 1961. |
| *MKGK* | *Matthäus-Kommentare aus der griechischen Kirche.* Edited by Joseph Reuss. Berlin: Akademic-Verlag, 1957. |
| NAB | New American Bible |
| NIV | New International Version |
| Norris | H. T. Norris. *The Berbers in Arabic Literature.* New York: Longman, 1982. |
| NPNF | A Select Library of the Nicene and Post-Nicene Fathers of the Christian Church. Buffalo, N.Y.: Christian Litera- ture, 1886–1990. |
| *OF* | John of Damascus. *The Orthodox Faith* |
| *On Monog.* | Tertullian. *On Monogamy* [*De monogamia*] |
| PG | Patrologia Graeca |
| SC | Sources Chrétiennes |
| *SEC* | Hippolyte Delehaye, ed. *Synaxarium ecclesiae Constanti- nopolitanae e codice Sirmondiano nunc Berolinensi,* 1902. Reprint, Wetteren, Belgium: Imprimerie Cultura, 1985. |
| *TT* | Isabella Sjöström. *Tripolitania in Transition: Late Roman to Islamic Settlement with a Catalogues of Sites.* Brookfield, Vt.: Avebury, 1993. |

# LIST OF
# ILLUSTRATIONS

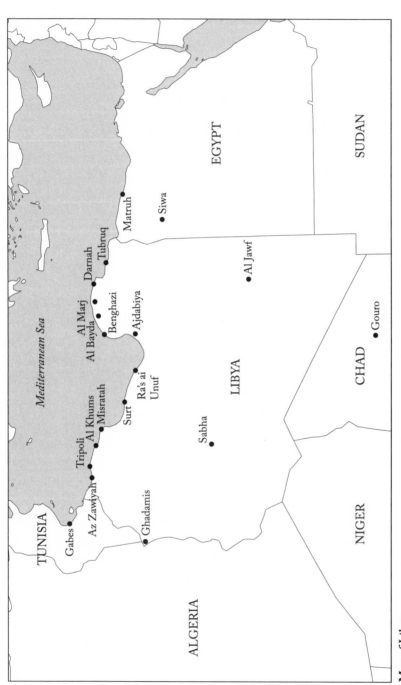

Map of Libya

# I

# A BURIED HISTORY
# AWAITING DISCOVERY

■■■

Christian believers living on the continent of Africa have a distinguished intellectual history that awaits their own discovery. But ironically in subtle ways they seem to have been barred access to it as a result of long-standing preconceived ideas and biases. So the early African heritage has remained sadly unnoticed even in Africa. Not only Westerners have ignored early African Christianity but also many African scholars and religious leaders themselves educated in the modern West under the premises of modern consciousness.

The decades since the African independence movements of the 1950s have been intently focused on condemnation of modern colonialist Christian missionary history. This justifiable indignation saturates African studies. It has been a legitimate and necessary phase.

Meanwhile at the same time in the last fifty years these independence movements have hardly glimpsed their own premodern, distinctly African Christian, texts. Yet these have remained the actual foundation of the durable worldwide Christian intellectual heritage.

Even my esteemed "black theology" friends and colleagues who have rediscovered many fertile aspects of "traditional African religion" seem to have consistently ignored the intellectual depth of the deposit of faith in early Africa itself.

## THE LEGACY THAT VANISHED

These African texts are among the most dear gifts, costly in blood, of the first millennium to this new third millennium. They are now lying at our feet unnoticed, and in our archives unread. They seem almost too near to us to allow us to get them into clear focus as uniquely African gifts. The rhetoric remains preoccupied with the outrage of anticolonial revulsion.

Meanwhile the precolonial jewel of ancient African history, almost entirely lost in the twentieth century, is being rediscovered in the twenty-first.

This gift is wrapped in the papyrus texts of the African church mothers and fathers. It is conveyed in the martyrs and classic scriptural exegetes from early Africa.

## HOW BLOOD WAS POURED OUT FOR THIS WITNESS

Confessors prepared to die for their convictions can hardly be ignored. Many have died.

Most of their names remain quite unfamiliar. Listen: Januaria, Generosa, Vestia, Donata and Secunda. Note that all these were women. These five were among the earliest African martyrs in A.D. 180. Other women who followed them are Perpetua, with a child in her arms in prison before she died, and Felicitas, who was eight months pregnant. We find them standing before an imperial judge in A.D. 203 in a lethal court trial whose proceedings have been shockingly recorded. Both chose faithful death in preference to a forced denial of the truth. There were many other martyrs, both men and women, whose names are largely unknown: Mina, Lucius, Theodorus, Cyrilla and Helladius. The last of these was burned to death in a furnace in Libya.

These names do not spring quickly off the tongue, but their African blood was shed on their native continent. They are all African saints just as surely as those who are better known, such as Cyprian, Leonides and Peter of Alexandria. Then there is Wasilla. The tiny town in Alaska is named after the early Christian martyr who died in Libya. Wasilla is the Russian name for Basilides. His story will be told in what follows.

Libyan tradition recalls that it was by a lake near Selena, Libya, near Al Bayda, that St. George slew the dragon. There are the vestiges of a huge monolithic church named for St. George. George is remembered throughout Western history in the names of British kings and thousands of boys speaking a hundred languages, and hundreds of paintings of a knight on a horse with a spear through a monster. But no one thinks of him as Libyan. The dragon yet to be slain is a crushed memory: No one remembers the place of George's victory.

Traditional African religion cares deeply about ancestry. But the believer's ancestry of Saints George and Wasilla has been forgotten.

Why did Libyans spill blood for the One who was the way, the truth and the life? The short political answer is colonialism, even as early as the second century A.D. The deeper religious answer is truth-telling in the context of endemic idolatry.

## THE SAINTS FORGOTTEN

African young people need a more accessible way of understanding the part played by these early African Christians based on their faith, tenacity and in some cases their remarkable intellectual intensity. That is why this story awaits retelling. The real histories of Libyan saints are far more dramatic than anything rhetoric or romanticism might add to them.

Christian scholars do well to leave it to the Muslim scholars to tell the story of early Islam in Libyan Africa. My modest task is to tell the story of Christianity in pre-Islamic Libya. Since it is accessible to historical inquiry, it does not require a particular hue of skin to tell it.

The story of Libyan Christianity provides a unique occasion to learn expressly about the faith once for all delivered to the saints of the Maghreb, and especially to the ancient saints of Libya.

This volume belongs to a series of books on early African Christianity. It is best seen in continuity with that series. It is the third in a series of interrelated studies:

1. *How Africa Shaped the Christian Mind*—the first of three books on early African Christianity—inquires into the ironic thesis that out of early Africa came brilliant intellects (Tertullian, Clement, Origen et

al.) and texts (philosophical, religious and moral) that would put a permanent stamp on Western European culture, later to dominate the whole of Western thought. It attempts to show that European and American intellectual history is far more indebted to African textual sources than is commonly acknowledged. Cappadocian theologians (Gregory of Nyssa and Gregory of Nazianzus) went to school on Alexandrian models. In Alexandria they found the crucial nexus of the intellectus where the idea of a university was most sharply conceived and effectively grasped, and where the idea of a complete library was virtually invented and largely manifested in its time. *How Africa Shaped the Christian Mind* shows that African Christianity developed core habits of mind in exegesis and conciliar Christian teaching in the first three centuries A.D. These habits would have lasting effects on the emergence of Western culture. From Africa came a sophistication in the study of sacred texts that led to consensual Christian doctrinal definition, philosophical experimentation and scriptural interpretation. From this sophistication came a steady stream of intellectual history from South to North, from Africa to Europe, from Clement and Origen to the Venerable Bede, from North Africa to Eurasian cultures and religion. The series thesis for further research was set forth in broad terms in this first book.

2. *The African Memory of Mark* advances and narrows the broad research project in relation to a decisively single person, by common tradition the sole apostolic founder of all African Christianity, Saint Mark. It focuses the broader thesis on one crucial figure whose influence has been unmatched in Africa, yet whose African identity has never been understood or explored in the modern West. It asks how Mark's life and works have shaped African consciousness. In all the glut of studies on Mark filling many board feet of library shelves, only a few touch on the birth of Mark in Libya and the death of Mark in Egypt, and if they do mention these, it is usually with disdain. *The African Memory of Mark* seeks a modest corrective based on recent archaeological and literary criticism, amplified by a wide-ranging cluster of implicit arguments.

3. This book, *Early Libyan Christianity*, is the third volume of this

series on early African Christianity. It focuses on the most neglected arena of early Christian studies, a vast land where Christianity flourished unnoticed for five hundred years—in the sprawling reaches of ancient Libya. Today it is still seldom mentioned in the international literature, and least of all in the North American literature. *Early Libyan Christianity* provides the occasion for retelling of the whole story of early African Christianity from a particular vantage point—Libya, its leading Christian characters and characteristics, its intellectual history, its rise and fall. Of the thousands of books on early Christianity, not once to my knowledge has the subject focused on a book-length treatment of Libya.

## HOW DID WE GET HERE? THE ROAD MAP

Chart 1 sums up the core of the research efforts of the Center for Early African Christianity in Philadelphia. The trajectory of our journey thus far can be easily visualized in three stages.

These three stages of recent inquiry reveal the early priorities of the core of the research effort undertaken by the Center for Early African Christianity. This study is a report on its third stage. More studies are planned.

Christianity has a very long textual history of notable intellectual contributions of Christians to early Africa in the first half of the first millennium. These venerable Christian texts have been largely ignored by contemporary African Christian theology and social history with only a handful of exceptions led by Lamin Sanneh (born in Gambia, Yale Divinity School), Bénézet Bujo (of Zaire, University of Fribourg), and Kwame Bediako (of Ghana, formerly University of Edinburgh)—all friends of the Center for Early African Christianity from its earliest stages.

The rich wisdom of early African Christian writings still has astonishing relevance for the problems of Africa today: issues of displaced persons, economic injustice, war, abuse of children and women, care for the poor and hungry, and many more. All of these issues appear repeatedly in the literature of early African Christianity. They have not ceased being vital issues today.

**Chart 1. The Early African Christianity Series**

| Title | *How Africa Shaped the Christian Mind* | *The African Memory of Mark* | *Early Libyan Christianity* |
|---|---|---|---|
| Descriptive Subtitle | *Rediscovering the African Seedbed of Western Christianity* | *Reassessing Early Church Tradition* | *Uncovering a North African Tradition* |
| Subject Matter | Exploring the thesis: *The major movement of intellectual history in the second and third centuries was from South to North, from Africa to Europe and Roman Asia* | Meeting the first saint of African Christianity: John Mark of Cyrene | Tackling the least attended, most neglected region: Libya |
| Disciplinary Backdrop | Intellectual history: how Europe's intellectual roots lie buried in Africa | New Testament studies: the Gospel of Mark, recalled in Africa as the founder of all African Christianity | African studies; regional studies; Libyan studies— buried under sand for a millennium, now breathing new life |
| Research Questions | Why have modern African studies neglected the patristic period? | Why is St. Mark the most neglected saint of early Christian studies? | Why is Libya the most neglected country of early Christian studies? |
| Unfolding the Task of Scholarly Research | Proposing the overarching thesis of neglect and promise of early African Christian history | Advancing the idea with its single most important figure: Mark | Narrowing the inquiry into a buried arena of the Christian past in Africa: Libya |
| The Issue | How Africa shaped Euro-American intellectual history | How St. Mark shaped Africa | How the memory of an entire population of Christian believers was forgotten in the West but remembered in Africa |

## WHEN LIBYA WAS CHRISTIAN

Libyan Christianity was formed in a nexus of cultures bordering on Egypt, Ethiopia and ancient Nubia, modern Sudan, ancient Darfur (part of Cush), Chad, and Roman Byzacena (southern Tunisia). Ancient Libyan Christianity had close affinities with Coptic Egypt and Coptic Ethiopia, and with the Meroe kingdom in Nubia (Sudan). They belonged intentionally to the community of worldwide believers who held to orthodox, apostolic, classic Christian teaching.

This study gives modern Christians an opportunity to learn about a historic people of faith—Christian believers of Libya. It is a subject about which most have heard very little, maybe nothing.

Test yourself by asking: Can I name one Christian teacher or biblical interpreter from Libya? If not, you are at just the point I was only two decades ago as I undertook the task of editing the exegetical works of ancient Christianity.

Libya is the most neglected of all the historic Christian locations in the ancient world that experienced over five hundred years of Christianity. That is why I have recently made it my first priority to focus on early African Christianity. Our time frame is the era from A.D. 1 to 1000—the first millennium of Christianity.

But in Libya itself there is less archaeological excavation, relative to its importance, than in any other North African country, and far less rigorous critical scholarship or theological or literary inquiry. There is less architectural investigation of Libyan Christianity than of Egyptian or Algerian or Tunisian or Ethiopic or even Nubian Christianity. This might lead one mistakenly to think that Libya has produced less architecture and literature or had far less intellectual impact on Western culture than these others. Wrong.

Those who visit modern Jerusalem or Istanbul or Antioch or Cairo will immediately see abundant evidences of early Christianity. But go to massive Libyan sites like Cyrene or Leptis Magna and try to discover evidences of Christianity. Most of it is hidden, buried or softpedaled. That was the problem that led to this study. If you go there and walk through the ruined ancient cities, you will discover how hard the Christian sites are to identify, despite their long and once prominent history.

But they are there. Consult the architectural literature in Italian, French, German, Arabic and Polish (regrettably little exists in English) and you will see what labor is required simply to dig out basic facts from inaccessible archaeological journals and older excavation reports in libraries widely scattered.

Christianity was once a significant presence in Libya during a specific period of time: from about A.D. 68 to A.D. 643. That is 575 years. Today less than 1 percent of Libyan citizens are Catholic Christians, along with a scattered but growing community of Protestants, evangelicals and Pentecostals, who for economic reasons come to Libya from the sub-Saharan south. Many have immigrated to the growing economy of Libya for business purposes. They come from the Sudan, Niger, Nigeria, Chad, the Central African Republic and much further south, all the way to South Africa. Christian faith is still surviving within a robust Muslim culture.

## THE NEWNESS OF OLD STONES: THE ARCHAEOLOGICAL TESTIMONY

There are at least a dozen historic archaeological sites in Libya that are truly spectacular. Among the most magnificent are Leptis Magna, Sabratha and Cyrene. But there are many others, as we will see.

In many dozens of towns of Libya there are remnants of early Christian history that have been buried for centuries under the sands and erosions of time. Most have only been partially excavated intermittently in recent decades. They have lain silent in an almost pristine state without having layer after layer of urban sprawl built on top of them. That is what makes the whole scene remarkable. The best place to learn of the huge number of these Libyan sites containing Christian remnants is the study by Isabella Sjöström, *Tripolitania in Transition: Late Roman to Islamic Settlement with a Catalogue of Sites.*[1]

Why did some of these sites like Sabratha and Leptis not have layers

---

[1]Isabella Sjöström, *Tripolitania in Transition: Late Roman to Islamic Settlement with a Catalogue of Sites* (Brookfield, Vt.: Avebury, 1993), hereafter *TT.*

of successive cities built on top of them? Many of them virtually ceased to exist over a thousand years ago with the Arab upheaval. They became grazing places or desert. Some were in remote parts of the African Mediterranean coast. Over the centuries their economies and military defenses became vulnerable. The Islamic victory was overwhelming. Alternative religious views would be hard-pressed to survive. Most Christians were expelled in A.D. 643 by the Arab surge.

At the university in Tripoli, I was tasked to simply rehearse a factual historical narrative. I was explaining to my Muslim audience what paleo-Christians were doing in Libya. Why were they there so long? What did they build and write and sing? Where did they go when they disappeared from Libya? What architectural and cultural artifacts did they leave behind?

## BREAKING BARRIERS

Libya is likely soon to see a significant increase of non-Libyan visitors and entrepreneurial business ventures. Many will want to see its spectacular historic Christian sites. Large-scale ancient Christian sites previously inaccessible to an American audience are gradually being made available by the sluggish opening of Libya to travelers. This promises to stimulate interest in future years toward further study of now obscure aspects of Libyan history, especially its five centuries of Christian history. While Canadians and most Europeans are currently allowed into Libya, it is still difficult for an American to get a reliable visa approval unless officially invited. Though hard to enter, it is becoming less so. It is gradually being opened to travel.

Everywhere Christian believers travel abroad, they want to know more about the historic and contemporary conditions of Christianity in those places. These often become major tour sites. This has been especially so in Ethiopia and Egypt, but to date not so much in Libya. If not closed, the door has been at least guarded. For decades a steady stream of European visitors (chiefly Spanish, French and Italian) have been coming to the major Libyan sites, but not many North Americans have been permitted. There will be many more in the coming years. Among these will be many who are curious to find evidences of the earliest centuries of Christianity in Africa.

Meanwhile Libya is still largely dismissed as an area of interest that could possibly be pertinent to world Christianity. Only a slight awareness exists among Christians that there are still Christian believers in Libya. These include Copts, evangelicals, Orthodox and Catholics. By law there are no overt evangelical mission activities in the usual Western mission sense. Islamic directives prevent personal evangelization. Freedom of assembly is limited and requires government approval. Property ownership is hard to get. Westerners should be warned in advance that if they pass out a pamphlet on a street corner, they risk arrest. But in practice there are highly committed Christian businessmen who are gathering along informal friendship networks and in small groups as house churches. They gather quietly and with full respect for Muslim law and religious practice. They receive Holy Communion quietly in neighborhoods where the call of the minaret is heard on loud speakers.

The evangelicals in Tripoli are largely composed of Arabic-speaking Africans who have been permitted to live in or visit Libya for business purposes, or who are there for economic reasons. Most are there with, but a few others without, government approval. Thankfully, the government permits the continued presence and limited freedom of assembly for the historic churches that have been in Libya for a long time: Orthodox, Coptic, Catholic, Anglican and to a lesser extent generic evangelicals. The standard methods of evangelism through relief efforts and schools that depend on support from abroad are not acceptable in Libya. It is ironic, however, that these very evangelical methods are now being widely adapted and utilized by Muslims themselves in the building of mosques and offering medical and educational services all over Africa. They hope to bring indigenous African leadership to Libya for training in Arabic language and sharia. A great many efforts at Islamic missions are occurring all over Africa with bountiful funding from the Saudis.

Many of the future Christian travelers to North Africa will have little or no awareness of how deep their ties already are with the ancient believers of Africa of the first millennium. They will not know how much classic Christianity has already learned indirectly from Libyan Christians over many centuries.

It would be a mistake to think of Libya as an impoverished Third World country. It produces millions of barrels of oil a day, has huge reserves of fresh water due to "the Great Man-Made River Project" and soon will have a major natural-gas line threading its way under the Mediterranean Sea to Europe. It is an oil-rich economy that until recently has provided free housing, free schooling, free medical attention and cheap power. When I asked an experienced African diplomat in Ethiopia which African nation has the most promising future, he instantly replied: Libya.

Despite chronic political tensions between Libya and the United States, the doors are being cracked opened provisionally for a form of communication much deeper than oil wells—between Western believers and believers in Libya. Believers are small in number but more resilient and dedicated than most of us in safe, narcissistic Western societies. Even now while these conditions are still forming, the Center for Early African Christianity has been seeking to increase the incentives for Christian scholars and laity in Africa to learn more objectively about Libya's Christian history. What follows is a report on my personal experience of dialogue and engagement with a Muslim academic audience in Libya as an American.

In order to protect innocent people I met in Libya, I will refrain from comment on current conflicts in Libya. My purpose in being there was to discuss ancient historical issues, not modern politics. The current fluidity of realpolitik in the region, however heart-rending, is not the focus of this discussion.

There is a torrent of interest today in Libya. May it stimulate renewed interest in the rich historical layers of Libya's Christian history.

## AFTER LOCKERBIE

I was afraid of stepping on toes when I first arrived in Libya. I half expected that my audience might be hostile, and if it turned hostile, a realistic and honest conversation might be impossible. I found exactly the opposite. Conversation was neither hostile nor impossible.

I had been asked to speak on the centuries of pre-Arab Christian history in Libya to Islamic university students and to the international diplomatic community. It happened to be at a time when the U.S. State Department was weighing a Libyan proposal for compensation on the Lockerbie settlement. The other hard news that accompanied my lectures in Libya was the accelerating relief crisis in Libya's neighbor, Darfur, now a part of the modern Sudan, but in ancient times a satellite of the Cush kingdom.

When I set foot on the university campus, I instantly began to feel this hunch: If they perceived me as a person who cared about their culture and history, which I did, they would want to listen. I sensed that if they could see beyond ideological stereotypes into the heart of a person capable of empathy for them, then we could build on that.

The first presentation of the key ideas of these lectures occurred in Tripoli, capital of Libya, in February 2008 at Da'wa Islamic University, and at the Church of St. Mary's in the medina near the old castle of Tripoli in the oldest part of that ancient Punic-Greek-Roman-Byzantine city. The university is recent in its founding, but the church was founded by the Franciscans centuries ago as an emancipation ministry to ransom prisoners and redeem slaves. Speaking in that church gave me goose bumps—the church is across the street from an ancient prison.

My invitation was quite specific: to speak in Tripoli on the early history of Christianity in the first millennium in Libya, prior to the Arab victory of A.D. 643 (= A.H. 21). The joint invitation had come from Da'wa Islamic University and Bishop Mouneer Hanna Anis, the Anglican Primate of Egypt with North Africa and the Horn of Africa. It was accompanied by generous cooperation of officials from the civil government. I came to Libya at a time when the long frozen political ice between Libya and the Western democracies was just beginning to thaw.

I observed this distinction: What Christians and Western historians call the "first millennium" is called by Muslims "the centuries before and after the Hegira of Muhammed." Whichever way you think of it, it is a period of about a thousand years—not a magic number but the decisive period in which the relation between Jews, Christians and Muslims was first being formed and tested.

## PARTNERS IN DIALOGUE

At the university I met students from all over Africa who were studying Arabic and sharia law. What they call sharia is largely a history of commentary on the Qur'an as it applies to judgments in the legal system. Since I had been working on the history of exegesis in the early centuries of Christianity for twenty years, I was fascinated to see how they were working on the exegesis of the Islamic sacred texts analogous to the patristic fathers, especially in relation to their social and legal consequences.

They brought respectful, thoughtful and penetrating questions to me concerning the part of Libya's history I have special interest in, namely, the extant evidences of a significant Christian presence in Libya from the first to the seventh century. Though some will assume that this is an utterly esoteric question out of an unknown period relevant to no one, others will instantly grasp its current relevance. I found the analogies intrinsically germane to the contemporary Christian-Muslim dialogue and to the deepest questions of African self-identity. That identity is what some in Francophone West African call the issue of Africaneity or Africanity (Africanité, Négritude, in reference to the works of the late Léopold Sédar Senghor, poet-president of Senegal).

To enter the arena of early Libyan Christianity is to venture into the least studied theater of patristic scholarship. Today's visitors to North Africa are hungry for more information. The terrain is a vast and baffling country. But more intriguing are the Judeo-Christian jewels buried in the antiquity of that region. Unexcavated Christian sites from the third to the eighth century promise to yield a rich new motherload for Libyan archaeology and history, as opulent as their oil fields.

I experienced in those students an ardent motivation and open desire to listen to a Western Christian voice that appreciated aspects of Libyan history and early African history seldom noted in Islamic circles over the last fifteen hundred years. Many students were not Libyan. They had come to Libya from all parts of Africa, including sub-Saharan

Africa. All were Muslims, mostly interested in law, political science and family counsel. They were eager to hear and go one-on-one with a Christian scholar from the United States.

The form of Sunni Muslim teaching and family values that prevails in Libya is not characterized by captivity to the Wahabist views that have been widely exported to Africa. Though politically reviled and stereotyped in the Western press, Libya's form of populist socialism is at the grass roots level a moderate, populist, family-centered form of traditionalist Islamic governance. Many Libyans think of themselves as fulfilling a mediating role between East and West, and between Europe and Africa. Many conceive their special national vocation as offering an irenic place for the integration of pan-African consciousness, and for the communication of classic Islamic values to the rest of the Mediterranean and the broader world. American exceptionalism views America as a country with a unique purpose. So does the Libyans' perception of themselves.

## GETTING THERE

In recent years it has been very difficult, almost impossible, to get into Libya and Algeria (as distinguished from Tunisia, Egypt and Ethiopia). Only when I was privileged to be invited as a historian welcomed by the scholars and leaders of Algeria and Libya to visit ancient Christian sites did I realized how much I had been missing. We received special protection by the Algerian and Libyan authorities for these visits, both along coastal cities and very far inland into the Atlas Mountains and the Green Mountains of Libya. This provided an unusual entrée into the ordinary life of North Africans. In pursuing this study I have found myself working with Italian, French, German and Polish archaeological reports as much or more than those in English. I came away with the conviction that in the coming decades there will be many Christians who will want to know more about Christianity in North Africa, and even to go there to get some visual sense of the vital presence of the Christian community in the earliest centuries of paleo-Christianity.

Earlier I had tried several times to gain entry into Libya. Once by car I reached the tiny border station where passports are reviewed. I was turned away while my Canadian friends were allowed to pass. I had a valid passport with a Libyan visa approved and stamped by the Libyan Consulate, but that was overridden because the U.S. State Department had unexpectedly stepped on Libyan toes a week before. On two other occasions I was promised entry with a European touring group, once by ship and once by air, but in both cases the project was unexpectedly closed to U.S. citizens.

In previous visits to the ancient Christian sites of Turkey and Armenia I had developed a conviction that the subcontinent of Anatolia was the crucial place for Christians to rediscover their classic past. The focus of that conviction has shifted toward Africa.

During the past two decades I have been able to lay my eyes on the huge scale of the remains of some of the earliest edifices of Christian history in Africa. These were found in Cherchell and Hippo in Algeria, Carthage in Tunisia, and many sites in Egypt. Only when I was able to travel widely in North Africa, including Libya, did I realize how lacking were my previous perceptions.

I had previously lived in Rome and Heidelberg for several academic seasons, immersed in European assumptions. I had traveled extensively by microbus camper from the Balkans through Lebanon, Syria, Jordan and Israel. I had trooped from Spain to Sweden, from Scotland to Hungary. I had visited Egypt three times before grasping the challenge of African Christianity as a problem of intellectual history. I had an unrecognized bias in my worldview. I had bought into the predispositions of the great Western tradition. But still I had not reached Libya.

In 2003 I was invited to join an academic group for archaeological study tours to Algeria and Tunisia. There I met scholars who told me about the wonders of Libyan architecture, but little about how it related to the Christian tradition. This fired my curiosity. In Algeria, Tunisia, Egypt and Ethiopia I was able to sense the lure of early African Christianity. But still not Libya.

In the great Christian sites of the Near East, in most cases there are working modern cities built on top of layers of ruined earlier Christian sites of the third to the seventh centuries. This contrasts with Libya, where there are many open archaeological sites that encompass large portions of the ancient city much as it was. So it is in Sabratha, Leptis and Cyrene. Unlike Alexandria, these have remained largely unbuilt upon, with many artifacts remaining in almost pristine condition. Many have been only partially excavated.

Only belatedly was I able to behold the monumental scale of intellectual acumen that had been first lodged in Africa, which would in due time shape Europe. That happened in Algeria and intensified in Libya. It was only in exploring the Christian layers of Tripoli and Leptis Magna that I recognized that someone must have the vocation to dig into on the most neglected of all ancient Christian lands—Libya. I was slow to recognize this calling as a challenge addressed to me.

## THE GUEST

Why then was I welcomed there under these divisive circumstances of visa blockage, Lockerbie, Darfur and ideological polarization? Because I was a guest. I experienced the heartfelt North African tradition of hospitality and cordial treatment of wayfarers at the table of the host. Through the offices of my esteemed friend Bishop Mouneer Anis, the Anglican Primate of Egypt with North Africa and the Horn of Africa, I was invited to Libya as a guest of the Libyan government. My generous and friendly government-sponsored driver and keeper was with me every step along the way. He kept me aware that I was moving through a system featuring a complete state-controlled monopoly of power, but one that was beginning to seek partnerships with free economies and democratic values.

I was determined to disavow any political interests whatever. My concern was limited exclusively to matters of historical analysis and interpretation. Yet it was immediately evident that simply by being there I was already empathizing with a subtle point of Libyan self-esteem—the positive rediscovery of Libyan history by an American. It did not take them long to connect my noneconomic and nonpolitical concerns with their practical sensibilities regarding future economic development of interests in tourism as an injector of capital into the contemporary Libyan entrepreneurial economy, though that was not my purpose.

The Libyan economy ranks objectively as one of the wealthiest in Africa, based on oil exports, which account for 95 percent of Libya's revenues. This income has been largely dispersed by a top down, socially planned system of distribution chiefly administered through government agencies, all essentially under the direction of one man, one family. Everything has been done on the basis of a political order that strikes me as deeply influenced by the socialist vision and Islamic communitarianism, softened by a strong dose of Sunni family ideals.

As an invited guest I had the privilege of not having to struggle for my civil liberties, unlike many of my hearers. I met some there who must have had great difficulty obtaining even a modicum of any noticeable measure of civil justice as defined in the West. For example, I met a young man who wanted advice about the possibilities of coming to North America to study theology. He had come from somewhere in central Africa. He had been serving in a tough self-giving ministry to the poorest of the poor in the most alienated and forgotten portions of the city of Tripoli. I was curious. I asked how he got there. I was stunned by the answer. He *walked* into Libya through the desert from the south. I did not ask from where. How he survived the long walk to Libya I cannot imagine, but my guess is that there is a great novel hidden in that young man.

I am trying to explain why I as a classical Christian theologian from the West who happens to be interested in the history of Libya, especially its Christian history, could receive such an open and welcome reception from governmental, diplomatic and university authorities. This happened without my being tempted to fudge on any basic commitment to consensual classic Christian teaching of Scripture, the classic doctrine of revelation, Christology or triune teaching.

They quickly grasped that their position was something like a family that unknowingly owns a gold mine. There is a part of their history that is like a hidden gemstone hoard that they have not yet quite noticed and have not really wanted even to look at, primarily because it is imprinted with a cross.

They were recognizing the simple fact that they have something in their country that they didn't even recognize as a value for them and that could benefit them by learning about it. They have this historic asset. If the world could get a glimpse of it, many would want to see it and touch it and be touched by it. It was not difficult for them to imagine the future stream of trade and commerce by ship, plane and automobile into Libya. As a Christian observer, I think of this opening as a beautiful potential gift of peacemaking and grace.

## CONNECTING

Some of these university students were for the first time hearing of the ancient Christian slice of Libyan history. They were curious and fascinated. They had no difficulty relating this ancient story to their own present Libyan and sub-Saharan African struggles.

I talked with many young Libyans who were eager to find their way into a principled international dialogue. They did not disguise their aspiration to become major players in technological development. They hungered for identity and recognition in the modern world. They aspired to be reasonable defenders of a moderated international vision of Islam. They were looking for a third way between the Wahabist jihadists and Western colonial accommodation. Western scholars have an interest in encouraging this dialogue.

The Libyans I met saw in ancient African Christianity some resources for moral renewal that might be very different from much of the stereotyped modern Christianity they had come to expect. The duration of the history of populist socialism in Libya is one century old. The history of Christianity in Libya spans five hundred years. It is under their feet.

No one asked me the dreary question that I so often get from American students: "Why study old things? Quickly give me the pragmatic reasons for studying history. And don't waste my time pondering it." But these students were Muslims. Hence they already knew a great deal about their own history. They had literally memorized much of it—a central feature of Islamic education: learning by literal recall of the sacred texts. Their entire system of legal reasoning is essentially a commentary on their sacred texts—the Qur'an and its earliest commentators.

In addition to this university audience, I also spoke to an international audience of diplomats and Christian believers living in Libya. This took place in the heart of the ancient medina in Tripoli, the historical epicenter of Libyan governance and culture. We met in a former Catholic church that has now been restored and offered by the governing authorities for use to the Anglican communion with its international congregation, which is largely composed of teachers, diplomats and refugees from all over Africa—truly a crosscultural audience. Some are cradle Anglicans, but most are not. They form an intensely believing community of Christians coming from all parts of Africa who adhere fervently to scriptural and classic Christian teaching. It was an unusual place to offer a public lecture on history—a seventeenth-century Catholic cathedral church built in the center of the ancient medina to serve prisoners and slaves.[2]

## UNEXPECTED OUTCOMES

The lectures in Tripoli were not intended to have political consequences. It was exclusively an event for Muslims and Christians interested in history. It became evident that the Libyan people have much to learn about hidden elements in their own history. The outcome was surprising to many. Most found that the history of Christianity is not intrinsically unfriendly to the future well-being of Libya. It is not alien to the emerging interests of continental Africa. They listened with intense interest and asked penetrating questions. They understood quickly the ways they might benefit from what I was saying about their own distinguished history.

Ironically, the only person I met while in Libya who was suspicious, challenging and hostile was not from Libya but from London—a Muslim intellectual who had a professional interest in surveilling and assessing press coverage. What I heard from him and him alone was a defensive Muslim outlook. That defensiveness did not come from ordinary Muslims in Libya. It came from London. I had something to learn from that: The problems we have with Libya are not so much from Libya as such but from defensive preconceptions of the supposedly inevitable clash of civilizations.

---

[2]Costanzo Bergna, *La missione francescana in Libia* (Tripoli, Libya: Stab. "Nuove arti grafiche," 1924).

## TAKEAWAY LEARNINGS

I come away from Libya as theologically orthodox and personally evangelical as ever. I experienced genuine warmth from the people of Libya.
I talked about historical resources from the continent of Africa that
have been neglected by European and American historians. All were
welcoming to me and open to dialogue with a total stranger. I learned
that a significant historical conversation with Islamic intellectuals in
Libya did not depend on them giving up their beliefs or me camouflag-
ing mine. It did not depend on looking for the lowest common de-
nominator between us so as to fog over real differences.

I showed attentive respect for their view of God's revelation without
making the veiled assumption that I had to change it in order to care
about them or be in dialogue with them. I did not have to give up something of my own conviction in order to be there with them in an empathic way. I was not asked to fudge to the least extent. Too much of the
interfaith dialogue over the last century has been based on modern assumptions that implicitly require equivocating on faith commitments.

I took away the feeling that the rest of sub-Saharan Africa would do
well to learn to listen more empathetically to what is going on in northern Africa, and vice versa. Sub-Saharan African Christians can benefit
by understanding, grasping and gratefully owning the ancient Christian narratives, treatises, sources, texts and thoughts that have borne
and nurtured in the historic multicultures of North Africa.

In the first millennium Christianity never got beyond the Sahara,
due to the immensity of the deserts and the oceans. But Christians
were certainly a significant presence in the first millennium of the history of the continent in the north. These earliest layers of African
Christianity decisively affected European Christianity and world
Christianity long before our modern world came into being.

## THE MOST IGNORED LAND HAVING FIVE CENTURIES OF EARLY CHRISTIAN HISTORY

The ancient Christian era in Africa has been profoundly misunderstood by academics. It has been underreported by historians and insuf-
ficiently excavated by archaeologists. *Libya is more ignored than any*

*country in the world which has experienced a half millennium of Christian history.* This is an extreme case of modern amnesia. The amnesia prevails more in the West than in Africa, but nowhere in Africa more than Libya. It is as if a posthypnotic suggestion had been triggered.

I have ventured into numerous castaway cultures, but none cast so far away from conventional awareness as Libya. Neither the present citizens of Libya nor astounded visitors to Libya have had a fair opportunity to learn about the ancient sites or texts of ancient Libya. This applies with all the more irony to the memory of the ancient Christian inhabitants of Libya—their art, architecture and ideas. Pursuers will soon discover, as I did, that this information is hard to find. Readers seeking to study this area will learn that it has an inaccessible bibliography that requires vast linguistic skills to master. This subject will not be penetrated by reading in English-only sources. It is hard to find any reliable resources in any Western languages other than Italian and French. This is evident from the footnotes.

These pages hope to provide for the first time in recent years a preliminary introduction to some of the neglected Libyan layers of the history of African Christianity. Typical visitors come to Libya with a burning desire to see the spectacular Greco-Roman sites. They will leave with astonishment, but with little or no awareness that Christianity ever existed in Libya. They will not find much usable information on great Christian sites in either typical travelers' handbooks or travel industry materials. And when they go to eager and well-meaning local guides, they should not be surprised if they hear little or nothing about the centuries of Christian history that are in many cases only a few centimeters under the surface. Those who fail to ask will not receive indicators of Christian basilicas, Christian symbols on doorposts and the inscriptions of a necropolis.

The result is an almost complete absence of an accessible body of literature on early Libyan Christianity. Limited sporadic exceptions may be found in Coptic and Ethiopic academic circles. There the Christian tradition has been planted so deeply and so well watered that it has survived lengthy droughts and hardships. Otherwise the bibliography at the end of this work shows the best that can now be offered. This bibliography will be extended and built on in the coming years.

The Libyan ingredients of this five-hundred-year story have never been properly told. The observer is forced to work very hard to dig out this information. When bits of evidence are found, they are in difficult languages like Coptic and Arabic. The archaeological reports are mainly in Italian, French, German and even Polish. Much more archaeological excavation remains to be done. Much of the evidence remains underground, only partially or inadequately excavated, and even if excavated, its significance not fully understood or digested.

## A WORLD FAR AWAY, A WORLD LONG GONE

When I returned to speak to a North American audience, I realized that never before had I faced such a self-chosen impediment in a book or public lecture: to speak on a subject about which there is minimal precipitating concern, which is hard to explain, and about which there is little predisposing motivation even to listen to its passionate concerns. These are all the things Mrs. Peterson, my high school speech teacher, warned me to avoid. So let the folly continue: I have chosen voluntarily to try to elucidate a remote topic in a sufficiently interesting manner that you will want to come back for chapter after chapter. That is my goal. But what passion fuels me toward such folly? What motive could make it so weighty and urgent to me? And maybe even to you?

Libyan Christianity epitomizes the struggle of world Christianity. What makes it so urgent? Its issues are arising in the most tense and conflicted part of the world. Libya is positioned in the front trenches of the battle lines of North-South hemispheric conflict, East-West cultural differences and Muslim-Christian religious predispositions. Understanding Libya may be as important to the future of Christianity today as it was in the third century.

Libya is to sub-Saharan Africans something like Alaska is to Americans: a vast, distant and intriguing space. Libya is the fourth largest land mass in Africa and the least known to North Americans. I confess that I am trying to coax you, woo you like a lover, into a place you might never otherwise want to go—into the fascinating orbit of a subject you probably do not think you even need to know—a world far away, a world long gone.

The irony of this disregard is seen when light is shown on the actual direction of intellectual creativity in the known world of the second through sixth centuries. The chief intellectual guides of North African Christianity have been studied by Christians all over the world, but seldom recognized as African. They have often been thought of as purely Hellenists or Byzantines, but not Africans. These African writers have been studied and pondered for centuries. Their voices have echoed in every subsequent generation of Christians. However, they have seldom been studied as indigenous Africans, as people shaped by that great continent that is not and never will be Europe or Asia.

A closer look shows that many of these early believers were indigenized Africans who were leading the way in the greatest intellectual and spiritual developments of the early Christian centuries. In those centuries basic ideas of North African Christianity, including those conceived and debated in Libya, have quietly become transferred to and embedded in European thought. They helped to define the Orthodox, Catholic and ecumenical consensus in Europe and the Americas, and ultimately in world Christianity. Here I am thinking of Christian writers of the African continent (not Libya alone) such as Cyprian, Origen, Athanasius, Didymus the Blind, Augustine and Fulgentius. All these are indigenous Africans, born and bred on the continent of Africa. North Africa is defined here as the region from the Red Sea to Morocco. More often than is recognized, the movement of human knowledge was often *from South to North*, from Africa to Europe, from the Maghreb and Nile north to Europe.

The conventional Eurocentric *misperception* is the opposite—that intellectual leadership typically moved from the North to the South, that is, from Europe to Africa. But a more careful inquiry into Christian intellectual history, contrary to this common assumption, shows that the main flow of intellectual leadership in that era was moving from Africa to Europe, that is, South to North. Libya contributed its fair share to that African vortex of intellectual vitality, as we will see.

It remains the task of a generation of future scholars, many of them from Africa, to restudy the rising tide of ideas flowing from Africa to embryonic Europe in the earliest Christian centuries. They will be acquiring the requisite language skills and academic temperament to unpack this neglected but ancient hypothesis. What must be overcome is our own inattentiveness to texts.

## AFRICAN ROOTS OF EUROPEAN IDEAS

Let one simple point sink in: the South to North flow of intellectual creativity. Once grasped, this movement of human knowledge is easy to trace through the liturgy, through scriptural interpretation, through dogmatic formation, through ecumenical consensus, through moral teaching and ethics, and through the study of the philosophy of history. All these had numerous and deep African roots, chiefly from Alexandria and Cyrene, but later from Leptis Magna, Carthage and Hippo.

What was first firmly established in the Nile Valley and the Maghreb became later widely confirmed as classic consensual Christian teaching. The seeds for the scriptural interpretations that became common Christian teaching were first sewn on the African continent. *The major movement of intellectual history in the second and third centuries was South to North, Africa to Europe, Africa to Asia.* This is markedly counterintuitive to the modern mind.

Separate studies are called for that detail the textual grounds of this counterintuitive thesis. Groundbreaking transmitters of culture from Africa north to Europe are easily demonstrable, but seldom noted. Here is the thumbnail version:

- Origen taught Gregory Thaumaturgus of Cappadocia.

- Tertullian first formulated early trinitarian teaching for the Latin world.

- Cyprian perfected a conciliar method that ever thereafter shaped the orderly formation of Christian dogma.

- Athanasius in exile brought the story of Anthony to Europe to stimulate the monastic movement everywhere.

- Latin translations of the New Testament were in Africa before they arrived in Europe.

- Leptis Magna likely was the original residence of the first African pope (Victor I) who preceded the first African emperor of the Severan dynasty (Septimius Severus).

- John Cassian brought the Pachomian model of ascetic community to Benedict of Nursia.

- Augustine offered a unified understanding of history to the formation of medieval Europe.

Seldom have these cultural attainments and intellectual insights been viewed as coming out of Africa or being refined in Libya, but our aim is to show the extent to which they were. I will, for example, provide evidence for the argument that Septimius Tertullianus was Libyan by birth and familial identity, as was the emperor Septimius Severus.

Christian monastic movements had a significant effect on the kind of education that Muslim leaders would later receive in their two greatest intellectual centers of African Islam: Kairouan (patterned after Scetis) and Cairo (patterned after Alexandria). By this strange providence the centuries of Christian presence in Libya have echoed through the subsequent generations of both Christianity and classic Islam through the passage-by-passage examination of sacred texts, through the patterns of North African education, and through conciliar debates on the moral life of piety and prayer.

## THEN AND NOW

Africa experienced the most spectacular growth of paleo-Christians, greater than Italy, France or Spain, in the third century. Most of that growth occurred in the Nile and Medjerda valleys, and great African cities from Alexandria and Cyrene to Leptis Magna to Carthage and Hippo. But a great deal of it occurred in villages and towns in the mountains and inland steppes. The seeds of these congregations were being planted in the earliest Christian centuries. The period of vast and terrible persecution of Christians was the very time of exponential growth of Christianity in Egypt, Libya and Tunisia.

The third through sixth centuries brought the apex of that growth. I will present archaeological evidence that shows there were hundreds of towns of Libya that had active Christian congregations during this period, continuing up to the Arab military victories.

Meanwhile today there is no continent on earth where Christianity is more vital and alive than Africa. African Muslim and Christian total populations now are almost equal—at a little less than a half billion each. The Christian population of Africa is now estimated at over four hundred million (48 percent of the total African population of 890,000,000 according to the Pew Forum). The World Religion Database estimates a current African Christian population of 495.8 million. Compared with world population growth, Africa's growth is very high. David Barrett in the World Christian Encyclopedia projects that by A.D. 2025 there will be 633,000,000 Christians in Africa.

It is illuminating to compare the first four centuries of African Christianity with the last four centuries of African Christianity. Both have been periods of exceptional growth, challenge, passion, intellectual ferment and moral enlargement. At times conversions have reached huge numbers with exponential growth. African Christians today have an opportunity to see their present religion from the perspective of two thousand uninterrupted years of classic Christian teaching. The story of African Christianity begins in the Nile Valley.

Today in North Africa there is little awareness of the exponential growth either of the first or last four centuries of Christianity. That minimal awareness will not turn around until the hard work of archaeological and intellectual history has been taken seriously by young Africans.

Christianity in Africa still appears to many as if it had no distinguished ancient history and no significant textual deposit. This is false. This low level of awareness of ancient Christianity is not only present in sub-Saharan Africa, but in northern Africa as well, where it might have been expected to be already quite deep. Nowhere is that special form of unawareness more firmly and intractably entrenched than in Libya.

In Libya we find an extremely lost past and an awesomely undecided future. It presents a prototype scenario of what is found in lesser form all over Africa: the amnesiac past and the uncertain future. This consciousness is commonplace in modernity. It is made by Western modernity and exported to Africa.

The massive area west of Egypt was in biblical times called Libya. However large in mass, it seems small in modern intellectual interest, the least examined historically. Yet among all ancient countries Libya possesses the richest store of unexcavated Christian artifacts. This treasury has embedded in it a spectacular ancient Christian memory of early apostolic Christianity. Its climate has preserved artifacts that have rotted away elsewhere. It is favorable to archaeological preservation.

The irony: a place that has ancient cultural and artistic monuments of unequaled wonder has left unexplored ancient Christian artifacts of the highest value. As we look over the lean bibliography of ancient Christianity in Libya, we might wrongly conclude that it would have very little of substance to offer the historian. This is why the exceptional number and quality of early Christian archaeological sites is so surprising.

So why is one of the most significant ancient Christian locations the least visited? One obvious answer for Americans is that it has been very hard to get visas. But Libya was also largely unvisited (except by Italians) in the days when visas were easy to obtain. Another possible answer is that it is truly insignificant. But that conclusion cannot be properly made until the evidence is considered. Try another thesis: Libya is unexplored because the logistic support for travel is limited. This is not convincing because other rustic and remote sites with all sorts of discomforts (Kilimanjaro, Timbuktu, Sinai) are constantly visited. The limitations of world-class hotels and transportation cannot become an excuse for historical ignorance. The more plausible answer is that the ignorance is based on cultural biases and stereotypes.

The value of Libya as a natural and paleological attraction is fairly well established, but the value of Libya as a place of Christian pilgrimage is not considered at all. Libya is seldom visited by spiritual pilgrims, and even less by those seeking to understand the history of human knowledge. A personal intervention—telling my own story—may help to grasp this irony.

## THE TRANSFORMING POWER OF AFRICAN CHRISTIANITY

It is true: my own personal faith has been reactivated through rediscovery of early African Christian faith. Ironic? In case you hadn't guessed, I confess: I am a white guy from middle America, born in the Dust Bowl of the Great Depression. What is a person like me doing talking about this unusual subject: the transforming power of African Christianity? I do not have exactly the best genes to talk about this. But that does not make the story any less worth telling. My own distinctive skin pigment is roughly the color of the Dust Bowl—somewhere between red clay and sandy loam. The DNA comes from Scotch-Irish, English, Scandinavian and Saxon ancestors. So what is a fellow like me doing in a place like this?

My field of research in recent decades has focused on the history of exegesis. This field asks about how the same sacred Scriptures were interpreted in different languages through changing generations. There are many eras of interpretation of stable sacred texts. I have been drawn especially to those written immediately after the earliest apostolic testimony—in the earliest period of Scripture studies, the first three centuries and more broadly the patristic era (A.D. 90–750). Ecumenical teaching was based on these foundations. It emerged as a result of consensus formation about what Scripture as a whole meant, as remembered by what the apostles wrote.

For years a side-bar interest has been the African ethnicity and catholicity of the earliest Christian interpreters of the New Testament. This sidebar has increasingly become a central feature of my research and writing in recent years.

## WHAT CHANGED MY LIFE

My life has in fact been massively changed—transformed, turned around, recycled—by decades of listening to the ancient Christian teachers as they listen to Scripture. During the last two decades, I have been privileged to be editor of the Ancient Christian Commentary on Scripture (published by InterVarsity Press). The complete twenty-nine-volume behemoth is now in print. The publisher tells me that it has more than six million words and has sold over five hundred thousand copies. Its three successor series have been inaugurated. Every passage of Scripture has been commented on in the patristic period. My senior years as a scholar have happily been poured into the study of these early writers on the African, Asian and European continents, each one commenting on each passage of Scripture, verse by verse.

What birthed the African branch of this effort is simple: Through years of selecting and editing, guiding and producing this patristic commentary, I learned, to my surprise, how so many of these earliest and wisest lovers and critical readers of sacred Scripture came from Africa. Africa has been the most fertile seedbed of intellectual depth in Christian reflection on Scripture. Other members of our international team began to note this as well. We were struck by the relative absence of this recognition, especially as it relates to modern Africa.

Out of this profound spiritual exercise of reading Old and New Testament Scripture as seen by African eyes, I have come to a new respect for the African mind, which means the larger African textual and intellectual tradition. These African teachers have already changed us all. This includes all Christians worldwide. Ever since Mark's Gospel was first read and preached on the African continent, this ferment has been at work. The most fruitful preaching and teaching and durable ecumenical consensus came from the Nile Valley and the Maghreb: from the north of Africa where Libya holds the central location bridging east and west.

From these great minds came a grasp of Christian teaching and common church practices in worship and the moral life that would be emulated wherever Christians later went—as far north as Norway and as far east as China, from Alaska to Mozambique. African Christians gave the whole historic church its earliest and deepest clarification of the mind of God in Scripture. They adhered faithfully to the preaching of the apostles, planting the Word and watching it grow on the continent of Africa. These African writings have since become the common patrimony of all Christians everywhere. Many crucial third-century questions were settled first in Africa through consensus by African church councils. The first Synod of Rome was called by an African pope from Libya.

Africa set the pace for the maturing of ecumenical Christianity. What was decided in North Africa by rigorous exegetical debate? The most sensitive issues of Christian teaching: Whether Jesus is truly God incarnate, whether the expected Christ has come, whether the Old Testament is best seen through eyes of its fulfillment in the New Testament. The consensual answers were often debated and formed first in Africa.

These decisions ultimately became widely accepted to believers in the North and East in Europe and Asia. Many of the most decisive of these intellectual developments in early Christianity were first exegetically contested, consensually defined and most profoundly understood on the African continent. These definitions were clarified and received as consensual classic Christian teaching generally in the Mediterranean world and in due time in Christian communities of the fourth century from India to Spain, and by the fifth century in the Rhine and Danube valleys. The whole *oikoumenē* of world Christianity is thus indebted to African intellectual acumen and persistence in consensus formation.

In the last several years a new phase of scholarship has been opening up for me and many others. Belatedly, my vocation is becoming clearer to me: helping modern Africans to better grasp what already belongs to them. As one step along this way I am focusing on how important and unrecognized the Libyan layer of earliest Christianity is. The intense exegetical debate over the eternality of the Son took place first in Libya, then in the Egyptian Delta and Meletian dioceses, and finally north all the way across Europe lasting for four centuries in the Latin West. Why did the Arian-Orthodox controversy start in Libya?

## PROVIDENCE PONDERED

Today the relationship between Christianity and Islam contains both threat and promise. The stakes are high, and this volatile situation has become an enigma for everyone, but more so for those living in Africa. The irony: both religions believe in providence but neither religion yet fully understands God's purpose in the other.

Christianity and Islam have been in steady tension since the 630s when Islam swept across North Africa. Since then they have remained in a very interactive and intense relationship, always echoing the previous crucible of Jews and Christians in ancient North Africa. Sometimes this tension has been creative, as in Kairouan, Tunisia, and in Córdoba, Spain. Other times it has been tragic, as in the ancient Pentapolis of Libya and in modern Darfur.

My conviction, though many will disagree, is this: The more seriously Muslim and Christian believers can together study the texts of each others' sacred writings, the more clear will be the understanding of the world in which the judge of history has placed us both today. Here we stand in the vortex of the decisive conflicts of our time. It indeed is a conflict of civilizations, but I prefer to name it theologically as a conflict between Christian and Islamic views of providence. The doctrine of providence is passionately held by both, but understood in conflicting ways. Much new intellectual energy needs to be put into this dilemma. It is a question of theology, not merely politics. Its resolution is most likely to come from African Christian readers of the Bible in dialogue with African Muslim readers of the Qur'an.

There is one manageable action both can take. The challenge for young global Christians today is to learn the languages that will enable them to read and understand these African texts of early Christianity and Islam. These texts will illuminate how the providence of God has led us to this unique point in history. These texts on both sides of the Christian-Muslim divide are intellectually demanding.

They are brought to unnecessary polarization when approached within the moral frame of reference of modern secularist prejudices. No realistic observer can adequately assess the current geopolitical dilemmas of Africa without taking into account this heavily laden religious history. This is illumined if the sacred texts are conjointly considered alongside modern economic and political considerations. These early African texts still have the capacity to reveal the human heart and the providential ironies of God's mercy and judgment as refracted through different lenses.

As modern Western persons, we come with a prevailing predisposition to ignore the past. Muslims do not have this disability. We do. We make the assumption that our modern way of understanding reality is normative and thus superior to all other worldviews. Regrettably we make these assumptions without having read and pondered the great ideas and wisdom of these sacred texts.

## THE BURDEN OF REDISCOVERY

Libya has a three-thousand-year-old culture and a ten-thousand-year-old paleological prehistory that has echoed through cultural formations that have shaped us today. Yet Libya remains Africa's most neglected arena of historical understanding. Libya arguably presents a distinctive expression of the African spirit. For most Africans, Libya's Africaneity is unquestioned. Libya is lodged in Africa. That is a geographic fact.

The Libyan leader Muammar Muhammad al-Qaddafi in his Third Universal Theory once actively tried to persuade the Pan-African leadership to consider Libya as the central headquarters of the Pan-African movement. Ethiopia won that contest. But it was close.

Why is Libya unique? Because it has had extensive experience being the midpoint of East-West conflict in Africa through two millennia. The drawing of an imaginary line through the middle of Libya in the times of Diocletian that resulted in two Libyas, one Greek and one Latin, is symbolic of this duality.

Historians may be mystified by the fact that this study is a broad essay in intellectual history and the meaning of history. It is not a historical analysis of factual evidence alone, though it is that. It is rather an attempt to place the long narrative of Libyan history in the perspective of divine providence. That is a problem of theology, which means the discernment of purpose in universal history. Libya presents an awesome challenge for the Christian teaching of providence. This excursion will take us from the New Testament Cyrenians to the Arians to the Vandals to the emergence of Islam. This may be a curiosity for historians, but it is a profound puzzle and mystery for Christian theologians.

Libya is a colossal land mass, fourth largest on the continent, exceeded only by Algeria, the Democratic Republic of the Congo, and Sudan. It joins together both mineral and technological resources, infused by both ancient and modern aspirations. It is a consciously Islamic state. It might be thought that there is little need to study or even remember Libya's five centuries of Christian history. But I will present credible reasons why Libya remains a key location for understanding early Africa's buried Christian history.

My special burden for historical rediscovery lies much deeper than the dynamics of political influence or economic wealth. My motivation hinges on the attempt to understand the meaning of universal history. This is what Jews and Christians, and many Muslims, call providence. The question is not simply the outcome of trade and commerce, though these may open the way for deeper forms of insight and communication. The deeper enigma for both Muslims and Christians lies with grasping God's purposes in human history. This is a common dilemma of all historical reasoning, and the soul of theology.

A separate chapter is subsequently dedicated to examining how Muslim and Christian views of providence echo, clash, harmonize and threaten each other. This issue constitutes the pivotal theological reflection of this study.

Libya has played an unseen role in the formation of my own Western culture. But that needs to be explained, step by step. Learning the story of Libyan Christianity has been for me humbling and surprising. Its current issues touch the heart of the encounter between civilizations today.

## FINDING FOCUS

The more I turned my attention to the study of the earliest years of African Christianity, the more I was moved by the uniqueness and brilliance of the early African intellectual tradition. Soon I had piled up so many notes and drafts on my own hunches and tentative learnings that I was forced to admit that I could only digest some small portion of its complexity. That is when I reluctantly realized that I would have to select some manageable slice of it.

Not until I was invited to Libya was that slice clearly cut for me as a question of vocation. Libya, the least studied, was ironically the most promising for future inquiry. I found the history, archaeology and art so multifaceted and intriguing that it would require a longer life than I have just to introduce it. In this study I have trimmed my scope to deal only with the earliest evidences of Libyan Christianity in the first millennium. Within this span, I am focusing on a few key sites and figures in Libya. In doing so, there is no pretense of exploring adequately the history of religions in Libya.

The five or six centuries of Christian presence are like ghosts in Libya. They are not self-evident to most observers. Visitors to Libya will see many stunning architectural remains of ancient Roman, Greek, Punic and Troglodyte Libya. But very little will come into focus that reveals paleo-Christian Libya.

You need a good eye to recognize the symbols of Christian presence that are hidden in many of these artifacts—the signs in stone of Alpha and Omega, and in mosaics of bread and wine, and the cross and the Christ-bearer (Christopher). The symbols of the great biblical narratives like Daniel in the lion's den, Joseph in Egypt and the good Shepherd are silently imprinted in the artifacts of pre-Islamic Libya. This inquiry hopes to train the eye to see more of what is there.

As a result it may at first appear that the Christian witness is entirely dead in Libya. But this is a blurred perception—the illusion of absence. This lengthy Christian history has left deep footprints. Though often buried, they are impossible to erase, and when recognized, hard to ignore.

There are many inland villages which now typically appear as if they had been forever Arabic in culture. Yet prior to these overwhelming Arabic influences that swept through in A.D. 643, Libya had known many sustained generations of indigenous Christian communities. They had for centuries been planting and raising families on African soil. Christian believers resided there long enough to become grass-roots Christian cultures, not just temporary outposts of visiting outsiders.

Much more information needs to be uncovered about Christian communities in Libya, especially its remote villages, monasteries and cities. This is why I point in detail in the appendix to known sites and indicators of Christian presence in Libya, especially in the interior and not merely the coastal region. Most have not been thoroughly excavated.

Scattered believers did endure in Libya. In some cases these were remote monastic communities. Some Christians did survive long after the decisive Arab victory in A.D. 643. But about many of these archaeological sites we have very little information. Many Christian churches of the fourth century became foundations for the mosques of the seventh, only slightly redesigned. They await further research. This information will doubtless be available at some future time through archaeological excavations and literary and epigraphic studies. The premise that God is completely through with Libya is as alien to Jews and Christians as it is to Muslims.

# 2

# LIBYA IN
# BIBLICAL TIMES

▪■▪

It should not be assumed that the Libyan presence in world history was unnoticed during biblical times. Libya was recognized as a great nation during the period of Judaic kings from Jeroboam to Herod. Israel's armies were aligned both with and against Libyans at various times, depending on international alliances.

Libyan history interweaves with biblical history. The Philistines who were conquered by the Hebrew tribes practiced a particularly abominable form of idolatry: child sacrifice. These were among the third wave of inhabitants of Libya, after the Libu and Greeks. The Philistines were judged by Jews as not worthy of the land of milk and honey. In this way Joshua and others were presumably justified in attempting to drive them out of Palestine.

## THE THEATER OF SALVATION HISTORY

Recall that all three Abrahamic families—Jews, Christians and Muslims—share a history of salvation that had its earliest beginnings right on the geologic seam of two continents: Asia and Africa—between Libya and Palestine. Just as primitive human history itself begins with the transition of migrant human populations from Africa to Eurasia, so does the history of salvation in the great monotheistic religions nest in the same nexus. Libya is within that nexus at its western margin.

Classic Christianity has its roots in the narrative history of peoples formed in the close linkage between two continents: Africa and Asia. They were connected by the Sinai Peninsula. This lively interface of continental plates has formed the backdrop for the most decisive events of salvation history.

The narrative of the Ethiopian eunuch refracts this interface. It tells of a high official who immediately after his baptism sets out for his native Africa. He appears to be headed to what was then the most southerly known land of Africa, namely Ethiopia or Cush (Acts 8:26-40). We meet him on the road to Gaza. Significance: the first known African to be baptized upon believing the gospel was an Ethiopian in transit from Asia to Africa, from the Negev Desert to the Upper Nile.

## The Libu Before the Coming of the Greeks

Long before the Greeks appeared in Cyrenaica in the tenth century B.C., the Libyans were known in Egyptian and Hebrew history as the Libu (variously rendered Ribou, Labu or in neo-Punic inscriptions as the consonants Lby or Lbt, or later by Romans, Laguatan), an ethnic identity mentioned also in Nilotic texts going back to the twelfth and thirteenth centuries B.C. This name sometimes appears in Hebrew Scripture under the name Lubim and in the Greek Septuagint as Libyes. Libya was from time immemorial a crucial segment of the world arena in which God's providential purpose was being worked out, according to the Hebrew prophets.

The Libyans also appear in Hebrew history under the name of Put (Putaya), the third son of Ham (Gen 10:6; 1 Chron 1:8). Jeremiah, Ezekiel and Nahum all make reference to the Lubim or the Put. The generic term *Berbers* (barbarians) is used to encompass many of the indigenous tribes along the northern coasts of Africa, including the ethnic identities of Libya from primordial times.

During the fifth year of Rehoboam (1 Kings 14:25-26; 2 Chron 12:1-10 [c. 925 B.C.]), the Libyan pharaoh Shoshenq I invaded Palestine, an event confirmed in a stela at Karnak, conquering the ancient Israelite fortresses of Megiddo, Taanach and Shechem. Libyan troops are recorded in Judeo-Christian Scriptures in 2 Chronicles

12:3 as among the armies of Shoshenq I (945–924 B.C.; in some biblical texts Shishak).

> Shishak king of Egypt attacked Jerusalem in the fifth year of King Rehoboam. With twelve hundred chariots and sixty thousand horsemen and the innumerable troops of Libyans, Sukkites and Cushites that came with him from Egypt, he captured the fortified cities of Judah and came as far as Jerusalem. (2 Chron 12:2-4 NIV)

The Hebrew prophet Shemaiah prophesized to Rehoboam and the leaders of Judah: "This is what the LORD says, 'You have abandoned me; therefore, I now abandon you to Shishak'" (2 Chron 12:5 NIV).

The pharaoh Shoshenq I was likely of Libyan Berber ancestry through his Libyan uncle Osorkon. Shoshenq I was founder of the Twenty-Second Dynasty. When Jeroboam fled from Solomon as reported in 1 Kings 11:40, he was received by Shoshenq. In Nahum 3:9 the prophet wrote that "Thebes trusted the mighty power of Ethiopia and Egypt; the nations of Put and Libya were her allies" (CEV). Nahum was condemning the Ninevites and prophesying that they would not be able to conquer Thebes, which was protected by armies beyond the Nile. Later in the days of Antiochus III the prophet Daniel would prophesy that "He will gain control of the treasures of gold and silver and all the riches of Egypt, with the Libyans and Nubians in submission" (Dan 11:43 NIV). This was presumably fulfilled when Antiochus invaded Egypt again, gaining control over the armies of Ptolemy V and over the Holy Land.

The people from Philistine Tyre had been "forced out of their homeland by civil strife," according to the Roman writer Sallust (*History of the Jugurthine War*). They found refuge in the coastal area around the sea of Syrtis in central Libya. *Syrtis* comes from the Greek word "to drag," in reference to the way the stiff wind dragged ships along the turbulent shores of the Libyan coast.

## ANCIENT HEBREW PERCEPTIONS OF PUNIC LIBYA

From the Hebrew Bible we learn that these same early Canaanites practiced a form of worship that featured child sacrifice to the God

Molech (Jer 32:30-35). In Hebraic sacred texts, they so offended Yahweh that they were viewed as abominable and made unworthy to remain in rightful possession of the land of Canaan. Punic child sacrifices had largely disappeared by the Christian period, but their evidences were left in sacrificial tombs of the Maghreb.

Six centuries before Jesus the Punic traders had already settled in Leptis. At times they were in flight from Judean conquests. The people of Israel had a relation of tension and often enmity to those Punic or Phoenician inhabitants of Palestine that preceded the Jewish diaspora in Libya. Its residues may have been felt in the Jewish populations that migrated to Libya. The early layers of the Punic form of Phoenician-Palestinian language and culture took deep root in Libya. The local laws that reflected some of those traditions were preserved and passed from Punic sailors to Carthaginian military leaders to Roman governors. By late Roman times only vestiges remained of Punic family names, language, law, city plans, traditions, culture and religion.

Alexander the Great conquered the multicultural Cyrani (Cyrenians) in 331 B.C., three hundred years after its founding in 631 B.C. Alexander died in 322 B.C. The Ptolemy dynasty of Alexander's leading general Ptolemy I began in Cyrenaica. Under Ptolemaic rule the five city states of the Pentapolis were in time integrated into a stable administrative unit.

In the aftermath, a hundred thousand people, mostly Jews, were captured as prisoners of war by Ptolemy in Palestine and the Near East. Many of these Jews were sent to Cyrene. It is likely from this experience-battered core of the Ptolemaic Jewish population in Cyrene that later the scholarly, rabbinic and internationally well-traveled mercantile Jews (such as Simon of Cyrene, Rufus, Alexander and Lucius of Cyrene [Mk 15:21, Acts 13:1]) derived in the first century A.D.

## THE JEWISH INGREDIENT IN LIBYAN ETHNICITY

It is pertinent to review the ethnic composition of Libya at the time the Christians arrived. The ancient city of Cyrene and its province of Cyrenaica embraced numerous ethnic identities beyond the Greco-Roman identities that founded and ruled it from 631 B.C. This cultural mix continued through the Jewish Revolt of A.D. 115 and following the Arab victory of 643.

Indigenous Libyan ethnicity before Christianity included the Garamantes, Berbers, Libyans, Marmaridae, Nasamones, Jews and Egyptian ethnics as well as the Greco-Roman ruling class. By the time of the emergence of Christianity, Libya already had seen six centuries (631 B.C. to A.D. 31) of recorded history in addition to its extensive paleohistory.

The immigration of Diaspora Jews into Libya occurred extensively during the Ptolemaic period (third through first century B.C.) and continued sporadically. Jews were present in Benghazi (Berenike) and Cyrene long before the Jewish wars with Rome. In Benghazi there are inscriptions that show the Jews were loyal to Tiberius, the Roman emperor, and that a synagogue had been constructed there during the time of Nero. However, the Jewish wars with Rome reached their apex in the period from A.D. 70 to 115 and following. By the time of Jesus and John Mark, there were many Jews living in Cyrenaica with intensified messianic expectations. Many of those Jewish families had become indigenized as Africans over two or three centuries.

Their number is not known, but we know that they had property and synagogues. We know that they were influential and they scrupulously carried with them their Jewish culture, food laws and festivals. Through a combination of forced expulsions and voluntary immigrations, and through sustained trade relations and family relations between Palestinian and Cyrenaic Jews, the Jews of Libya became well adapted to Libya while yet remaining devout Jews.

## LATE JUDAIC CONTRIBUTIONS TO LIBYA: JASON OF CYRENE AND HIS LIBRARY

The Jews of Cyrene and Egypt were credited with keeping and preserving Hanukkah in the liturgical cycle. This demonstrates that provincial events in Africa influenced God's people in Jerusalem. According to 2 Maccabees 1:9, Jews were instructed; "Now see that you keep the festival of booths in the month of Chislev, in the one hundred eighty-eighth year" (in the Roman Empire's reckoning 124 B.C.).

Second Maccabees was best preserved by the faithful Jews in Libya, notably by Jason of Cyrene. The story of the Diaspora Jews was narrated by Jason of Cyrene in five volumes, of which 2 Maccabees is a brief summary. Jason of Cyrene wrote of one named Solomon who "founded a library and collected the books about the kings and prophets, and the writings of David, and letters of kings. . . . In the same way [one named] Judas also collected all the books that had been lost on account of the war" (2 Macc 2:13-14). These were *long-inhabiting indigenous African Jews* with names like Solomon, Jason and Judas. They preserved many major episodes of Jewish history. The Jews were not latecomers to Africa. They preceded the Arab conquest by seven centuries. Many subsequent migrations (Nilotic, D'mt, Sabeans, Ge'ez and later the Dutch, Indian, etc.) both into and within Africa would be absorbed into African culture. Why would these later be regarded as indigenous African cultures in the areas they migrated to, but the Jews would be more often considered nonindigenous?

The scholarly Jewish tradition of Cyrene is epitomized by Jason of Cyrene. He was a Diaspora Jew who composed the work on which 2 Maccabees is based. By this act of rekindling, this historian from Cyrene preserved the continuity of Jewish history in the period after 167 B.C. During this time, because of the wars, some of the sacred books of Israel had been temporarily lost. They were gathered and reconstituted in a library in Cyrene by Jason.

The preface of the compiler of 2 Maccabees reports that there was a larger version of this history. The Apocrypha or Deuterocanonical books of the early Christian canon recall:

> All this, which has been set forth by Jason of Cyrene in five volumes, we shall attempt to condense into a single book. For considering the flood of numbers involved and the difficulty there is for those who wish to enter upon the narratives of history because of the mass of material, we have aimed to please those who wish to read, to make it easy for those who are inclined to memorize, and to profit all readers. (2 Macc 2:23-25)

The compiler of 2 Maccabees continues with an explanation of the difference between primary historical research, such as that of Jason of

Cyrene, and secondary reporting of that research such as 2 Maccabees: "It is the duty of the original historian to occupy the ground, to discuss matters from every side, and to take trouble with details, but the one who recasts the narrative should be allowed to strive for brevity" (2 Macc 2:30-31). Jason of Cyrene was the "original historian" preserving the documents of the narrative summarized in 2 Maccabees. Jason worked from a library of original sources, many not preserved. He had to consider every angle. That library existed in Cyrene.

All Jews of subsequent centuries have benefited from the rabbinic library in Cyrene of the period of Jason of Cyrene. He lived about 100 B.C. and wrote his history of the Maccabean times down to the victory over Nicanor (175–161 B.C.). Jason's purpose was to set forth a providential reading of the history of the whole period, showing how God purified the temple and restored his faithful people. In doing so, Jason became "the earliest known composer of stories that glorify God's holy martyrs" (NAB, introduction)

The longer documentary history of Maccabean Judaism was written in Cyrene. It tells "the story of Judas Maccabeus and his brothers" in their campaigns against Antiochus Epiphanes, and "the heroes who fought bravely for Judaism," detailing how they "regained possession of the world-famous temple [and] liberated the city" of Jerusalem. If so, present-day Judaism owes much of its memory of late Judaic Palestine to Libyan Jews.

## THE PRIMORDIAL GREEK FOUNDING OF CYRENE

Ancient Cyrene became the chief multiethnic city of Africans between Alexandria and Carthage. Its setting is a spectacular view between the Green Mountain (Jebel Akhdar) and the Mediterranean Sea.

On the nearby plateau and steppes were indigenous Libyan tribes of very ancient origin. There were rock-face carvings as early as 12,000 B.C. in Libya showing large animals being hunted. Carbon-14 dating shows that some of the stylized polychromatic paintings of human figures date to 8000 B.C. These human figures with rounded heads appear in red, yellow and green pigments. Paleolithic representations of horses and carts go back to 1500 B.C. The nearby Geramantes tribes mentioned by Herodotus were using horses and carts by the fifth century B.C. Paintings of camels appear about the beginning of the Christian era. The Sahara region was undergoing gradual desertification.

The founding myth of Cyrene places the gods of Homeric renown at center stage. The Greek goddess Kurana (or Kura or Cyrene) was a nymph princess in Libyo-Hellenic mythology who slew giant beasts. She is portrayed wrestling and killing large animals like lions with her bare hands.

Cyrene was linked romantically with Apollo, who is remembered in Greek mythology for his adventurous and amorous behavior. The founding legend of Cyrene tells of a time when Apollo was riding his centaur and encountered a beautiful young girl fighting a lion with her bare hands. Apollo fell in love with her and abducted her in a golden chariot to the site that would bear the name of Cyrene in Africa, where the Temple of Apollo would memorialize this event. Apollo had carried Cyrene "beyond the seas to the unequaled gorgeous gardens of Zeus to make her queen of the cities where you will bring together people who will come from an island to live and prosper over a fertile plateau." The attractive Cyrene was promised a well-watered place where she could enjoy her hunting in the green mountains. There Cyrene bore Apollo a son, Aristaeus.

These gardens were around the spring of Cyrene on Jebel Akhdar in Libya. This was a place where the earth would yield three abundant crops per year: the first from the fields near the shore, the second from the hills, and the third from the mountains. The reason for the founding of Cyrene was famine in the Greek islands. The command to go to Africa was given by an oracle. This became living history with the movement of immigrants.

Herodotus in his history relates the parallel story of the troubles of the people of the island of Thera (Santorini). The island's geography placed it within the orbit of the Spartan kings of the Peloponnese. Economic crisis forced the islanders to move to a different place to live. They came to Libya to survive. The history of the founding of Cyrene is shrouded in myth and mystery, but a myth having a factual basis in the migration of peoples to Africa in the seventh century B.C., the period of Amos and Hosea. Large migrations have been a feature characteristic of much African history. The story of migrants and displaced persons resonated with the earliest Christians who arrived in Libya, who said their citizenship was in heaven.

In the history of Herodotus (4.150-58), a detailed account is preserved of the colonization of Cyrene. Herodotus himself had visited Cyrene sometime after 440 B.C. According to his narrative, colonists from the island of Thera had consulted the oracle at Delphi during a time of economic stress due to overpopulation, drought and forced immigration. Lead by Gernus, who was accompanied by Battos, they traveled to Delphi, where the oracle commanded them to found a new city in the idyllic location of Libyan Africa. Gernus answered the oracle of Apollo saying, "I am an old and feeble man. How could I start this kind of journey?" The oracle answered that Battos could lead the people to the new place and that Apollo would be there protecting them.

They were led by Battos first to a small island south of Crete in the Gulf of Bomba—the island of Platia—which they found hazardous and insufficient for colonization. So they proceeded on, heading due south to the coast of Africa to a point east of the modern city of Derna at Aziris, where the Berber tribe Giligami resisted their presence and told them about another more fertile land further west. That place further west turned out to be Cyrene. In the founding myth we see how the ancient oracle provided a legitimizing framework for the sacred foundation of the city. When Battos died, his tomb became a place of veneration, where the agora was built and where the two main streets of the city came together: the Sacred Way or Skyrota, and the Street of King Battos, which goes from the agora down to the valley where the Byzantine Christian basilica to the east would later serve as a place of worship until the arrival of the Arabs.

The historic date usually assigned to the founding of Cyrene is 631 B.C., a date generally confirmed by Laconian pottery finds. There conditions were very favorable to the building of a permanent colony near the sea with superb agricultural and defensive advantages. The horses of Cyrene would become famous. They would be used for elite cavalry.

They grazed on spacious grasslands near Cyrene. The people found the topography easy to defend from the slopes of the Acropolis of Cyrene. Herodotus described it as a place of plentiful water—as if there were holes in the sky. The annual rainfall of 600 millimeters and the presence of heavy dew made agricultural conditions favorable, and Cyrene became a productive agricultural center, a trading center and political center for central North Africa.[1]

## CYRENE IN PRE-CHRISTIAN ANTIQUITY

Cyrene had been a world-class intellectual center as early as the fourth century B.C., during the time of Plato and Aristotle. Cyrene's intellectual leadership was evidenced by such figures as Theodore the geometer, Callimachus the poet, the philosophers Carneades and Aristippus (Aristipos), and Eratosthenes the scientist. Writers from Cyrene were among the figures that became voices in the Socratic dialogues of Plato.

Cyrene was a place of invention and discovery. The poetry, science and philosophy of Cyrenaic thinkers were accessible in the academic centers of Macedonia, Greece and Cyprus, far predating Rome's ascendancy. Cyrene produced a school of thinkers who set forth a doctrine of moral cheerfulness, focusing on happiness as a rational quest. The intellectual heritage of North Africa was a staple influence on Greek thought going back to the fourth century B.C. Libyan Jewish and paleo-Christian writers would extend that pattern.

The preeminence of Cyrene as an early African intellectual center was established at least a century prior to the founding of Alexandria. When there was no city of Alexandria but only a small village, Cyrene was providing a daring model for independent academic inquiry that would later appear in Alexandria and much later would shape the very idea of the European university. Cyrene was already an academic center of philosophy, mathematics and literature a century before the found-

---

[1]Martin Bernal has presented evidence that Cyrene was earlier identified with the Black Athena in *Black Athena: Afroasiatic Roots of Classical Civilization*, vol. 1: *The Fabrication of Ancient Greece, 1785–1985* (New Brunswick, N.J.: Rutgers University Press, 1987). This controversial thesis has been critiqued by Mary R. Lefkowitz, *Not Out of Africa: How Afrocentrism Became an Excuse to Teach Myth as History* (New York: Basic Books, 1997).

ing of the museum in the city of Alexandria. Cyrene was considered the Athens of Africa, with scientific and intellectual activity thought to surpass Carthage in most gifts excepting naval technology.

By 440 B.C. the Cyrenaic dynasty of Battos was supplanted by a quasidemocratic government that featured a bicameral legislature—a senate of 101 and an assembly of 500, which would later be a classic model for that adapted in the U.S. constitution.

In the *Stromata*, when Clement of Alexandria was commenting on biblical examples of women of unfettered, mature faith, such as Judith, Esther, Susanna and Sarah, he attached a remarkable list of pagan women of ancient literature whom he thought had shown anticipatory elements of the life of perfect love. Among these women was Arete of Cyrene (7.19), who personified civic virtue in the mind of this early Christian teacher.

## SORTING THE FIVE LAYERS OF CYRENAIC ARCHAEOLOGY

Cyrene is one of the most complex archaeological sites in Libya due to its irregular topography and its complex mixture of histories and archaeological strata in five major layers—Libyo-Punic, Greek, Roman, Byzantine and Arabic.

The Greek and Libyo-Punic layers lie underneath the Roman layer. The Roman layer lies underneath a heavy layer of Byzantine fortifications and Christian period remains. The ancient site of Cyrene requires some modicum of archaeological awareness to get a grasp of the complexity of these strata and to identify specific features of the Christian sites.

Sadly, the standard travel literature emphasizes the older Greek and Roman history, not the later Paleo-Christian and Byzantine remains, which fuels our major interest in these pages. Visitors to ancient Cyrene normally begin at the northeast gate near the modern roadway settlement of Shahat and follow a trajectory around the circumference of the great ancient city, ending again at the northern gate, where there is a sculpture and archaeology museum. But in this trajectory little is likely to be said about the Christian layers of Cyrene.

These five major layers of archaeology are found scattered through five different geographical sections of the sprawling site of Cyrene: the ancient market and agora, which includes the Sacred Way; the paleo-Christian and Byzantine archaeological remains; the Temple of Zeus, one of the most colossal temples in the Greek world; the Acropolis and the Sanctuary of Apollo; and the nearby funerary inscriptions of the necropolis.

The focus of our interest is the fourth of these archaeological layers (Roman and Byzantine) and the paleo-Christian geographical sector and the necropolis. There the evidences of early Libyan Christianity have lain buried for centuries, now faintly exposed to view.

## THE IRONIC SYMBOL OF SILPHIUM

By the fifth century Cyrene had become a growing city of tens of thousands of people, with livestock and agricultural production. This production was concentrated in the culture of a now extinct plant called silphium. This was a medication that was in high demand as a purgative antiseptic and was thought to be an aphrodisiac. It was thought to stimulate race horses and was used as a spice for seafood. This herb was reputed to grow only in Cyrenaica.

Cyrene found that it had a world monopoly on this particular highly sought-after commodity. Silphium became the emblem of the city, stamped on its bronze and silver coins and featured on its royal crest. Cyrene became an international trading center based on their monopoly on this highly prized medicinal plant. This monopoly held fast through the centuries of the Greek dynasty, Ptolemaic dynasties and well into Roman antiquity. Its extinction remains a point of dispute among environmentalists and historians. At one time it was thought to be as valuable as silver. It soon was rendered extinct, probably due to its unpredictably high value. While it lasted, this was a highly favored commodity that needed prudent and efficient marketing.

But the irony is compounded: It has been argued that the international mercantile Jews who migrated to Cyrene played a part in the marketing of silphium, due to their international network of traders around the Mediterranean. Thus the irony of silphium is twofold: it was considered medicinal, but ultimately played a role in the economic crisis of the city that many captive Jews had been sent to. Providentially viewed, the distribution of silphium encouraged the formation of a type of Diaspora Judaism that was highly international in outlook, whose descendants would play a decisive role in taking the Christian gospel to Gentile Antioch, as we will see.

# 3

# THE CYRENE-
# JERUSALEM LINK

## EARLY CHRISTIANITY IN CYRENE

■■■

Irenaeus gives us our first documented testimony of Christians residing in Libya before A.D. 180. Watch carefully for the Libyan reference
embedded in this oft-quoted text from *Against Heresies*:

> The Church, though dispersed [throughout] the whole world, even to the
> ends of the earth, has received from the apostles and their disciples this
> faith: [She believes] in one God, the Father Almighty, Maker of heaven,
> and earth, and the sea, and all things that are in them; and in one Christ
> Jesus, the Son of God, who became incarnate for our salvation. . . . The
> Church, having received this preaching and this faith, although scattered
> throughout the whole world, yet, as if occupying but one house, carefully
> preserves it. She also believes these points [of doctrine] just as if she had
> but one soul, and one and the same heart, and she proclaims them, and
> teaches them, and hands them down, with perfect harmony, as if she pos-
> sessed only one mouth. For, although the languages of the world are dis-
> similar, yet the import of the tradition is one and the same. For the
> Churches which have been planted in Germany do not believe or hand
> down anything different, nor do those in Spain, nor those in Gaul, nor
> those in the East, nor those in Egypt, *nor those in Libya*, nor those which
> have been established in the central regions of the world. But as the sun,
> that creature of God, is one and the same throughout the whole world, so

also the preaching of the truth [shines] everywhere, and enlightens all . . .
that are willing to come to a knowledge of the truth. Nor will any one of
the rulers in the Churches, however highly gifted he may be in point of
eloquence, teach doctrines different from these (for no one is greater than
the Master); nor, on the other hand, will he who is deficient in power of
expression inflict injury on the tradition. For the faith being ever one and
the same, neither does one who is able at great length to discourse regarding it, make any addition to it, nor does one, who can say but little dimin-
ish it. (*Ag. Her.* 1.10.1-2, emphasis added)

Irenaeus in the same sentence is talking about where churches are
already *planted* and *established*. These two verbs make it clear that the
reference of the whole sentence is to places where churches are already
situated and in place. He is naming specific locations about which he
has some knowledge. Libya is among these places.

Irenaeus is clear: These Libyan Christians, however different culturally or linguistically, held to the same doctrines taught by the apostles themselves. That faith has, in Africa, been carefully preserved. No
Christian would be so arrogant as to "make any addition to it." Wherever it is taught, this faith penetrates cultures, changes them, but remains the same in its sacred apostolic texts: the four Gospels and letters
of Paul. No leader in Libyan Christianity, even as early as A.D. 180
would dare depart from the sacred texts or add to them or subtract from
them, as the Gnostics did. The Christians of Libya and Gaul belong to
a single family, "as if occupying but one house." The family believes as
one. The international community has "one soul." From Africa to Gaul
these teachings are in "perfect harmony."

How long before A.D. 180 did it take for a church in Africa to be
planted and established? After that, how long did it take for the word
to reach Irenaeus? When Irenaeus says its existence has been "carefully
preserved," we wonder for how long? A cautious estimate might be one
or two generations. If so, Irenaeus knew that *Libya had established
churches by about A.D. 150.* Where was this record "carefully preserved"?
Likely in Rome or Lyon. At the time of Irenaeus there existed documentation preserved in a safe place that references Christian communities in Libya some time before A.D. 180.

## EVIDENCE OF CHRISTIANS IN THE "CENTRAL REGIONS" OF AFRICA

Even more stunning is the next phrase. Immediately after referring to *"those in Libya,"* Irenaeus pointed also to those Christian communities "which have been *established in the central regions* of the world." What central regions of what continent?

Could the reference here be to apostolic believers somewhere in the interior of Africa? This seems likely when we note the geography and the literary sequence of lands. Since these "central regions" follow immediately after Libya, it is sensible to imagine that Irenaeus was referring to Christians living deeper in the continent of Africa.

The geographical sequence is entirely reasonable: Spain, Gaul, the East, Egypt and Libya—and then the "central regions." All of these are semicircular in order around the Great Sea, beginning with the most natural point for Irenaeus to start his circle: Spain. Immediately after Libya the circle comes to an end in his reference to the "central regions" in the plural.

Irenaeus is apparently pointing in a clockwise orderly sequence including Libya and then referring to somewhere else nearby and immediately after Libya. There is good reason to wonder if these "central regions" are in sub-Saharan Africa or the upper Nile, due to their placement in the order of nations known to Irenaeus. If he had been thinking of Proconsular Africa, it does not seem likely that he would have chosen the term "central regions," since Proconsularis is coastal. Hence it seems much more likely that Irenaeus was thinking of some lands south of Libya. This could be pointing toward Numidia, Nubia or Ethiopia. Or perhaps by sea to Somalia. Does this suggest further inquiry into the timing of the arrival of Christianity in the upper Nile? African writers will recall that the sources of the Nile stretch all the way to Kenya and the Congo, and wonder if the earliest dates for Christianity in central Africa need to be restudied.

Irenaeus was quite specific in knowing about ecumenical Christians in Libya in the second century A.D., who held to the same apostolic faith as those in Gaul, Antioch and Jerusalem. Note that these churches were assumed by Irenaeus to be not recent but *established* in A.D. 180.

On what sources would Irenaeus have depended in learning about these Christians living and witnessing in Libya? Likely from Alexandria. Recall that Irenaeus himself had come from the Asia Minor. He was writing his classic work, *Against Heresies*, from a far-off inland location: the Rhone Valley of southern Gaul—in Lyons. He was far removed from Africa. But he belonged to a world community.

It is obvious that Irenaeus was reading African sources of all kinds, especially those that had drifted away from or defied the apostolic consensus. He was quoting contemporary sources written on the African continent. His chief opponents were writing in Africa at that time. They were the Gnostics—those like Valentinus and Basilides. These Africans were the main reason he was writing *Against Heresies*.

Whether he was reading sources particularly from Libya is speculative, but it would be premature to rule that out. Recall also that he is not talking about Gnostic beliefs alone, but more crucially here describing orthodox, consensual ecumenical apostolic Christian teachings, and contrasting them with nonconsensual views. If the embryonic Sabellians and proto-Arians that would soon arise in the Pentapolis of Libya were already being talked about, it is likely that Irenaeus would have gotten wind of it.

## WAS IRENAEUS IN TOUCH WITH LIBYAN CHRISTIANS?

How did Irenaeus learn so much about early African Gnosticism? Clearly he was well informed. The Mediterranean constituted a fairly small world when traversed by sea. Libya was no more out of the reach than Spain for itinerant early Christian teachers like Paul, Justin Martyr and Irenaeus. It is conceivable that Irenaeus himself may have visited the African continent to gather information on Christian heresies.

The works of Irenaeus were known in Africa very soon after they were written. This is evident from their being quoted in Africa by the time of Tertullian (writing in the 190s). Getting from Smyrna or Lyons to Cyrene would have been no more difficult than getting from Smyrna to Lyons. Irenaeus was familiar with other writings from the continent of Africa, such as the *Letter of Barnabas* and the *Gospel of the Egyptians*. Since Irenaeus knew of apostolic Christian believers in Libya before

180, and since he was curious about heresies, it is possible that he may have been informed about the proto-Sabellian and proto-Arian debates in Libya.

Mediterranean trade and travel along Roman roads and sea lanes were well established during this period of the pax Romana, the peace under the umbrella of Roman supremacy. Pantaenus of Syracuse reportedly took the good news from Alexandria all the way to India before A.D. 200, according to Egyptian tradition. That could have meant the great subcontinent of present India or the Indus Valley or the Arabian peninsula, but it could also have referred to lands as far south as Somalia or Nubia.

Of all the nations of Africa, the ones most favored for trade were those with coastal cities from Carthage to Oea (Tripoli) to Alexandria. They had more opportunity for international exchange of goods, services and ideas. Libya had seven of these coastal cities: Tripoli, Sabratha, Leptis, Ptolemais/Barce, Benghazi, Teuchira/Taucheira and Apollonia. It had more Mediterranean ports than Egypt. That put Libya in touch with the rest of the world. Irenaeus's reference to orthodox Christians in second-century Libya was not mere speculation or hearsay. Since he was scrupulous with evidence, he must have had some substantiation for his choice to mention Libya as a place where Christian teaching was harmonious with apostolic teaching.

## A WELL-TRAVELED PATH

The record is well established: Both Jews and Christians traveled easily and frequently between Africa and Asia by both sea and land. Both Jewish and Christian histories have crossed back and forth between the Holy Land of salvation history and Africa. So did the Cyrenaeans reported in Acts.

Familiar New Testament names associated with Cyrene include Mark (according to African memory) and the remarkable mother of Mark (Mary), Simon of Cyrene, and probably others such as Simon the Black and Lebbaeus. A viable case can be made that Libyan Christianity dates back even before Irenaeus to first-century figures like

Lucius, Rufus and Alexander, and above all Mark.[1] The sons of Simon of Cyrene, Alexander and Rufus, were apparently known personally by Mark.

How quickly the gospel spread between Jerusalem and Cyrene to inland Numidia remains speculative, but reasonable inferences point to the mid-second century, and no later than the arrest of the believers of Scilli. Written records of Roman court procedures against Christians place African martyrs as far west as Scilli in Numidian Proconsularis and Madaura in inland Numidia (Eastern Algeria). These records go back to A.D. 180. But these communities of faith must have been vibrant for some time earlier than 180 to penetrate as far into the Medjerda Valley or the Numidian inland as they had by that time. This pushes the entrance of Christianity in Numidia back at least to the middle of the second century. It must have taken some time for the trajectory of Christian witness to move to such a remote inland location. If they were firmly planted in the interior of Numidia before 180, how did they get there?

Which alternative fits best? (1) The martyrs of Madaura and Scilli were African born. (2) They came from the East (Egypt or Libya). (3) They came from the north (Italy or Gaul). Among Western historians the opinion is uniformly either (2) or (3) but never (1). In my view (1) is most likely, due to their inland location.

If they were not African-born, then the topography may resolve the question: It is highly likely that Christianity had arrived at some port city such as those in Cyrenaica or Tripolitania or Carthage before they arrived in the interior highlands of Numidia. But how much earlier before 180? At least a generation, it seems, which would mean by about A.D. 150.

Just trace with your finger on a map the course of the Medjerda River upstream from Carthage west; it will then be evident that a potential trajectory of Christianity from Utica or Carthage to the earliest African martyrial place names like Madaura in Numidia is conceivable. These are along the same roads that Augustine would travel two

---

[1]See Thomas C. Oden, *The African Memory of Mark* (Downers Grove, Ill.: IVP Academic, 2011), chaps. 3–5.

centuries later, in the 370s. Madaura, where Augustine went to school before he studied in Carthage, may have had a memory of Christian martyrdom there over two hundred years before his time.

The most natural hypothesis is to suppose that the earliest Christians of Numidia would have sailed or traveled overland from Diaspora Jewish communities of Cyrenaica and Tripolitania in Libya to Proconsularis and Numidia. It is less plausible to suppose they must necessarily have come from Rome. It is even less likely that they would have leaped over all the port cities of Libya between Alexandria and Carthage. That would take time.

It would be implausible to argue that the martyrs of Scilli (location unknown but likely in Numidia or Proconsular Africa) would be unequivocally ready to die for the faith if they had only appeared in North Africa as late as A.D. 180. That is when they refused to yield their sacred Christian texts to profane authorities. It is likely that the texts they withheld were at least Paul's letters and Mark's Gospel, already translated into a rough form of rudimentary African Latin. The premise that Christianity could not have arrived in Libya before the third century requires some extreme rationalization. The greater likelihood is that it came decades earlier.

Was this Bible of the martyrs of Scilli in Latin or Greek? It could have been in Greek, but in the Medjerda Valley it was more likely cast in a rough African form of Latin vernacular perhaps predating or serving alongside the embryonic versions of the Vetus Latina. Codex Bobiensis preserves an early Latin version. We know from Tertullian that most of the Bible was translated into Latin by A.D. 220 (*Ag. Prax.* 5, *On Monog.* 11). That task was largely completed within about twenty years after the Scilli martyrs were tried and slain.

There is a simple inference that can be made from the toughness of this community of faith that produced martyrs who already had in hand a Latin Bible: *It must have taken time for the African predecessors of Scilli to produce both the Latin Bible and the community of faith willing to die for it.* The alternative is the imagination of a community falling from nowhere out of nothing.

The puzzle of the beginnings of Maghreb Christianity is: Where did this community come from? How long had it been there? In my view there is no compelling reason to rule out the presence of Christianity in the coastal cities of North Africa such as Carthage, Apollonia and Leptis as early as apostolic times, and in their surrounding neighborhoods by A.D. 100–150 or even earlier.

## EARLIEST LIBYAN CHRISTIANS

Most Western historians have taken for granted that Christianity must have been smuggled into the Roman Maghreb via either Alexandria or Carthage. Using Clement and Tertullian as evidence for Christianity in Africa by the 180s A.D., these historians looked skeptically on most contrary evidences prior to Diocletian.

Other alternatives are more plausible but seldom considered. The hypothetical evidences of a much earlier date are worth reviewing. They include the following:

- The Libyan speakers at Pentecost could have returned to the Libyan Pentapolis as early as the 30s A.D.

- The Cyrenians involved in the mission to Antioch could have returned to Cyrene by the 40s A.D.

- The Christians of Libya could have been native-born Libyans who, upon traveling to any of the ports of the Mediterranean, could have heard the good news and brought it back to Libya.

- If Mark preached in the Pentapolis before his death in Alexandria, with numerous converts and the appointment of an apostolic successor, then the arrival of Christianity in Libya could have been in the range of A.D. 40 to 68.

The speculation that Libyan Christianity almost certainly must have come from either Alexandria or Carthage may be too quick to foreclose against these simpler alternatives.

We are trying to establish a probable date for early Christianity in Libya. In my view the answer is unknown and unknowable, but the likelihood of its being in the 30s A.D. is higher than the usual date given of the 300s A.D.

## THE FLIGHT TO EGYPT AS PROTOTYPE OF PROVIDENTIAL REFUGE

The interface between Palestine and Egypt is prototypically symbolized in the Gospel narrative of the flight of the holy family to the Nile Valley—deep into the continent of Africa. As if by anticipation, the infant incarnate Lord thereby brings a foretelling of the gospel in the form of hope to all of Africa. From time immemorial Africa has been a customary place of refuge for all those troubled in Judea. So it was for the infant incarnate Son in flight. In African memory Jesus spent some of his earliest days in Africa in flight from Herod (Mt 2:13-18).

This story bears deep truth not just for Coptic Christians alone or black Africans alone or Byzantine Christians alone, or Nilotic Christianity alone, or Nubian or Ethiopian Christianity alone, but the whole body of Christ the world over. There are early pilgrimage sites with ancient archaeological remains up and down the Nile Valley. There are innumerable ancient churches, oratories and monuments built in the fourth, fifth, sixth and seventh centuries throughout the Nile Valley that celebrate the presence of the holy family in Africa. Why is this two-continent interface crucial to salvation history?

Those who visit today's Coptic Museum in Old Cairo will find the remains of a fort that dates to Roman times, built on the site of previous Egyptian and Persian fortifications. This site was in Egyptian history nicknamed "the battlefield" (Kheraha = Cairo) precisely where modern Cairo sits today. The same battlefield has been fought over since Persian times. It had decisive military significance. It is the point where the one great Nile turns into the many streams of the Delta. It became a key location for the protection of those in flight. That precise location has been a refuge for Jews and for Christians over many centuries. An ancient synagogue and the earliest churches in Cairo are located in the immediate area. The interpretation of 1 Peter 5:13 may be the exegetical key to seeing its importance for Peter and Mark.

The traditional memory of the Cyrenaic Christian story is filled with narratives of flight, including Mark's family from Cyrene to Jerusalem and Mark from Alexandria to Cyrene, then to Alexandria, then the forced flight back to Cyrene, then back to Alexandria. Add to this the hypothesis that Mark fled with Peter, after his miraculous escape from prison (Acts 12), to the safest place in Egypt at Old Cairo. This prompts two hypotheticals: Mark's birth in Libya and Mark's accompaniment of Peter were in some way related to Old Babylon in Cairo. For a preliminary exploration of these two hypotheses, see my book *The African Memory of Mark*.

## LIBYA EMBRACED WITHIN NEW TESTAMENT SALVATION HISTORY

Several Gospel narratives place Libya within the orbit of New Testament salvation history. Harking back to the Exodus, Africa has never been a secondary or insignificant partner in the history of salvation. This profound connection is indicated in five discrete New Testament narratives:

- The cross of Jesus is carried through Jerusalem by an African from Cyrene in Libya.

- The zealous generation of Lucius of Cyrene, John Mark of Cyrene and Rufus of Cyrene show that Christianity had clearly attested embryonic connections with the Libyan region of the African continent.

- The Pentecost event provides a telling recollection of Cyrenaic Christians in Jerusalem already right there among those touched by the Spirit at the birth of the church in Jerusalem.

- Immediately after Pentecost we have Luke's record of an activist cluster of Cyrenaic Christians in Jerusalem. Some of them soon were headed toward Antioch. All of these narratives are considered by early African Christians as a preparation for the gospel to come to Africa.

- According to African memory, Mark was born in Libya.

To draw these threads together into a single cord: *If* the cross of Jesus was dutifully taken up and borne by an African from Cyrenaica; if the Africans that appear in Luke's narratives in the Acts of the Apostles presuppose some kind of preconnections with the African continent; if there were known Africans present at Pentecost from Libya; and if Cyrenians took a leadership role in the first missionary activities in Antioch and Anatolia, *then* Libya is rightly viewed as within the orbit of salvation history narratives found in the New Testament. With all these vectors merging, it is fanciful to insist that Christianity did not reach Libya earlier than the third century. Yet this is a common assumption among many historians.

These five narratives are symbolic of this world-historical setting: the crossroads between two continents. They symbolized, then and now, that the Christian witness reaches out between people of different continents. This was established early in Jewish and Christian history flowing back and forth from the Near East to Africa and back. This stream has continued steadily through every generation of Africa since the incarnation, all the way to the living testimony of the remnant of believers of Libya today who have survived persecution in Libya. These celebrate their solidarity with the over 400 million believers (nearing a half billion) in the larger continent of Africa.

## LIBYAN APOSTOLIC CONTINUITY

Christianity in Libya bears the marks of apostolic continuity of every generation since Simon, Lucius and Mark in the first half of the first century. Since the times of Pentecost, Lucius, Mark, Apollos, and the Ethiopian eunuch, no century has lacked some form of baptism and Christian testimony in Africa. Someone already resident in the Nile Delta had to be there to teach the Scriptures to Apollos and interpret them as relating to John the Baptist and the Anointed Servant Messiah to whom Apollos pointed. These first-century African witnesses to the coming of the Anointed One have continued to flow without cessation in every subsequent period of African history.

Modern historians have puzzled over the question of where the largest populations of the earliest Christian believers appeared and were first concentrated. All agree that they were numerous in Syria and Anatolia. The other place where there was a major early concentration of believers, just as committed, just as large, and equally influential was Africa. Records of persecutions and memorials of martyrs before Constantine were especially large in Africa—from Egypt to Mauretania.[2]

---

[2]For a map of early church and martyrial locations, see Henry Chadwick and G. R. Evans, eds., *Atlas of the Christian Church* (London: Macmillan, 1987).

The key African cities were Alexandria and Carthage, but the next most crucial cities for Christian mission would be those of the Libyan Pentapolis and Tripolitania.

Theirs is a true story. It needs to be accurately rediscovered and modestly retold, not as a political ploy but as a story of inner certitude and faith commitment. Those who wish to rediscover this community do more than honor the dead. They bring light to a forgotten, still-living community of faith. They offer a ray of hope for the future of all believers in North Africa.

Anyone digging into the case of early Libyan Christianity may feel like a relentless detective coming across tiny bits of circumstantial evidence confirming a hunch. For centuries the vulnerable Libyans had no defense attorney to speak up for their longsuffering. They have long awaited some voice to attest the beauty, holiness and saintliness once found so vigorously among Christians all over the North of Africa. But that voice cannot have a Western accent. It must ultimately come out of the heart of Africa. Young Africans must step up. They will be best prepared to credibly speak on behalf of the virtually voiceless minority in Libya.

## THE EUROCENTRIC MISREADING

A small cadre of academics has worked actively to disvalue early African Christian orthodoxy. At their center have been the aggressive skeptics of the scholarly tradition following Adolf von Harnack and Walter Bauer. Their legitimacy is coming to an end. Some have made academic careers out of demeaning the continuity and integrity of classic consensual Christian teaching to which Africa contributed so decisively. Libya provides an occasion for reversal.

The cities on the coast of Africa have been treated as if they were merely extensions of Greco-Roman cultures. This disregards their multigenerational African indigeneity prior to Constantine. Thus their intrinsic Africaneity has been overlooked. Eurocentric misreadings of African Christianity have been consistent in underestimating the scale and importance of indigenous Christianity in these African cities, in part due to bias or silent bigotry.

The documentary evidence that Mark preached and died in Egypt (Eusebius, *CH* 2.16), for example, has not until recently been taken seriously by modern writers. More poignantly, many more of the earliest African Christians are unknown and unnamed. Many, many more were tortured, killed and had no voice. They are not known to us but they were there, likely in larger numbers that even Eusebius attests. These sources remain discounted by Eurocentric gatekeepers. European Enlightenment skepticism about Mark reaching Africa is closely connected with the myth of the dark inaccessibility of Africa. This myth does not adequately account for the entrepreneurial creativity of Diaspora Jews with their international networking or for the evidence of established coastal sea lanes.

More common is the "late arrival fantasy"—the persistent, narrow and Western-centered category mistake that African Christianity began only with modern Western colonialism. Equally familiar is the widely assumed premise in North Africa that Islam has more authentic claims to Africaneity than Christianity. This has the false but common premise that Islam arrived in Africa before Christianity and is more native to African soil than Christianity. The simple reason for this common mistake is that Christianity is viewed as a European product.

The equation of Christianity with imperialism misunderstands its deeper spiritual motivations and hence much of its actual history. It reduces the history of salvation to political and military causes. This view of causality, excluding intellectual, religious and liturgical factors, is a distinctly modern habit. The modern myth of the recent entry of African Christianity through colonialism as an extremely late arrival is an anomaly that cannot be found anywhere in the literature until the nineteenth century. What in modern historiography has caused such myopia? Western hubris. These hypermodern assumptions are untenable. Libya is a decisive test case for reversing these historical misinterpretations.

Oral traditions such as those regarding St. Mark have been largely dismissed by Western historians while they were nursing their own advocacy interests. "Modern chauvinism" is a generous way of speaking of this persistent neglect of relevant sources of the African oral tradition. A fuller inquiry into the history of paleo-Christianity in Libya, which has never yet been adequately investigated, is necessary for a new start in this arena.

The first step: to explore the paleo-Christian presence in the Jewish Quarter of Cyrene. Christian *presence* is a theological concept that arises out of the Christian mission and spirit, as seen in its ministries of witness and compassion. *Occupation* has political and military meanings not necessarily associated with the reality of Christian presence. My interest is not with political concerns. Rather it is with the remarkable fact of a continuing Christian presence in Libya from the first to the twenty-first centuries, despite all political obstacles. That is a fact recognizable only within the Christian narrative of God's revelation and its texts.

## THE EARLIEST CHRISTIAN PRESENCE IN CYRENE

There are strong connections between the messianic Jews of Cyrene and the early Christian community in Jerusalem. There is abundant evidence of this, drawn from diverse sources and quarters, but together they make a compelling constellation of evidence.

The evidence points toward widespread primitive *messianic Jewish and proto-Christian presence in Libya in the first century, first in Cyrene (with the Cyrenaic Jews known to be in Jerusalem early in the first century) and by the second century in Tripolitania and Leptis*. If so, it is possible to speak of seven centuries of Christian presence in Libya, understood as the first through the seventh. But it is more prudent to speak of clear documentation of the five hundred years between about 180 and 680, that is, between Irenaeus and the massive Arab victory.

The beginnings of Christian presence in Cyrene go back to the origins of Christianity itself in Jerusalem. The story of this Jewish-Cyrenaic-Jerusalem connectivity begins with a familiar figure in the Gospel narrative: Simon of Cyrene, first found in the Gospel of Mark. We meet him and other Cyrenaic Jews in Jerusalem. Soon these Cyrenians take us directly from Jerusalem to Antioch, Cyprus and Anatolia. These are Cyrenaic Jews who believe in the risen Jesus as Lord.

The first written transmitter of the Gospel was Mark, who by common memory in Africa was also from Cyrene in Libya. The John Mark of traditional African memory found his way to Jerusalem as a messianic Jew from Libya prior to the crucifixion of Jesus. Most in the modern West have not even heard of this narrative, which if they had been born in Coptic Africa they would know in detail.

From Jerusalem we meet Mark and other Cyrenaic believers repeatedly in the New Testament accounts in Antioch, Cyprus, Anatolia, Ephesus, Rome and in due time, according to African tradition, back again to Libya and finally to Alexandria. Note that it was only after Mark's return to Libya, where reportedly he performed many miracles and made many converts, that he is called by an angelic voice to go to Alexandria. There he establishes the church of Alexandria and faces martyrdom by dragging.

The primary evidence for a reexamination of Mark begins with a closer look at the relations among four texts: Mark 14, Acts 12:12, Romans 16:13 and 1 Peter 5:13 (a preliminary attempt has been made in *The African Memory of Mark*, chaps. 4–6). This correlation prompts further examination into the literary, material, archaeological and epigraphic evidences that confirm or challenge traditional views of Mark and the Jerusalem Cyrenaic Christians.

## ROBUST CONNECTIONS BETWEEN CYRENE AND JERUSALEM

Persons from Cyrene or associated with Cyrene appear often in the Gospel narratives, notably Mark. Luke's narrative in Acts recounts the presence of the Cyrenaic community in early Christianity as well. These Cyrenaic accents are heard in the most crucial of times: the institution of the Lord's Supper, the crucifixion, Pentecost, the commissioning of Paul and Barnabas to their first missionary journey, and Mark's subsequent ministry.

A prosperous Jewish trading community resided in Cyrene more than two hundred years before Christians arrived. Messianic Jews formed the core of the earliest Cyrenaic Christian community. The term *Cyrenaic* refers to the all territories of the Pentapolis in the vicinity of Cyrene in northeastern Libya.

This Jewish expatriate community on the continent of Africa was originally composed largely of Jewish war prisoners and displaced persons fleeing from war and persecution or by forced deportations. Before this the Jews of Cyrene were nimble seagoing commercial traders along with some local Jewish artisans and some brilliant scholars in Cyrene. The Jews had a history in North Africa long before the Diaspora of A.D. 70. Remains of pre-Christian Jewish communities of merchants and traders were found in Tipasa, Carthage, Djerna, Cyrene and Alexandria. By the time Christianity was first spreading to Libya (A.D. 30–330), there were known Jewish synagogues in many locations in North Africa. These include Tingis (Tangiers) and Volubilis in present-day Morocco, Sitifis, Cirta, Hippo Regius, Lambaesis in Algeria, Utica, Carthage and Hadrumentum in coastal Tunisia.

There were longstanding Libyan Jewish communitie settled in Oea, Leptis Magna, Berenike, Ptolemais, Cyrene and Apollonia.[3] Some were found far in the interior, where we have epigraphic evidence of Jewish burials. Before the destruction of the second temple, the faithful of these Jewish communities of Africa took part in the time-honored practice of returning to Jerusalem for great festivals of the Jewish year such as Passover and Pentecost. The Jews of Cyrene regularly sent pilgrims to Jerusalem for seasonal festivals.

Jews of Cyrene remained staunchly Jewish while living in Africa. Libyan Jews with trading interests had good reason to learn Greek, and many knew Hebrew, Aramaic and Latin. If Mark was interpreting Peter's message to a Roman audience, he must have known Aramaic, Greek and Latin. By New Testament times the Cyrenaic Jews had established a Diaspora-based Libyan congregation in Jerusalem, which we read about in Acts 6:9. Some of them became quite early drawn into the ministry of Jesus. Among them was the remarkable mother of John Mark. In time this congregation became divided between those who were offended by Jesus and those who were drawn to him in faith.

In the ensuing years after the life, death and resurrection of Jesus, many Christian communities would emerge out of the messianic be-

---

[3]Eli Barnavi, ed., *Historical Atlas of the Jewish People* (London: Hutchinson, 1992).

lievers already planted in those Jewish communities in Cyrene and in Diaspora synagogues scattered around remote towns of Cyrenaica. Most were in commercial trades, some far-flung and seaworthy and worldly wise, with close connections in Cyprus, Alexandria, Caesarea Palestina and Antioch. All of these were places where the earliest Christians would emerge alongside these Greek-speaking messianic Jews. They were among the core of those who were intentionally spawning faith in Jesus Christ to Gentile hearers wherever they went. They were proclaiming this good news, proclaiming it first to their Jewish colleagues but also in time to Gentiles.

The transition of Christianity from a Jewish sect to a Gentile and Jewish Christian movement transcending Judaism owes a great deal to messianic believers from Cyrene. We don't know exactly how and in what time frame it happened, but this transition to Greek was made easier by messianic believers from Cyrene. The evidence lies embedded in the text of Acts.

## SIMON OF CYRENE

It is not an irrelevant feature of the Gospel narrative that it was a foreigner, an African, who was forced into service by the Roman soldiers on the way to the crucifixion. They needed someone to carry the cross. In order not to offend a volatile crowd, they chose a foreigner. Jesus had taught that those who are forced to go one mile should be ready to go two (Mt 5:41). By this means the vanquished could take the initiative away from their captors and turn evil intent into good effect. Simon embodied the second-mile teaching intuitively.

The soldiers had the right under Roman law to order subjugated and colonized people to carry heavy loads as evidence of their compliance. Simon of Cyrene was present in the crowd through which Jesus went on the way to the crucifixion (Mt 27:32; Mk 15:21; Lk 23:26). He was required to assist Jesus in bearing the cross. Simon's cross-bearing came to signify substitutionary sacrifice. Early Christian writers saw Simon as a *type*, picture or model through which the meaning of revelation was illustrated historically.

The early Christian exegetes such as Clement, Origen, Tertullian and Didymus looked for the spiritual meaning of the texts, having established its plain or historic sense. They found profound meaning in the narrative of Simon of Cyrene. They were intrigued by the biblical prototypes embedded in the narrative.

Ephrem the Syrian grasped the irony that the *first cross-bearer*, following Jesus, was an outsider from North Africa, that he was stopped in his tracks on his way as a bystander, that he was a Diaspora Jew who had come back from far away on a pilgrimage at a feast day in Jerusalem (*Commentary on Tatian's Diatessaron* 20.20). Similarly, Leo the Great noted that *the wood of the cross was borne by an outcast*, just as Jesus was crucified "outside the city gate" as an outsider (Leo I, *Sermon* 59 [46].5;[4] Heb 13:12). The Old Testament prefiguring of this was Isaac, who was required by Abraham on God's command to carry the wood which would be lit for he himself to be sacrificed on the holy mountain (Gen 22:1-24).

But why was an African chosen? Was this wood involuntarily placed upon the back of Simon of Cyrene because he was defenseless and a member of the underclass? Despite it being a forced requirement, "It was only right that that they should have *given the wood of the cross voluntarily to the Gentiles*," since the leaders of the Jews had clearly "rejected the coming of him who was bringing all blessings. In rejecting it themselves, in their jealousy, they threw [these blessings] away to the Gentiles" (Ephrem, *Commentary on Tatian's Diatessaron* 20.20).[5] Simon took it up voluntarily, though he had been at first compelled.

Cyril of Alexandria remembered that Isaiah had prophesied that "the government will be on his shoulders" (Is 9:6 NIV). Thus the cross was being borne by two persons on the day of the crucifixion: Jesus, who was truly God and truly human, and Simon of Cyrene, a wayfarer from Africa. It is not inconsistent that the three accounts of Matthew, Mark and Luke complement each other (Cyril of Alexandria, Fragment 306, *MKGK* 262-63, emphasis added): "*Jesus bore the cross part way, and Simon took up his cross and followed him the rest of the way.* For

---

[4]The sermons of Leo I (the Great) are numbered differently in various critical editions. The number preceding the brackets is the sermon number found in CCSL and the common English translation of NPNF. The number within brackets is the sermon number found in SC.

[5]Quoted in Arthur A. Just Jr., ed., *Luke*, ACCS NT 3 (Downers Grove, Ill.: InterVarsity Press, 2003), p. 357.

the Savior carried the cross, and having met the Cyrene about half way, they transferred the cross to him." This embodies the teaching already anticipated in Jesus' teaching of sacrificial service, which would be ultimately expressed as cross-bearing. "Now *the cross has become the means by which he governs*" (Cyril of Alexandria, Fragment 306, *MKGK* 262-63, emphasis added). Since his kingdom is not of this world, he governs through transcendent and spiritual means. Origen reflected on the two bearers of the cross: "It was *fitting not only for the Savior to take up his cross but also for us to carry it*, doing compulsory service" as an expression of a fitting response to grace (Origen, *Comm. on Matt.* 126, emphasis added).

Faith would come to the Gentiles, to whom the cross of Christ was not to be shame but glory. It was not accidental therefore but symbolic and mystical that while the Jewish rulers were raging against Christ, *a foreigner was found to share his sufferings* when "he was unable to walk" (*Gospel of Nicodemus* 10.1, emphasis added).

This event took place after "they went out of the Praetorium" (Chrysostom, *Homily on the Paralytic* 3) on the way to Golgotha, when *the burden was shifted from Jesus to Simon.*

> It was not a Hebrew or an Israelite but a foreigner who was drawn into service for the Savior in his most holy humiliation. By this transference the propitiation of the spotless Lamb and the fulfillment of all mysteries passed from the circumcision to the uncircumcision (Heb. 13:12), . . . with the cessation of the old symbolic victims, a new victim was being placed on a new altar. The cross of Christ was to become the altar not of the temple but of the whole world. (Leo I, Sermon 59[46].5)

"Simon of Cyrene therefore was carrying the instrument of this great triumph in his arms. He was *a partaker of the Passion* of Christ, so that he might be a partaker of his resurrection" (Chromatius, *Tractate on Matthew* 19.5, emphasis added).

None of these are throwaway remarks. They are studied reflections of leading exegetes on Simon of Cyrene. All of those quoted were significantly shaped by the African school in Alexandria, with its focus on the confluence of types of biblical images.

## OTHER CYRENAIC JEWS IN THE NEW TESTAMENT

A rough headcount shows that there was a long list of Cyrenians involved in the New Testament narratives. The connection between Cyrenaic believers and the Gospel story goes back to:

1. Simon of Cyrene, known by all who heard the crucifixion story.

2. Less remembered are two of Simon's sons, Alexander and Rufus, involved in the Jerusalem Christian community in the first century (Mk 15:21; cf. Rom 16:13). Since their father is explicitly known to be from Cyrene, it is a fair inference that they too were from Cyrene or had family connections in Cyrene, and that their Cyrenaic family was known personally by John Mark, author of the earliest Gospel.

3. Then there is an important leader in early Christianity called *Lebbaeus*, whom Matthew names as the tenth of the twelve apostles. Lebbaeus (Greek *Lebbaios*), whose surname was Thaddaeus (Mt 10:3),[6] who may have been the same person as Jude or "Judas son of James," (NIV, or "James's relative Judas," Weymouth; or "Judas the brother of James," KJV). This individual is mentioned in both the apostolic lists of Luke 6:16 and Acts 1:13. Early African tradition holds that he was numbered among the seventy disciples. The name itself may refer to a Libyan origin or familial connection (from Leba or Libu, ancient name for Libya). According to early African tradition, Lebbaeus was sent to preach the gospel in Libya and became the first bishop of the Pentapolis under the apostolic direction of Mark himself. Although the documentary evidence for the origins of the Libyan apostolic succession have been destroyed, the later memory connects first-century Cyrenaic believers with Mark himself.

And there are more:

4. Jews from Cyrene were unmistakably present among the Pentecost believers, as reported in Acts 2:10: On the day of Pentecost we hear of people coming to Jerusalem from various "parts of Libya belonging to Cyrene." This designation likely embraced a general area around

---

[6]The ms evidence for "Thaddaeus who was called Lebbaeus" versus "Lebbaeus who was called Thaddaeus," or simply "Thaddaeus" or "Lebbaios," is discussed in Bruce M. Metzger, *A Textual Commentary on the Greek New Testament* (New York: United Bible Societies, 1971), p. 26.

the city. What language did they speak at Pentecost? The language of their homeland was Libyo-Punic. It was likely their heart language that was being understood when the Spirit descended as with tongues of fire upon the earliest church. Since Luke's narrative was in Greek, and since Greek was already noted or assumed among the languages active at Pentecost, it would have been redundant if it were Greek, in listing speakers of *other* languages at Pentecost.

These Cyrenaic Jews were given a worldwide mission at Pentecost. That mission certainly included Libya. More so, the worldwide mission of the church through the Spirit was in no small part initiated by the Cyrenaic voices among the circle of disciples.

Readers of the New Testament will recall that the Punic-Phoenician people of Tyre and Sidon had willingly come to hear Jesus and beheld his healing miracles (as reported by Lk 6:17) in the times of his earthly ministry. So now they were coming in the times of apostolic witness to his risen lordship.

5. Jews from Cyrene were present at the stoning of Stephen (Acts 6:9).

6. Then there is Lucius of Cyrene, who is first mentioned in the New Testament in company with Barnabas, Simeon called Niger (Latin *niger* = the Black), as well as Manaen and Saul. They are prophets and teachers of the earliest church at Antioch (Acts 13:1).

7. By the time of the writing of Paul's letter to Rome, there were a number of believers living in Rome. Paul announced his travel plan to them—"to go to Spain and visit you [the Roman Christians] on the way" (Rom 15:28 NIV). One of them was named Rufus. Whether this is the Rufus, son of Simon of Cyrene, mentioned by Mark and Luke is conjectural, but need not be ruled out, and all the clues point in this direction.

8. More explicitly, in his letter to Rome, Paul affectionately greeted "Rufus, chosen in the Lord." He also spoke personally and warmly of the mother of Rufus, "who has been a mother to me, too" (Rom 16:13 NIV). Why would Paul speak of the mother of Rufus of Cyrene as if she were a mother to him? The personal warmth of this greeting suggests some very close relationship that may have prevailed be-

tween Paul and the Cyrenaic circle of messianic Jewish families in Jerusalem before the crucifixion. This makes it tempting to imagine that Mark's mother and Rufus's mother and Paul could have been joined together by deep ties of either friendship or family.

## NORTH AFRICAN MESSIANIC JEWS LED THE WAY TO THE UTTERMOST PARTS OF THE EARTH

Since distant Spain was already on Paul's itinerary, there is no reason to think it impossible that Paul or Mark or Lebbaeus or Barnabas might have also had in mind the even less distant coast of Africa for evangelization. Libya was as accessible by sea as Spain. Christians were already residing in Rome before Paul and Mark arrived in Rome in the mid-60s A.D. There is no compelling reason to rule out the hypothesis that Christians were arriving in the port cities of Libya—closer than Rome to Jerusalem—near the same time or shortly after, which could be anytime between A.D. 45 and 65.

The first disciples were taught by Jesus that they were called to take the good news to the uttermost parts of the earth—his last words to his disciples before his ascension. They would know when to begin when they received the Holy Spirit. "You will receive power when the Holy Spirit comes on you; and you will be my witnesses in Jerusalem, and in all Judea and Samaria, and to the ends of the earth" (Acts 1:8 NIV). The launching of this mission was almost immediately after the empowerment of the Spirit at Pentecost, where Libyans were known to be present.

The question remains: Why so many Libyans? We have already met more than a half dozen key figures from Cyrene explicitly identified by name in Mark and Luke-Acts, and more by indirect inference. If Simon of Cyrene is identical with Simeon the Black, as many have argued, then it is evident that believers from Africa were involved in the very founding of the Christian community. More surprising is the unexamined datum that the Africans in most of these earliest cases were from Libya:

1. An African was present on the road to the *crucifixion*.

2. Africans were present in the Cyrenaic synagogue in *Jerusalem*.

3. Africans were present in the first missionary journey north toward *Antioch* predating Paul—to Samaria and Antioch.

4. An African—the eunuch from the court of Candace baptized by Philip—was present in the first missionary journey south toward *Ethiopia.*

5. Africans were present in the debates leading to the major decision about *circumcision* for Gentile believers.

6. Africans were present in the growth of the first *international* church in Antioch.

7. Africans were present in the preparation and *ordination of Paul* to be an apostle.

8. Africans were present *in Rome before the arrival of either Peter or Paul.*

All these were from Libya, excepting the eunuch. Each has left textual evidences in the sacred texts. It is likely that Simon of Cyrene and his two sons and wife, and Lucius of Cyrene, and probably Mark of Cyrene and his uncle Barnabas were all important players in this story. More particularly many came from Libya's chief intellectual center—Cyrene—perhaps the least likely place for God to awaken the beginning of a worldwide mission.

Why were so many Libyans involved so early at such crucial points of transition? Evidently, to many African believers, this was an indication of God's providential design. The alternative hypothesis is implausible, that it was purely an accident that these people from these remote places were planted at the right time and in the right place to engage in a once in a lifetime mission.

# 4

# THE CYRENAIC CORE
# OF EARLY CHRISTIAN
# LEADERSHIP

■■■

Jews from Cyrene were active disputants in controversy with the martyr-to-be Stephen. He had a Greek name, but that was not unusual in Cyrenaica. "Stephen, full of grace and power, did great wonders and signs among the people. Then some of those who belonged to the synagogue of the Freedmen (as it was called), Cyrenians, Alexandrians, and others of those from Cilicia and Asia, stood up and argued with Stephen" (Acts 6:8-9).

Remember that Paul of Tarsus was himself from Cilicia. Whether he was one of those who "stood up and argued with Stephen" is impossible to determine, but he clearly was present at Stephen's martyrdom. This episode shows that regardless of whether or not they became disciples of Jesus, Cyrenaic Jews in Jerusalem were keenly attentive to the earliest missionary developments of embryonic Christianity. They questioned Stephen, but "could not stand up against his wisdom or the Spirit by whom he spoke" (Acts 6:10 NIV 1984).

Before Stephen's martyrdom, a controversy was already underway among the Cyrenaic Jews in Jerusalem. They were actively engaged in the debate about who Jesus was and what his death and attested resurrection might mean to all Jews everywhere. This debate surely must have occurred within a few months after the resurrection.

The African Jews of Jerusalem were not docile or passively waiting for high priestly signals. They were zealous activists. Some of them "stirred up the people as well as the elders and the scribes" (Acts 6:12 ). Some of them agitated both the lay population and the temple leadership. Some were so perturbed with early Christian preaching that they had Stephen arrested, brought him before the Sanhedrin, and presented false witnesses against him (Acts 6:12-13). Their charge: "For we have heard him say that this Jesus of Nazareth will destroy this place and will change the customs that Moses handed on to us" (Acts 6:14). This implied that Stephen was embarrassing some Cyrenaic Jews of Jerusalem so much that they brought deadly charges.

## THE RELEVANCE OF THE AFRICAN MISSION TO CURRENT AFRICAN CHRISTIANITY

Does this imply that Stephen himself was a Cyrenian Jew? Many evidences point in this direction. If so, consider the implications for early African Christianity. Consider its consequences for Africa's role in the earliest Christian mission.

If so, the first Christian martyr was from Libya even before Mark! Before James and Peter as well. The blood of martyrdom would later become the seed of the church. That maxim was first written by another African—Tertullian—who himself may have been born in Leptis Magna in Libya.

Did a primitive readiness for martyrdom in Christian witness arise in Africa, the continent that suffered the most during the Severan persecution of A.D. 202–203? Africa was the scene of the worst excesses of the Valerian persecution that beheaded Cyprian in Carthage in A.D. 257, and the Diocletian persecution of A.D. 303–305 that beheaded Peter of Alexandria.

If the first Christian martyr to follow the martyrdom of Jesus was himself an African, what does that mean to the African church of the first century and today? Why has such a decisive question been ignored? In any case, the narrative of the first Christian martyr indicates that messianic Jewish Cyrenians from Africa had something decisively at stake in the controversy that followed Jesus' death. If Stephen was

Cyrenian, the first world missionary outreach to Samaria and Antioch was immediately incited by the commitment unto death of an African believer whose roots were in Libya.

Did Africans receive Christianity from Europeans? No. Did Europeans first receive the good news from African voices? Probably, yes. If this could be explored in fuller scope it could be important to the self-respect of African Christian believers today who have been taught that Christianity is European in origin.[1]

This prompts further inquiry into the evidence for Stephen's identity, and whether his last plea to the outraged crowd may provide a major clue to the dynamics and motivation of the mission of the Greek-speaking messianic Jews who would go to Antioch, some of them certainly from Libya (notably Lucius of Cyrene and Simeon called Niger [Acts 13:1]). Was their relation with Stephen as a fellow African?

## A CLOSER LOOK AT THE CYRENAIC SYNAGOGUE IN JERUSALEM

The Jews of Cyrene had their own independent synagogue in Jerusalem (Acts 6:9; cf. Mt 27:32; Acts 2:10). They appear to have been closely allied with other Diaspora Jews from Alexandria, as well as those from Cyprus, Cilicia and Asia. This gives reason to wonder if Saul of Tarsus himself may have been one of these Cilician Jews angry about Stephen and committed to utterly destroying Christian witnesses. This picture fits his description prior to his vision on the Damascus Road. Does this imply that Saul of Tarsus and Stephen may have known each other, possibly from their participation in the same "synagogue of the Freedmen (as it was called)" (Acts 6:9). The synagogue had argumentative and zealously committed voices, not unlike that of Saul of Tarsus (Acts 6:10).

It is also curious that most of the coworkers with Stephen have Greek names, such as Philip, Prochorus, Nicanor, Timon and Parmenas—not unusual for Diaspora Jews living in Cyrene over many generations.

---

[1]An excellent start has been made in this direction by Kwame Bediako, *Theology and Identity: The Impact of Culture upon Christian Thought in the Second Century and in Modern Africa* (Oxford: Regnum, 1992).

These "Hellenists" or Greek-speakers (Acts 6:5-9) included Cyrenian Jews and proto-Christian believers. All had connections with the Diaspora. One of those named was a proselyte from Antioch. It is probable that some of these Cyrenaic believers returned from Jerusalem to Libya to spread the new faith. This is a conjecture, but not unlikely.

Messianic Jews of Cyrene before Simon and Stephen believed that God was preparing the nations for his soon-to-be-coming kingdom. Jesus proclaimed the coming reign of God and showed himself as the definitive sign of its coming. Some find it hard to believe that even before the conversion of Paul, there were Christian believers in Jerusalem actively engaged in Christian mission activity, as we see from the narratives of Stephen (Acts 11:19-20; 13:1).

There were clearly two types of Christian witnesses from the Cyrenaic synagogue of Jerusalem: those who spoke to "no one but Jews," and those who "began to speak to the Greeks." Some of the latter were from Africa. Parents of African children do well to encourage their children to memorize Acts 11:20: "But among them were some men of Cyprus and Cyrene who, on coming to Antioch, spoke to the Hellenists also, proclaiming the Lord Jesus."

Why is this sufficiently important for African children to memorize? Because it makes it clear that the first Christians in Antioch included Africans, and they were the ones who first communicated with the Gentiles or Hellenists. This is a decisive moment in the history of Christianity, and foundational for the history of early Libyan Christianity. Here the Christian mission turns irreversibly toward the Gentile world. The outcome was extraordinarily blessed: "the Lord's hand was with them and a great number of people believed" (Acts 11:21 NIV 1984). Ponder the consequences: men of Cyrene (from Africa) were intimately involved in the earliest spread of Christianity beyond Jerusalem.

Given this fact it is ironic that the academic guild has so long ignored virtually any thought of evidence of any form of African Christian presence before the martyrs of Scilli (A.D. 180). This is before Peter was delivered from prison. Note the chronology: before Peter found his way to Antioch, these men from Cyprus and Cyrene, doubtless including Barnabas, were scattered by the persecution of Stephen. They "trav-

eled as far as Phoenicia, Cyprus and Antioch" (Acts 11:19). Although
the text does not yet name Mark, he will be named in the next chapter
(Acts 12:25). Hence there is good reason to ask whether Mark was with
Barnabas in Antioch before Peter was imprisoned in Jerusalem. It seems
so in the light of the text that makes clear that *Mark was brought back to
Jerusalem by Barnabas and Saul.* "Brought back" from where? Likely
Antioch. This prompts the thought that the intertwining of many future sympathies between the Alexandrian and Antiochene patriarchates may have long roots in Mark himself.

## AFRICANS LEAD THE WAY TO APPLYING THE
## GREAT COMMISSION TO NON-JEWS

This provides stunning evidence for the premise that Cyrenians were
among the first to act assertively on the belief that the lordship of Christ
called for the worldwide fulfillment of the Great Commission to non-
Jews. They were clearly among the earliest disciples involved in an extended Christian mission beyond Palestine.

Acts 11:20-21 has profound ramifications for early African Christianity. They were already proclaiming the gospel to the uncircumcised.
Not only observant Jews but also non-Jews who had ears to hear the
gospel were now brought into the fold. The text shows how the Christian mission moved from Jerusalem to Cyprus, Cyrene and Antioch
through African leadership. In these cities there was a convergence of
Diaspora interests. When Greek-speaking Jews from Cyprus and
Cyrene began to proclaim the gospel to non-Jews of Antioch, a major
watershed had occurred. The salient difference was that in the early
phases no one was hearing the gospel *except Jews.* But it was these
Christians of Cyprus and Cyrene who "spoke to the Hellenists also."

Why is this of significance for global Christianity then and now? It
shows that Jewish messianic believers from Cyrene in Africa, who already had a cosmopolitan, international and mercantile background,
were among the first to grasp and implement the relevance of the ministry of Jesus of Nazareth for all humanity. They grasped lucidly that
the gospel was addressed not to Jews alone but to those speaking Greek
and other languages heard at Pentecost. They already had international

experience with the Gentile thought world. They quickly comprehended their special vocation.

This soon became such standard apostolic doctrine after Antioch that it is hard for us today to see that within its context it was a daring and courageous move prompted by the Spirit and enacted by Africans along with other believers from Cyprus and Cilicia. Cyrenian Christians appear to be the first believers to keep the Joppa vision of Peter alive. They embodied it in practice. In this way African Christians made a decisive difference in the remaining history of the church. Thus what Acts 10 promises, Acts 11 fulfills. This crucial transition was initiated by Libyans, along with Cyprians. This Cyrenaic contribution has hardly been noticed in the vast literature of Eurocentric historical inquiry.

Here is the crucial sequence: We learn from the meeting of Peter with Cornelius in the previous chapter, Acts 10, that Gentiles were to be the recipients of the gospel as well as the Jews. Acts 11 shows how Peter's vision was carried out—by Greek-speaking Diaspora Jews from Cyrene, from Africa, specifically from Libya—even today still the most ignored arena of early Christianity. Acts 10 promises that through the vision of Peter with Cornelius, Gentiles would receive the Holy Spirit. But the first record of Jewish Christians taking concrete steps to go to Gentile lands with the gospel beyond Jerusalem and Samaria, and as far away as Antioch, was carried out by believers from Cyrene, Cyprus and Cilicia. Among these believers surely there were women and families, such as the families of Mark and Simon and the relatives of Barnabas.

It was out of the circle of early Cyrenaic Christians and those associated with them that Barnabas and Saul were ordained to special service to the vast Gentile world to the north. These Cyrenians would be soon found in Antioch, praying and fasting, when "the Holy Spirit said, 'Set apart for me Barnabas and Saul for the work to which I have called them'" (Acts 13:2), in which they were accompanied by Mark. Was Paul ordained or commissioned by a community of believers that included Africans? Likely so, if Mark or Simon or Lucius were among those in the Antioch church praying and fasting.

## THE AFRICAN MEMORY OF MARK

My present purpose is to show evidence for the Cyrenaic core of leadership that launched the international mission of Christianity. This core had at its center a young leader named John Mark. As early as the narratives of Mark 14 and Acts 6 and 12, this young man appears to be at the center of the Jerusalem-Antioch pivot, under the guidance of Peter. These texts are fully explored in a previous book of mine, *The African Memory of Mark*.

Mark, who had begun his ministry with Peter and the Twelve in his own home in Jerusalem, and who was soon engaged with Paul and Barnabas in their first missionary journey. The closeness of Mark's relation with the circle of both Peter and Paul establishes him as one of the most trusted persons in the highest apostolic circles.

What was Mark doing in Antioch? Antioch was the first major leap along the way to the proclamation of the gospel to the whole world. Recall that Peter has already had this vision of the coming reign of God for all people, for the Gentiles, for pagans who have ears to hear. Mark was there in Antioch with Paul praying and fasting to begin this mission. The disciples at Antioch were making a momentous decision: to obey the command of Jesus and the prompting of the Spirit to go to the whole world.

But note who else is present in Antioch: the Cyrene-Cyprus leadership core has resurfaced. Mark is found again in the crucible of decision making in Antioch, along with "the prophets and teachers" there. Their names are there revealed: "Barnabas, Simeon who was called Niger, Lucius of Cyrene, Manaen a member of the court of Herod the ruler, and Saul" (Acts 13:1). Again, the Cyrenaic Levitic rabbinic family of Mark shows up in the leadership of this group, with Barnabas, Mark's cousin or uncle, and another Christian teacher from Cyrene, Lucius, and another unknown leader who may have been African, Simeon called Niger, along with the great Saul of Tarsus.

The evidence of Mark as present in the earliest Christian mission to the north from Jerusalem to Antioch is that Mark was embedded among the other Cyrenians referred to in Acts 12:25 where it is reported that "Barnabas and Saul returned to Jerusalem and brought back with them John, whose other name was Mark." They had already been engaged in their mission to the north. As they were completing it, Mark was "brought back with them." The evidence that Mark had accompanied them is found explicitly in the text that Mark was "brought back with them." How could he be brought back with them unless he had been accompanying them?

The time frame of this return of Mark to Jerusalem was the public speech of Herod to the people of Tyre and Sidon. This passage on Mark's return to Jerusalem is wedged in between the episode in Tyre and Sidon and the event of Saul's and Barnabas's being set apart for work in Cyprus and beyond, accompanied by John Mark.

What gave these Cyrenaic messianic Jews readiness and special competencies to undertake the international mission required by Pentecost along with Paul? Mark is consistently remembered in New Testament texts as well as in proto-Coptic sources as an internationally traveled figure. He shows up in Jerusalem, Antioch, Cyprus, Ephesus and Rome, so why not also the world's most cosmopolitan city, Alexandria? With these traveling proficiencies, it is likely that he spoke Aramaic, Greek and Latin. If the author of the Gospel of Mark was able to translate and write for Peter and accompany Barnabas and Paul into various Greco-Roman cultures and communicate with multilingual audiences in Cyprus, Pamphilia, Colossae and Rome, it is reasonable to conclude that he must have been proficient in several languages.

The premise that Mark knew some Latin is supported by the presence of many Latinisms within the Gospel and his role in serving as Peter's interpreter in Rome (as reported by Papias). Mark was likely translating Peter's Aramaic into Greek and Latin, depending on the audience. We infer from Mark's idioms that the Jews of Rome probably knew some Greek, but they needed Mark's help on turns of phrases and place names that they might not understand. Mark inserts these explanations in his Gospel. This suggests his multilingual competence.

Mark's writing style shows that he had a no-nonsense, practical, cosmopolitan Jewish education, but with a special gift: he was especially adept in international communication. This would not have been uncommon for a leading rabbinic family of prosperous Cyrene. The son of an observant Diaspora Jewish family, Mark would have been thoroughly familiar with the Greek version of the Old Testament (the Septuagint) and probably some Hebrew. Those who imagine that Cyrenaic Jews would have had trouble with Greek may not have considered the pre-Christian ethos of Cyrene as the intellectual center of the Pentapolis, where Greek had been the official language since the seventh century B.C.

If he and his mother lived intermittently in Jerusalem, it is likely that Mark would have also known basic Aramaic. However it happened, it seems clear that Mark became proficient not only in Aramaic but also in a low or popular form of Greek and probably Latin—these were the chief international languages of his time. Mark wrote his Gospel in the straightforward form of the popular Koine Greek, which was commonly employed all around the Mediterranean as the everyday language of international commerce. Mark had no aspiration to produce a high literary work of pretentious scholarly quality. His purpose was to write a plain account in a forceful manner for ordinary seekers and believers. It is marked by simple directness, vivid scenes and rich depth of feeling, without relying on literary artifice.

If Mark was in Rome when Peter was there, interpreting for him, as attested by Papias, then he presumably would have been using both Latin and Greek. It was this young man, Mark, who was sufficiently proficient in languages that he could interpret Peter's Aramaic to a Roman audience.

Mark likely wrote the Gospel in Greek in Rome for the whole Greco-Roman Gentile world. The cream of intellectual leadership of that world was already gathered together in the greatest cosmopolitan city of those times: Alexandria in Africa. That is where Mark ultimately would be headed. It is consistent with this international identity that Mark had two names, as seen in Acts 12:12, 25; 15:37: John, a Hebrew name, and Mark, a Latin name.

## THE MISSION OF MARK WITH BARNABAS AND PAUL

The youthful Mark from Africa made his way effortlessly into all the continents of the known world: Asia, Europe and Africa. He was chosen to assist in the starting of the Christian mission in the Asian continent (symbolized by Antioch), and then later traveled to the heart of Europe (symbolized by Rome). The next stop logically would be (according to the African narrative) Alexandria. To tell the story of Libyan Christianity is first of all to tell the story of John Mark of Cyrene, a son of Libya. I will be tracing his trajectory.

Mark was chosen to start the Christian mission in Asia (Antioch) in the company of the Paul and Mark's relative—Barnabas (Acts 13:5). Following the Spirit's direction, they embarked from Seleucia, the seaport of Antioch, and sailed to Cyprus (c. A.D. 47–48), the home of Barnabas. With Paul, Libyan believers were the earliest Christian missionaries to extend the mission to a place where they had familial and religious contacts. They set about proclaiming the good news to Jewish synagogues at Salamis and all over the east coast of Cyprus.

Crossing the island of Cyprus, they arrived at Paphos on the west coast. There the sorcerer Elymas sought to resist their witness to proconsul Sergius Paulus. Paul then caused Elymas to be struck with temporary blindness. Astounded by what had happened, the proconsul became a believer (Acts 13:4-12). From Paphos, Mark sailed with the first missionaries to Perga in Pamphylia in Asia Minor, where Mark, after a dispute, left them and returned to Jerusalem (Acts 13:13), a departure that left some hard feelings. When Paul wanted Barnabas to join him for a second missionary journey, and when Barnabas thought Mark should come along, Paul resisted, viewing Mark as one who had "deserted them in Pamphylia and had not accompanied them in the work" (Acts 15:38). This was serious enough to cause Paul and Barnabas temporarily to separate. Barnabas then took Mark with him again to Cyprus, and Paul went back with Silas to Syria and Cilicia (Acts 15:39-40).

At a later date, Mark rejoined Paul in Rome, where he assisted him in the upbuilding of its church. When Paul sent his greetings to the Colossians, he commended Mark: "Aristarchus my fellow prisoner greets you, as does Mark the cousin of Barnabas, concerning whom you have received instructions—if he comes to you, welcome him" (Col 4:10).

Suppose the African version is reliable: that a talented young believer from Libya had close associations with both Peter and Paul in the formation of the church of Rome. Suppose the event of the first Christian Pentecost occurred in his mother's own house in Jerusalem. Suppose the first Christian mission was inaugurated with the help of Cyrenian Jews in Jerusalem. If so, the Libyan messianic Jewish community who believed in Jesus was present from day one in the history of the church: in its founding sacramental institution, in its reception of the Holy Spirit at Pentecost and in the shifting of the attention of the church to the wide world of non-Jews.

If so, there could be little doubt that the Libyans were deeply engaged in the earliest layers of first-century Christian leadership. If so, it becomes a moot question as to when Christianity arrived in Libya, since it was present in the core circle of apostles from Pentecost. Even if only one of those several hypotheses were demonstrable, then the Libyan presence in early Christianity could not be easily dismissed. Yet it has been left unnoticed by mainstream Euro-American scholarship.

The most viable of these hypotheses is that Cyrenaic African Jews of Jerusalem were indeed the core of the first missionary journey that would eventually lead to Rome itself, and then back to Africa. My task is to present both confirmatory and circumstantial evidence of this conclusion.

## THE INTERWEAVING RELATION OF MARK WITH BOTH PETER AND PAUL

However they may have quarreled in Pamphilia, ultimately Mark became highly trusted by Paul. Paul spent his last days in a jail in Rome where he wrote the second letter to Timothy. There Paul was still hoping for a visit with Mark in the ensuing winter. Writing to Timothy, Paul said, "Get Mark and bring him with you; for he is very useful in serving me" (2 Tim 4:11 RSV). Paul is writing from a Roman jail. He knows his end is coming soon. His life is already being poured out in his final sacrifice.

Why does Paul want Mark at his side? Paul appears to be preparing for his departure. He is readying his final testimony. It is a time when

Paul asks that Timothy should bring his manuscripts. What manuscripts? Did they include Mark's version of the Gospel as Peter's teaching? It should not be ruled out.

Paul yearned to go to Neapolis for winter. He wrote to Timothy: "Bring Mark along. I have need of him." Something about Mark proved to be uniquely important to Paul at the end of his long and eventful journey. Ironically, at the beginning of Paul's mission he had sent Mark away. Now Paul was asking for him. If they were together in Rome, their visit would be cut short by Paul's martyrdom. Paul had found Mark useful. Now he was planning the next steps ahead for the next mission of the Spirit for Mark.

Was that next step to Alexandria? It is likely that both Peter and Paul would have agreed in principle that someone should take the gospel to Africa. It is unthinkable that this obvious challenge would be ignored by either Peter or Paul. Who would take this message to Africa? Who better than Mark? It had best be one who came out of Africa and knew its idiosyncrasies. Mark was the obvious one to do it.

This prompts further reflection on the identity of another neglected leader in early Libyan Christianity, namely, Lucius of Cyrene.

## MAJOR CYRENAIC VOICES IN THE EARLIEST CHRISTIAN MISSION TO GENTILES

Lucius of Cyrene was one of those who provided leadership for establishing the church in Antioch (Acts 13:1). Lucius was one of those "men of Cyrene" reported earlier in Acts who first took the gospel beyond Jerusalem to Antioch:

> Now those who were scattered because of the persecution that took place over Stephen traveled as far as Phoenicia, Cyprus, and Antioch, and they spoke the word to *no one except Jews*. But *among them were some men of Cyprus and Cyrene* [among them Barnabas and Mark] *who, on coming to Antioch, spoke to the Hellenists also, proclaiming the Lord Jesus.* (Acts 11:19-20, emphasis added)

The text of Acts suggests that the earliest Cyrenian Christian believers were the first to preach Jesus as Lord to the Greeks. Lucius was one of those described as either a prophet or teacher, along with Barnabas and Simon the Black. These were the chosen vessels—chosen by the Spirit—who were called to lay hands upon Barnabas and Saul for the first missionary journey of Christians beyond Antioch.

Mark was right there in this vortex of leadership. Ponder this as if with African eyes: Mark, Lucius of Cyrene and Simon the Black were all together in Antioch, praying and fasting and participating in the Spirit's mission to send chosen vessels for the first missionary journey. Note that this African core of missionaries *preceded Paul* in gospel witness. In fact they ordained Paul (Acts 13:3).

Lucius of Cyrene may have been one of the congregation to whom Peter preached on the day of Pentecost (Acts 2:10). Though the text does not reveal it, by tradition in the Orthodox Synaxarium, Lucius of Cyrene is remembered as the first bishop of Cyrene following Mark.[2] If so, this would have placed a Christian bishop in Cyrene in the first century. If not, they would not be long delayed.

Another tradition reports that one named Lucius was in early times the leader of the church of Cenchreae, where Paul and Phoebe ministered. Phoebe was the deaconess who delivered Paul's letter to the Christians of Rome. It remains disputed as to whether this Lucius is the same Lucius as the kinsman of Paul who was greeted in Romans 16:21 by Paul, where Paul's relative Lucius was with him sending greetings to Rome joined by his other relatives Jason and Sosipater. Whatever the specific identity of Lucius, it is clear from every reference to him that Lucius of Cyrene was a notable and respected leader of the church at Antioch as reported by Luke (Acts 13:1).

If order of reporting represents seniority, as usually presumed, then the order of the Antioch leadership was clearly stated in Acts 13:1: "Barnabas, Simeon called Niger, Lucius of Cyrene, Manaen (who had been brought up with Herod the tetrarch)" (NIV 1984). Then note whose name appears at the bottom of the list: Saul. Barnabas had gone to Tarsus to seek out Paul for this service. Paul took on leadership only after being commissioned by Barnabas and Lucius.

---

[2]*SEC*, p. 295; Michael J. Walsh, *A New Dictionary of Saints: East and West* (Collegeville, Minn.: Liturgical Press, 2007), p. 372.

If there were Jews of Cyrene at Pentecost and others who carried the gospel to Antioch (Acts 11:20), why wouldn't it be also expected that some of the Cyrenians would plan to bring the gospel back to their own home country of Libya in North Africa, where convinced messianic Jews were already active?

Note how many Cyrenaic Jews appear in the New Testament—minimally at least a dozen. But maximally there easily could have been many more first generation Cyrenaic Christian families involved in the ministries in Jerusalem and Antioch.

By inference these could also have included John Mark and the mother of Mark and her brother Barnabas, and perhaps also Stephen. But with more certainty than these there was Lucius of Cyrene. From this comes the feasible inference that remains spurned by conventional scholarship: "We may assume that some of the Cyrenian pilgrims took the gospel back to Cyrene, for the Christian Church was established there at an early date."[3] In my view there is little doubt that post-Pentecostal Christianity came to Cyrenaic Africa at a very early date and soon spread among both Jews and Gentiles throughout Cyrenaica and Tripolitania.

Coptic historians hold that Mark returned from the mission in Italy back home to Cyrene, where he converted many Jews and Greeks, and subsequently went to Alexandria where he preached and founded Christian communities. Coptic tradition holds that upon his last return to Cyrene, Mark appointed Lucius of Cyrene as the first ordained leader of Cyrene. The annals of Patriarch Eutychius preserved in Arabic relate that the bishops of Alexandria, from St. Mark to Demetrius, his eleventh successor (d. 231), were assisted by ordained elders in administering their churches. If so, there was a steady succession of Pentapolis bishops, including Lucius. After Lucius of Cyrene, however, there is an absence of reports of bishops in that region before the first half of the third century, probably due to lost or destroyed records.

## THE CYRENAIC OSSUARIES IN JERUSALEM

Archaeological evidence confirms some aspects of the literary reports

---

[3]*ISBE* 1:845.

of Cyrenaic Jews in Jerusalem. Hebrew University archaeologist Eleazar Sukenik in 1941 discovered a rock tomb in the Kidron valley in southeastern Jerusalem. Sukenik would later famously acquire the first Dead Sea Scrolls for the state of Israel. The pottery of the Kidron tomb carbon dated to the first century A.D. In these ruins they found a first-century ossuary, which is a stone funeral casket or bone box of one named Alexander, son of Simon. This was found along with eleven other ossuaries. After remaining for some time in the burial cave, the dried bones would be placed into an ossuary. This tomb belonged to a Cyrenaic family living in Jerusalem. Some were killed or exiled in the Roman destruction of Jerusalem in A.D. 70.

Some of the fifteen inscriptions on the ossuaries were of names particularly common in Cyrenaica, so the tomb may have belonged to a Jewish family that came from Cyrene. The inscription on one says: "Alexandros (son of) Simon." On the back is another more revealing inscription containing the *Alexandros* in Greek, and then an atypical word (QRNYT or quranut or cyrenut) which investigators think must have referred to the Hebrew for "Cyrenian" (QRNYH). While there is no way to demonstrate conclusively that this particular Simon was the same person mentioned in the Bible, it appears quite possible: "When we consider how uncommon the name Alexander was, and note that the ossuary inscription lists him in the same relationship to Simon as the New Testament does and recall that the burial cave contains the remains of people from Cyrenaica, the chance that the Simon on the ossuary refers to the Simon of Cyrene mentioned in the Gospels seems very likely." Pieter Willem van der Horst writes, "if indeed they were Cyrene, there is at least a good chance that we have here the ossuary of [Alexander] the son of the man who carried Jesus' cross."[4] In Mark 15:21, Alexander and Rufus were reported by Mark as sons of Simon of Cyrene. Paul greeted Rufus in his letter to the Romans (Rom 16:13).

Even more intriguing is the inquiry into Simon the Black or "Simeon called Niger," who accompanied Lucius of Cyrene to Antioch.

---

[4]Pieter Willem van der Horst, *Ancient Jewish Epitaphs* (Kampen, Netherlands: Kok Pharos, 1991), pp. 140-41.

## SIMON OF CYRENE AND "SIMEON CALLED NIGER"

Over many years scholars have debated whether Simon of Cyrene and Simeon called Niger (= Neesher) of Acts 13:1 might be one and the same person. There is a convergence of data that suggest an affirmative answer. It is based on the confluence of eight facts or probabilities:

1. The names Simeon and Simon are varied spellings of the same name.

2. It is Mark alone of the four Gospel writers who earliest provides this unique and personal information about Simon of Cyrene: He was the father of Alexander and Rufus (Mk 15:21). Other Synoptic writers may have learned from Mark that Simon was from Cyrene.

3. If other arguments from Coptic historians should prove correct that Mark was from Cyrene, and Simon came from Cyrene, that would make more plausible that Mark alone of the three Synoptic writers knew Simon and his sons personally. The hypothesis is that Mark and Simon had ethnic and cultural affinities with the same Diaspora Jerusalem synagogue referred to in Acts 6:9—at that time messianic and activist.

4. It is an anomaly that "Simeon called Niger" had a Jewish name. *Niger* is Latin for "black." This would fit the ethnic profile of a Jew known within the circle of disciples to be from Africa, and perhaps (though not necessarily) having darker skin. Whether he was the same person as the cross-bearer remains debated. We do not know, but what is clear is that Simon of Cyrene has a Jewish name, also spelled Simeon, and that he was a foreigner traveling to Jerusalem at feast time. In any event we must posit some reason why this Simeon was called Niger.

5. It has been overlooked that there is a mountain in Libya named Niger in the Garama region.

6. Remember that Jews had resided in Cyrene for three hundred years. The skin pigment of Berber Jews is unspecific, but could range from light to dark.

7. We know that Simon of Cyrene was a visitor to Jerusalem, remembered in a personal fashion by Mark and perhaps by Paul. We know

that Simon called the Black was first mentioned as being among the "men of Cyrene" (Acts 11:19-20) who first undertook the mission to Greek speakers in Antioch and Cyprus. Saul of Tarsus himself had cultural affinities with these "prophets and teachers." Some common link bound together Saul and the Cyrenians.

8. Simon the Black was a leader in a church founded by Cyrenians.

These vectors point in the same direction: Simon of Cyrene was likely called Simon the Black.

## THE MOTHER OF RUFUS

Finally the most astonishing component of all these bits of evidence has only been mentioned in passing: Paul knew very personally a Rufus as well as "the mother of Rufus." So intimate was this relation that the great Paul said she had been "a mother to me also" (Rom 16:13).

Thus there is no compelling reason to rule out the possibility that this Rufus could be the son of Simon of Cyrene, likely himself an African by birth. Rufus's mother then would have been the wife of Simon of Cyrene, who bore Jesus' cross as reported by Mark, who by African tradition was himself from Cyrene and probably knew the family of Simon.

What was the time frame in which Paul knew the mother of Rufus as a mother to himself? It was not in Rome, since Paul had not yet been to Rome. It is likely that this warm relationship occurred while both were in Antioch, where he had gone from persecutor to convert to apostle. Was it Simon's family and the circle of Cyrenians at Antioch that took Paul in and nurtured him along at some point? The circle included Simon the Black (likely Simon of Cyrene), his wife and Rufus, and a major leader of the Cyrenaic group, Lucius. Was Paul nurtured to vocational maturity in Antioch by the very one who had been startled to be unexpectedly required to carry the Lord's cross? A speculative hypothesis, but not impossible.

David Kosobucki has drawn together this circumstantial evidence in a consistent gestalt:

So now we can begin to connect the dots into a possible history:

Simon of Cyrene became a believer in Jesus Christ and his sons were well-known in the early church. He later travelled to Antioch and helped get the church there started. His wife and sons were with him. In Antioch he received the nickname *Niger*, "the black guy" for being a dark-skinned Jew. . . . He was later joined in Antioch by Paul (then Saul of Tarsus) and, later yet, John Mark, who both got to know and love him, his wife and sons. Years later, after Simon's/Niger's death, his wife and son Rufus were living in Rome. They were prominent in the church there in part because of the unique role Simon played in the Gospel story. Writing to a Roman audience, Mark mentions Rufus and Alexander, because he and the Roman church knew them personally. Paul, writing to the Romans, greets Rufus and his mom for the same reason.[5]

## THE STRENGTH OF PARALLEL INFERENCES

Though these are inferences that go beyond a strict evidentiary criterion, they are plausibly inferred from the conjoint pattern of a series of texts. This is what the early exegetes called *analogia fidei*, reasoning from uncertain texts toward clear texts, as viewed in a cohesive matrix of related texts.

In Mark 15:21 "we read of one Simon a Cyrenian who was compelled to carry the Cross of Jesus on the road to Calvary; and he is described as the *father of Alexander and Rufus*." William Barclay explains:

> Now if a man is identified by the names of his sons, it means that, although he himself may not be personally known to the community to whom the story is being told, his sons are. To what Church, then, did Mark write his gospel? He wrote it to the Church of Rome, and he knew that it would know who Alexander and Rufus were. Almost certainly here we find Rufus again, the son of the Simon who carried the Cross of Jesus.[6]

The point: the conventional majority who think of paleo-Christianity in Libya as coming along quite late in the third or fourth

---

[5]David Kosobucki, "Simon of Cyrene and Simeon Called Niger," *Palmer St. Parentheses ()*, October 28, 2008, <http://dckoso.wordpress.com/2008/10/28/simon-of-cyrene-and-simeon-called-niger>.

[6]William Barclay, *The Letter to the Romans*, rev. ed. (Philadelphia: Westminster Press, 1975), p. 215.

century, and those who think of Libya as having virtually no Christian history until Synesius, must consider these tests if a fair judgment is to be made.

Did Africa receive the gospel from Europeans? No. Did Europeans receive the gospel from Africans? Likely. Did Europeans receive the gospel from Libyans? Likely. Then did African intellectual history influence European intellectual history? I think so, and the earliest layers of evidence are found in the confluence of New Testament texts pertaining to the transition of Christianity from Jerusalem to Antioch and beyond to Rome. The embryonic clues are all there in Simon the Black, who carried the cross, provided core leadership for the church to Antioch and possibly for Paul himself, and whose family went on to Rome prior to Paul's arrival there.

# 5

# LIBYAN VOICES IN
# CHRISTIAN HISTORY
# BEFORE NICAEA

■■■

In addition to those New Testament figures mentioned previously in the writings of Mark, Luke (Gospel and Acts), Paul and other apostles, there are several pivotal figures in early Christianity whose names intertwine with Libya. The Christian leaders we have yet to discuss are found in sources following the New Testament. There were many Libyan voices in Christianity before the Council of Nicaea in A.D. 325.

Now the spotlight turns to the generations that followed the Cyrenians of the New Testament. We are here making a pivotal transition from first-century Libyan Christianity to those who shaped Christianity in Libya after the apostles had all passed away. My purpose is to set forth the signs of the intellectual vitality in the early Libyan Christian tradition.

## KEY PLAYERS

The key players in this drama are all vigorous and robust characters: Pope Victor the African, the theologian Tertullian, the archheretics Sabellius and Arius, the early Libyan saints such as Wasilla (Basilides) and Theodore, and the poet-philosopher-Bishop Synesius—all unique characters. One was a surprise individual personality from Libya who became pope of Rome. Only one of these is well known in Christian history: Tertullian. Two archheretics from Libya turned out to have had tremendous leverage on the formation of the early ecumenical consensus, even if by challenging it.

The names of most of the martyrs and confessors of Libyan Christianity have been lost. Once remembered, they are now forgotten. The records are buried or unnoticed. But we have good reason to think that there must have been many more than extant records show.[1]

The last Libyan Christian of high significance was a poet and diplomat who was elected bishop of Cyrene: Synesius. His philosophical reputation survives as a Neoplatonic thinker, but his Christian identity has been largely ignored. He will be treated in chapter six as a post-Nicene figure. All of these witnesses will be woven into the narrative ahead.

The identities of many of these figures are still debated by Western scholars, especially as to their precise place of origin. In cases where there is ample reason to place them in Libya, I will set forth the evidence, and for the plausibility of their Libyan identity. These claims have been made more credible by recent ethnicity studies, sociological analysis, funereal epigraphy and archaeology.

It is hard for modern people to imagine the startling power exerted by Libyans in the last decade of the second century—the 190s A.D. It is counter-intuitive to think of a Libyan pope, or a Libyan emperor of Rome or a major Christian theologian from Libya. Yet all this happened in the single decade of the 190s. All influenced the future of Christianity.

All these Libyan vectors came together in the last quarter of the second and the first quarter of the third centuries (A.D. 175–225). During this time the pope of Rome was an African, and the emperor, Septimius Severus, founded an imperial Roman dynasty that would extend from A.D. 193 to 235. Also during this time Quintus Septimius Florens Tertullianus was the leading theologian of the Latin world. All three had family connections within a single city, Leptis Magna in Libya. While they flourished, Leptis flowered into the most magnificent and monumental city of the world.

Leptis Magna was the richest city on the Mediterranean, gleam-

---

[1]W. H. C. Frend, *Martyrdom and Persecution in the Early Church* (London: Blackwell, 1965).

ing with power by the sea. The Septimius family were the Saudis of the Roman Empire at the time of its greatest prestige. Into this family was born Tertullian around 155–160, who became a brilliant lawyer and rhetor before becoming the first Christian theologian to write in Latin. He was the son of the military elite. His education was unexcelled—probably first in Leptis Magna, then in Rome, and finally in the practice of law, rhetoric and teaching in the leading city of Roman North Africa—Carthage.

Tertullian

## POPE VICTOR THE AFRICAN

The pontificate of Pope Victor I began in A.D. 189 and lasted until 198, a time of crucial changes in the relation of the Greek East and the Roman West. It is likely that both Victor and Severus came from Leptis Magna in Libya and studied or served for significant times in or around Rome—Victor for the church, Severus for military service.

Few Westerners have ever heard of Victor I. Only those who diligently pore over the history of calendars and ancient hagiography (the history of saints) would ever have heard of him, and even then little is known of him by the experts. Few historians have made anything much out of the stunning fact that there was a time when the whole Western Latin church was led by an African pope.

Victor I was born of an elite African Roman family, gens Gaius, and is generally acknowledged by secular historians as of African birth and descent. Christian tradition remembers him as bishop of Libya. Victor's period of leadership of the Latin Church overlapped with that remarkable time when the whole Greco-Roman world was ruled by an African emperor, Septimius Severus, born in the same city of Tripolitania in Libya—the still magnificent monumental city of Leptis Magna—the great city (magna) on the port and watercourse (Leptis) of the natural harbor of Leptis.

Victor and Severus exercised great influence at the same time. Did they know each other? Given the small size and interwoven family politics of Leptis, it is hardly likely that they would not know each other. Leptis had more wealth and power than population. It had vast international prestige with a remote and relatively small crosscultural populace. Leptis was not such a huge city that its most conspicuous Christian leader would have been unaware of its most famous international citizen. Being of two prominent families of Roman descent and of the military elite, they could hardly be imagined to be unmindful of each other. The likelihood of their knowing each other quite well is increased by the coincidence that both of these striking leaders were also living in the capital city of Rome during the apex of their public careers and arena of influence. Two elephants in one closet is hard to imagine, but even harder if they did not notice each other.

After the conflicted reign of Commodus as the emperor of Rome came the relatively peaceful reign of the emperor Septimius Severus (193–211). At the time of his accession an African pope had been already sitting on the Chair of Peter for four years. According to some accounts Pope Victor had been the former bishop of Leptis Magna. Whether this was seen as a coincidence or providential act, it proved significant in the history of Christian persecution. The fact that Victor became pope four years before Severus became emperor makes it harder to argue that Severus may have advantaged Victor than that Victor may have advantaged Severus.

The indicators that point to Libya as Victor's native country require putting together a number of inferences, but they are based on reasonable evidence. Taken together these clues become something between plausible and compelling. The leading indicators include the following.

Victor is best known for his role in the crisis of the dating of Easter—in particular, insisting that it should always fall on the Sunday following 14 Nisan rather than on 14 Nisan itself, as it was observed in the East. That fact places him more plausibly on the Latin side of the East-West divide. This corresponds to the fact that Leptis was on the Latin side of the East-West divide in Libya. Hence there may have been geopolitical or personal reasons for a conjunction of interests between Victor's ecclesial leadership and the Severan political leadership.

Victor knew and used both Latin and Greek, but favored Latin. After his elevation, he led the worshiping community in the Latin language. Since Libya is the only North African country that has both Latin and Greek traditions streaming together, it is more likely that his place of origin was west of the Gulf of Sirte, but not as far west as Byzacena. This would locate him most likely in Tripolitania, and even more specifically in its crown city of Leptis Magna, where the Latin language was linked with imperial influence. Sabratha or Tripoli would have been less likely, since they were not as much favored by Rome. Libya was at this time a part of Roman Africa, not a province of Egypt. This makes it more likely that Victor came from the Latin-speaking form of Christianity, hence from some location west of Egypt, but not so far west as to lose the capacity for Greek. Greek was not a major working language of commerce or daily political administration in Proconsularis or Byzacena.

The timing of Victor's reign is closely correlated with the ascension to power of military leadership coming from Leptis Magna. This could be accidental, but more likely has an explanation in personal and political affinities. By process of elimination, all these indicators point to Leptis Magna more than either Carthage or Cyrene or Alexandria. Several corroborating reasons correlate with these.

Victor's chief interest and apparent vocation was in resolving longstanding differences, especially those that were scandalous to the unity of the whole international Christian movement, the *oikoumenē*, the catholicity of the church. This required diving into the most neuralgic of these differences: chiefly those between the Latin and Greek traditions. Both he knew well. His unusual election as bishop of Rome was likely due to his ability to navigate in both. The dating of Easter had long been a chief concern. As a Latin and Greek speaking African, he favored the use of Latin in the Eucharist, where the unity of the body of Christ was refracted in the unity of the political order in Rome.

His decade of leadership was a pivotal time of change. Until Victor's papacy, the church in Rome had been celebrating the Eucharist chiefly in Greek. Victor officially changed the language of the Roman mass to Latin, playing a decisive role in introducing the worshiping community in the West to the Latin language. Latin was the normative language of Christian Scripture and worship in the part of the African Church Victor came from. In Africa the Greek Septuagint Scriptures and New Testament were first translated into Latin. The rising influence of the Latin language in the history of the church dates significantly to Victor. The continuity of Latin Eucharist has lasted through most of the subsequent centuries of the Latin tradition. Victor's active advocacy of Latin had vast consequences for unity of the Western church and for the history of liturgy. Pope Victor pried open the way for the Latin language to be used normatively in the West.

Another more subtle evidence of his Africaneity is a matter of temperament and character. It has to do with the decisive tone of African leadership patterns. Military models of supervision prevailed in Roman Africa, and nowhere more than Leptis. It required a great deal of confidence to confront these longstanding cultural and linguistic differences. The Greek language symbolized an intrusion and a political nuisance when seen within the Latin-speaking congregations of the West.

From what sort of cultural ethos did the robust confidence of the three African leaders (Victor, Septimius Severus and Tertullian) arise? It may be that Latinized Africans of elite Roman families living in tough Berber territories developed a high level of determination, ambition, brain power and self-confidence. All of these behavioral tendencies are sharply expressed in the character of these three: Victor, Septimius Severus and Tertullian. They are remarkably similar—outspoken and self-assured. All were decisive, confident, blunt and at times brusk. They were not shy about either their African roots or their Latin language. This is what makes the coincidence so intriguing. Western Christian history and liturgical practice have never been the same since their time.

In addition, there are a number of hints that Victor must have had a personal relation with some members of the family or court of both Commodus and Septimius Severus. The question naturally arises as to whether Victor might have relied on personal or familial support from the influential gens Septimius of Leptis Magna. The evidences of relative tranquility may suggest that he himself was successful in building a relation of confidence with the new emperor from Leptis Magna. The period of Victor's leadership was one of unusual peace between the Roman emperor and the bishop of Rome.

For these reasons it seems reasonable to refer to his birthplace guardedly as specifically unknown, but more likely Libya than elsewhere, and among Libyan cities, more probably Leptis Magna than any other. Thus Pope Victor of Africa becomes a major figure in the story we are trying to tell of early African Christianity, especially with respect to its most neglected region of Libya.

The canon of Scripture that appeared in the Muratorian Fragment was written in the years just before or during Victor's pontificate. This was among the first synoptic indications of the books of Scripture approved in the Western church for public reading in worship services. These books had probably been read in public for some time before Victor, but until then they were not defined by a canonical list that presumed to be catholic in nature.

According to Jerome, Victor was the first major Christian author to write in Latin. He was an older contemporary of Tertullian, who is often credited with being the first Latin writer to produce a major corpus of theological writings. It is ironic that the first African pope sewed the seeds of unity to the West by permitting and later requiring Latin to be used in the liturgy.

The documentary basis of the judgment that Victor was African hinges on the ancient official record of *Catalogus Liberianus* (A.D. 352–366), later *Liber Pontificalis*, which reports that Victor was a native of Africa, the son of Felix. He thus has the distinction of being the first African pope. Though his precise date of birth is unknown, we do know the approximate time of his leadership of the Roman Church. He succeeded Pope Eleuterus in A.D. 189.

Eusebius's chronology puts the beginning of Victor's episcopate in the tenth year of the Emperor Commodus (A.D. 189). Eusebius does not state directly the duration of his episcopate, but says that Victor was succeeded by Zephyrinus about the ninth year of Severus (about A.D.

200). This would mean that his papacy lasted about ten or eleven years through the changes of two dynasties (*CH* 6.21). Most conclude that Victor held office from 189 to about 198 A.D.

Jerome, in his Latin translation of Eusebius's *Chronicon* (and in *De viris illustribus* 34), assigns Victor ten years. "Victor, thirteenth bishop of the Roman city, the writer of certain opuscula on the paschal question and others, ruled the Church ten years under Severus"). In the Armenian version of the *Chronicon* it appears as twelve years.

During this time we see the footprints of Tertullian in Rome, while Pantaenus, Clement and Origen were all stirring in Alexandria. These are the leading Christian thinkers of the Severan period. They are all characterized by immense creativity and energy. If my intuition is right that Tertullian was born in Leptis Magna, he would have been born shortly after the birth of Victor I and Septimius Severus, all in the same city, at the apex of its creativity. It is not accidental that Tertullian heads the list of the most influential earliest African Christian teachers.

The core of African Christian intellectual leadership was formed by A.D. 180–220. Born about the middle of the second century, Tertullian would have been a younger contemporary of Victor, Severus and Pantaenus, and likely an elder contemporary of Clement and the younger Origen. These were all intellectually vigorous leaders of the emerging continent of Africa. The Christian teachers would lead in the developments of doctrinal, moral and exegetical theology in a way that shaped all subsequent Christian teaching. Their work would constitute the seedbed of European and Western Christianity, first planted in Africa and only later transmitted to Europe.

## CHRISTIANS IN THE IMPERIAL COURT OF COMMODUS

These decades of optimal influence followed the severe persecutions of the early 180s (Scilli, Lyons, Alexandria). Victor's episcopacy marked a more favorable relation between the church and imperial power. During this time there were Christians who were serving in the imperial court, according to Irenaeus (*Ag. Her.* 4.30.1). Commodus was co-emperor with his father Marcus Aurelius from A.D. 177 to 180, and sole emperor from 180 to 192. He is known to have employed a Christian believer named Prosenes, whose gravestone epitaph has been preserved (De Rossi, *Inscriptiones christianae urbis Romae*, 1:9, no. 5).

These were the unusual years of an African bishop of Rome and an African emperor of Rome. During this same time we see the rapid rise of the young rhetor and legal scholar Tertullian to intellectual leadership of lay believers in Carthage.

Now enter two women who played an admirable role in encouraging this era of peace. Both were prominent woman of the imperial court: Marcia, companion or wife of Emperor Commodus, and Julia Domna, wife of Emperor Septimius Severus. Both stories are complicated, but despite the grisly intrigues in their family and palace life, there remains compelling evidence that they had warm connections with Christian leaders and teachers who had privileged entré into the palace life. Both of their stories interweave with the history of early Libyan Christianity, as we will see.

The career of Emperor Commodus was stained with blood, narcissistic fantasies, greed and corruption.[2] Commodus at first continued the persecution of Christians under the decree "Sacrifices should be made to the gods and to the statue of the emperor Commodus." Many Christians proved ready to face the trial and offer up their lives in good conscience. Apparently through the efforts of his companion (concubine or mistress) Marcia, Commodus was drawn toward a more conciliatory view of Christians, contrary to his predecessors. It appears that there were many Christian advocates at the court of Commodus. Marcia was in active communication with Victor, bishop of Rome. This began a brief but welcome interval of reprieve and comparative immunity from overt persecution. This may point to the bridge-building outlook of the African pope Victor in Rome among Roman Christians. Marcia had a cordial attitude toward some Christian believers who were present in the Roman court and palace network.

According to the testimony of Hippolytus (*Philosophumena* 9.12) Marcia had been instructed by a Christian presbyter named Hyacinthus. In order to be a teacher welcome in the imperial court, he must

---

[2]Dio, *RH*, bk. 73 (LCL 177); Herodian, *HE*, 1.16-17 (LCL 454).

have been well learned both in the art of diplomacy and in the Christian ethic of service to the needy, especially those in prison. Under his tutelage, mercy for prisoners became Marcia's special cause of conscience. Whether she affiliated herself overtly with the Christian faith remains debatable. But she surely was an activist on behalf of the imprisoned and suffering Christian leaders who had been exiled to the mines. Christian believers regarded Marcia as "one who loves God" (*philotheos*; *Philosophumena* 9.7). This could have implied either a seeker or someone inwardly drawn toward the righteous life who was willing to give Christians a voice and who was seeking life with God. Imprisoned Christian confessors, including some bishops and priests, had long been languishing as prisoners in the mines of Sardinia. They found an effective advocate in Marcia. Through her efforts Christian prisoners were released from captivity.

Marcia summoned Pope Victor to the imperial palace in Rome. She asked for a list of the Roman Christians who had been condemned to forced labor in Sardinia. The pope delivered the list. Marcia obtained the pardon from the emperor. Marcia then sent the presbyter Hyacinthus to Sardinia with an order of release for the Christian confessors. Among this group of prisoners was a confessor who later would become Pope Callixtus (Callistus, Callistos).

Victor served as pope during this most opportune and favorable time. This occurred in the closing years of the reign of Commodus (180–192) and the early years of Septimius Severus. Eusebius wrote that "during the reign of Commodus, our affairs took an easier turn, and, thanks to the divine grace, peace embraced the churches throughout the whole world" (*CH* 5.21). Until the reign of Septimius Severus (193–211), persecution was local and sporadic. Victor's leadership is marked by a merciful lull in the intense persecutions that had been flaring intermittently in the decade after 180, following the horrible executions that occurred in Africa at Scilli and Madaura.

This calm was a fact, but it is accompanied by a speculative conjecture: Could that lull have been due to a friendship or family connection between Victor and Septimius Severus? Though this simple hypothesis has never been rigorously investigated, it remains intriguing and plausible. It should not be taken off the list of possibilities. This unexpected quiet period may have been the outcome of an unfreezing of the relation between Roman emperor and Roman pope. Victor and Septimius may have come not only from the same city, but from leading families of the same city. This seems like grist for a fantasy "historical novel" more than as history, but the indicators make it plausible. Start with the notion that two families from elite circles in Leptis had boys who were acquainted and whose acquaintance was renewed in Rome. One was from a family of military genius, and the other from a family who had believed the good news of Christianity. They both knew how to get things done. Victor's years marked a turning point in the role of the bishop of Rome, the relation of Christianity to the emperor, to the future of the Latin language and to the East-West divide.

## CHRISTIANS IN THE IMPERIAL COURT OF SEPTIMIUS SEVERUS

Born in Leptis Magna in A.D. 145, Septimius Severus was the son of Publius Septimius Geta, of Libyan-Punic ancestry. His mother was Fulvia Pia, of Italian Roman ancestry. Two of his cousins served as consuls under emperor Antoninus Pius. His native language in Leptis was Libyo-Punic, but he was also educated in Latin and Greek, which he spoke with a slightly awkward accent. His cousin Gaius Septimius Severus was appointed proconsul of the Africa Province in A.D. 173. Unpopular with the Roman Senate, Septimius Severus raised his own army of 50,000 and camped at Albanus near Rome. In 191 Severus received from the emperor Commodus the command of the legions in Pannonia. Upon the murder of Pertinax by the Praetorian Guard in 193, Severus's troops proclaimed him emperor at Carnuntum (in modern-day Austria), whereupon he hurried to Italy to make a successful bid for imperial power.

Christians were found in the Severan court and possibly in his family. Severus credited a Christian named Proculus with a miraculous cure. Proculus was retained in the Severan court. Tertullian reported that Septimius's son Caracalla (also known as Antoninus or Antonine) had a Christian wet nurse (*Ad Scapulam* 4).

During this time, Christians were not being systematically harassed and intimidated by Roman officials. Christianity had significant growth in the capital city. Many were converted from among the families of those who were distinguished for wealth and noble descent (Eusebius, *CH* 5.21). Tertullian emerged in Carthage as an activist spokesperson for Christian discipleship. Even when the Severan persecution in Carthage was resumed about A.D. 200, Tertullian appears to have been given a pass. Why? Maybe family or military connections. Tertullian enjoyed a more secure identity, less harassed than others like Perpetua.

The African pope Victor also found an ally in Julia Domna, the second wife of Septimius Severus, who succeeded Commodus. She was the mother to two subsequent Severan Roman emperors, Caracalla and Geta, who also had family ties in Leptis Magna, the likely home town of Victor and Tertullian. Julia Domna maintained cordial relations with Christian leadership both in Syria and Rome. Julia had special intellectual interests in Christianity and its best minds. Indeed Julia sought out Origen for his wisdom, or at least to test the intellectual mettle of his mind. Julia Domna was the daughter of a pagan priest named Bassianus. Her family came from the elite of Syria, where she had grown up in an environment where there were many Christians. They had established good relations with Julia Domna. She was an intelligent and talented woman who wielded considerable influence during her husband's reign and virtually administered the empire for her sons.

In telling the story of Libyan Christianity, there is a good reason to research and recall the links between Victor I, Septimius Tertullianus and the family of Septimius Severus. They illustrate the vitality of Latin Christianity not only in Leptis but also in the Roman world, and its influence quite early, not only in Libya but also in Rome. Now we focus on the outcomes of the reign of the African pope Victor.

## Victor's Role in the Search for Unity

Victor had the good fortune of being pope during this peaceful time of church-state relations. This may have made it possible for him to devote more of his time and energies on Scripture studies, liturgy and

East-West relations in the church. During this time Pope Victor was able to firmly establish the supreme authority of the bishop of Rome in church matters in the West like never before.

The claims of the primacy of the bishop of Rome had already been expressed as early as the *Letter of Clement* (bishop of Rome, 88–97) to the church at Corinth. They presumed that the bishop of Rome as successor to Peter was acting as acknowledged leader of congregations of Christians wherever Rome had influence, including Greek-speaking areas to the east. The implicit claim, still to be contested, was that the bishop of Rome was the rightful leader of Christians in the entire empire. Since all roads led to Rome, it was a natural place for early ecumenical Christianity to look to bring proximate unity to the interpretation of the apostolic testimony. A hundred years after Clement I, Victor I would seek to ensure Latin as an ecclesial language on par with Greek and the practices of the Western liturgical calendar as normative for the whole church.

Victor inherited a gnawing question between the Eastern and Western churches: When does the whole church celebrate Easter? Rome celebrated Easter on the Sunday following the fourteenth day of Nisan. Asian churches celebrated Easter on the fourteenth day of Nisan itself, the day before Jewish Passover. The Eastern practice was called Quartodecimanism in reference to the literal fourteenth day. Victor sought a resolution of these differences, yet in the course of the debate revealed his strong preference for the Latin, Western and North African practices. Eastern bishops resisted.

Despite Victor's reputation for being a partisan, his driving passion was for church unity. He was distressed by the continuing differences between East and West in an otherwise united ecumenical consensus. Victor solicited the opinions of all the churches as to how to resolve the difference. When sufficient support developed for the Western view, Victor declared Sunday to be the official day of Easter to be observed both East and West.

Many Christians from Asia were living in Rome. It must have been discomforting for Asian Christians to celebrate Lent and Easter at a different time than Western Christians. This controversy had been long recognized, but now began to boil. The West thought the East should accede to Rome. Seeking to restore the unity of Christian liturgical practice, Victor was determined to put a stop to this incongruity and lack of consensus. He ordered Polycrates, bishop of Ephesus, to hold a council of Asian bishops and requested that they follow the Western custom of celebrating Easter on Sunday. He repeatedly called on the bishops of the province of Asia to abandon their custom and to accept the Western practice. In his characteristic certitude, he bluntly warned that if they refused, they would be excluded from the Eucharistic fellowship of the church. Victor then called the first Roman synod for the purpose of establishing the celebration of Easter on Sunday. The Eastern bishops would not abandon the tradition they had received. This prompted Victor to excommunicate those who resisted his ruling.

The abruptness of this action was offensive to the Asians. Irenaeus urged Victor to show moderation with the bishops of East. Irenaeus reminded him that his predecessors had not opposed the Sunday observance of Easter, as was fitting, but had not broken off friendly relations or communion because they followed another regional custom (Eusebius, *CH* 5.23-25). Irenaeus pointed out the needless tragedy of cutting off from catholic unity the great see of Ephesus. The issue festered. Victor would become known for upholding Western, Roman Christian traditions over those of the East.

Victor's era revealed the growing influence of the bishop of Rome. Victor appeared to be acting as the mediator and spokesperson for the whole church, East and West. The outcome was ironic: the first African pope became best known for supporting the Western Latin bishops on this matter. Yet the deeper story here is that it took an African pope of strong and determined character to raise the issue, not avoid it, and to seek first to mediate it in a conciliar way, and then to seek to actualize the unity of a diverse church when the differences persisted. This left long-lasting wounds. In his passion to unify the church Victor played a crucial role in its division.

It is regrettable that after Victor's death the persecutions would resume in the latter period of Septimius Severus (202–211). Is there a correlation between Victor's reign, which had little persecution, and Severus? Did their Leptis background make way for this peace? These questions are speculative and unexplored, but they remain plausible conjectures. Severus permitted the reinstatement of the persecutions of Christians in this later period. Under the proconsul Scapula in 211, these persecutions raged, especially in Africa. The Severan persecutions were terrible in Numidia and Mauretania, but worst in Egypt and the

S.VICTOR I.*Afe* *Felicis filius, creat* *die i.Iunij ann.194,* *Sedit an.9.mens.* *i. dies 28.Pasfius* *die 28.Iulij a'.203* *Vac. Sed. dies 11.*

**African Pope Saint Victor I**

Thebaid, where a larger rebellion threatened. But Libya was largely spared.

## SABELLIUS AND THE LIBYAN CRUCIBLE WHERE APOSTOLIC TEACHING WAS TESTED

The unity of Christian doctrine was first sorely tested in Libya. For a while Libya was the most neuralgic of all joints of the body of Christ. At the time the African church was taking root in the Pentapolis of Libya, it was going through some rigorous trials. Cyrene was the place where this ordeal began. In the generation after Tertullian and Victor in the Latin part of Libya, the same aggressive leadership was taken up by the Greek East. The first challenger to apostolic leadership was Sabellius of Cyrene (fl. 215–230).

Basil of Caesarea (*Letter* 207) reported that Sabellius was a Libyan. He is remembered as an ordained presbyter of the church of Cyrenaica, according to Theodoret of Cyr (*Haer. fab. comp.* 2.9). Our scant sources of Sabellianism are those in Hippolytus (*Philosophumena* 9.6), Dionysius of Alexandria (*Letters*), Callixtus and Athanasius, as well as later references from Epiphanius (*Heresies* [or *Panarion*] 62). None of those who reported his views were favorable to them. So regrettably our knowledge of both Sabellius and Arius is still largely drawn from the writings of their opponents. From the outset Sabellian views were suspect and divisive. Of his life virtually nothing is known other than his probable time and place and the controversial core of his views. My modest purpose here is to show that Libyan theology was experimental and controversial much earlier than is usually acknowledged.

Cyrene was an intellectually sophisticated city uniquely prepared for research and inquisitive probing. After centuries of cerebral leadership in Africa, its history much older than Alexandria, Cyrene was by this time nursing a spirited competitive sibling relation with Alexandria, the younger brother. Cyrene was always ready to challenge Carthage and Alexandria. Many of these double dares came first from Libya. Cyrene quickly spawned prickly approaches to scriptural interpretation.

In the arena of scriptural exegesis, the two earliest and most divisive controversies on the person of the crucified Lord arose first in Libya: Sabellianism and Arianism. However much they were later reviled, both Sabellianism and Arianism arose as serious proposals for catholic Christianity to consider as orthodox. The faith that was commonly received from the apostles was in the long run generally held to be the most reliable core of Christian truth. But in these earliest centuries of experimentation it needed meticulous testing to make it stronger. Sabellius and Arius of eastern Libya provided those challenges.

Both of these highly contested views first arose in the diverse and argumentative cultural matrix of the Cyrenian Pentapolis. This attests to the spunkiness, curiosity and, to some extent, intellectual vitality of the early Christians in the Pentapolis. They were creative, but in the context of emerging orthodoxy, creativity is not a virtue. Innovation is a substitute word for heresy (= whatever is allegedly "improved" in apostolic teaching).

This problematic "creativity" first appears in Cyrene, where the earliest stirrings of African Christianity had begun even in New Testament times (with Lucius, Simon and the family of Mark). The Sabellian novelty soon moved its sphere of influence from Libya to greener pastures in Alexandria, Carthage and Rome. After due examination Sabellian teaching was almost universally repudiated in ancient ecumenical Christianity. All the faithful who understood their baptism could easily recognize it as not a part of the faith once for all delivered to the saints. Though Sabellius apparently taught later in Rome, his proposals were first debated and popularized in Cyrenaica in the third century.

Sabellian exegesis is one of the first examples of the Africa-to-Europe (South to North) thrust of intellectual momentum in the third century. Libya was an active player in the formation of early Christology, even if its contribution came in the form of offering options that were later rejected consensually. But the orthodox also reasoned that paradoxically these distortions also were part of God's gracious purpose of testing the church's teaching foundation. They thought that the providence of God had permitted these speculations in order to examine and assess the strength of the heart of Christian teaching: faith in the Son of God, who was truly God without ceasing to be truly human. The flawed exegesis of both Sabellius and Arius became in due time classified as nonconsensual, anomalous and thus heretical. At length both were firmly rejected by church councils. But they thereby accelerated the process of consensus formation. Their challenges required the orthodox to engage in the exegetical labor of comparing Scripture with Scripture to distinguish the center from the circumference.

The desire for faithful correspondence with worldwide Christian teaching—the rule of faith of the one, holy, catholic and apostolic church—was sustained in Libya throughout the periods of persecution, though challenged most severely. The diverse cultures and intellectual traditions in the Five Cities proved to be most fertile in producing these audacious challenges of scriptural interpretation, even if proven wrong.

## THE PROBLEMS FOR THE *OIKOUMENĒ* ELICITED BY SABELLIUS

The Libyan presbyter named Sabellius was one of the first teachers of an entirely novel point of view concerning Jesus' identity that was in due time rebuffed by the worldwide consensus. But the brazenness of Sabellius would in turn elicit a searching investigation of scriptural teaching on the person of Jesus, whether he was God or man or the unique theandric mediator, truly God, truly human.

These curious ideas of Sabellius were sufficiently thought-provoking to come into conflict with two of the most widely esteemed figures of his day: Pope Callixtus (= Callistus) and Patriarch Dionysius. Pope Callixtus was the bishop of Rome (d. 223), the see of Peter and the Western church. Patriarch Dionysius (A.D. 247–268) was the pupil of Origen, who became head of the catechetical school, and later was elevated to become Patriarch of Alexandria in the see of Mark, and hence spiritual guide of all African Christians. Their duty was accurately to teach the faith once delivered to the saints. What Sabellius was saying caused both primates deep concern.

The viewpoint debated under the name of Sabellius needs to be carefully set forth. Sabellianism is the belief that God the Father, God the Son and the Holy Spirit are three modes or aspects of God. The ecumenical consensus affirmed that God is one, but in accord with Scripture distinguished between the person and work of the Father, the person and work of the Son, and the person and work of the Holy Spirit.[3] The Son and Spirit are of the same nature as the Father, truly God.

According to Sabellius, God is known in three fundamental activities or modes, appearing successively as the Father (the Creator and Lawgiver), then as the Son (the Redeemer), and only later as the Holy Spirit (offering new life to believers). This places in question the eternality of the Father, Son and Spirit.

The central proposition of his reputed teaching was that Father, Son and Holy Spirit are the same, not distinguishable in voice and function as in Scripture—these three names thus being attached to one and the same being. God has become known in three apparently sequential or consecutive manifestations or energies. This distorted view of the triune teaching of Scripture is sometimes called modalism or modalistic monarchianism. It is monarchian because it emphasizes the oneness of the triune God declared in Scripture at the cost of denying the eternality of the three persons in baptismal practice. It is modal in that it suggests that the One God has successively revealed himself first as the Father in creation, then as the Son in redemption, and then as the Spirit

---

[3]Thomas C. Oden, *Classic Christianity* (San Francisco: HarperOne, 2009), pp. 520-25.

in sanctification and regeneration—merely "modes" of appearances. Since Sabellians explained their position by saying that the Father, the Son and the Holy Spirit are *not three persons but three functions or modes* of a single divine person, they were called "modalists."

Sabellius left his native country of the Pentapolis for the capital of Rome in the early third century to argue his case there before the highest ecclesiastical authorities. There he became the leader among modalistic monarchians. In Rome Hippolytus condemned Zephyrinus, the bishop of Rome, for not sufficiently resisting the idea. Later Hippolytus refused to submit to Zephyrinus's protégé and successor Callixtus I. Sabellius was later refused Communion by Pope Callixtus in A.D. 220. The resistance of Sabellius to the eternality of the Father, Son and Spirit led to his condemnation. The heresy was formally anathematized by a synod of Rome in 262. The notion that there is change within the Godhead was viewed as a contradiction to the consensual view of the unity and unchangeableness of God (Epiphanius, *Heresies* 62).

The party of Sabellius continued to persist in Rome for a considerable time, seeking to withstand Callixtus. In the Roman schools of Epigonus and Cleomenes it was taught that the Son is identical with the Father. But the presbyter Hippolytus was successful in convincing the leaders that the modalistic doctrine taken in its strictness was contrary to Scripture. Callixtus saw himself under the necessity of defining a mediating formula designed to harmonize the trinitarian and the modalistic positions. The mediation formula proposed by Callixtus became the bridge by which, in the course of decades, the doctrine of the Trinity was refined in the Western church.

The development of consensual doctrine in the East after Origen (from 260 to 320) was powerfully influenced by its sustained opposition to Sabellianism. Meanwhile the Sabellian doctrine itself during these decades underwent many changes in the East and blended into various philosophical expressions. In the fourth century this and the allied doctrine of Marcellus of Ancyra were sometimes combined.

The fact that the Sabellians did not completely vanish is seen in the recent history of gender language debates. In the 1970s North American theology labored through a weighty dispute over nongendered language about God that caused some to eschew entirely the classic triune language of Father, Son and Spirit. They preferred to limit God language to nontrinitarian terms such as the oblique reference to God as Parent, Child and Spirit of love, or the operational language of God as Creator, Redeemer and Consummator, or similar formulations. This left triune teaching without any personal names or identities that would imply gender. These debates show that modalism or Sabellianism has still lingered in modern theology.

All who diminished the eternal deity of Son and Spirit came to be called Sabellians. The wider African orthodox Christian consensus rejected Sabellianism because it failed to preserve the personal distinguishable relationships between the Father, the Son and the Holy Spirit. The most telling blow against Sabellianism was that it could not make sense out of the prayer life of Jesus, which hinged on the distinction between Father and Son.

The Sabellians contended that God is three only in relation to the world, appearing only in "manifestations" or "modes," or aspects, or energies, or phases of a single divine reality. If so, the unity and identity of God are such that the Son of God did not exist before the incarnation, contrary to the apostle John (Jn 1). If the Father and the Son are one person, not distinguishable, then it was implied that the Father suffered in the flesh on the cross. This is the error that became known as "Patripassianism." If Father, Son and Holy Spirit are all merely "modes" of a single divine person, it would follow that the Father, being the same person as the Son, suffered and died on the cross. This is contrary to the apostolic witness that the Son (not the Father) died on the cross as one who was fully human without ceasing to be the Son of God.

The experimental Sabellian type of exegesis was still spreading through Cyrenaica into the mid-third century (Eusebius, *CH* 7.6.1; 7.26.1). There ensued a long struggle with both Sabellianism and Arianism. Consensual Christian teachers from widely different places in Africa (including Cyprian, Dionysius, Athanasius and Augustine) all had to argue astutely to show Sabellian limitations. They showed that neither Sabellian nor Arian exegesis could be consistent with apostolic teaching.

## TERTULLIAN AND SABELLIUS

The teachings of Sabellius of eastern Libya were vigorously opposed by his formidable western Latin counterpart: Septimius Tertullianus, or Tertullian. The embryonic forms of proto-Sabellian teaching go back to the times preceding Tertullian (c. 155–c. 222) and Hippolytus (170–235). Sabellius had already created a widespread controversy as early as A.D. 195. Both Tertullian and his later contemporary Hippolytus strongly objected to this experimental, erratic form of exegesis. Hence an embryonic form of Sabellianism must be posited as present in Libya before the time of Tertullian, regardless of how it may be named. Tertullian attests of an early period in North Africa when Sabellian concepts, he said, prevailed among many.

Sabellian views were excoriated by Tertullian, just as they were condemned by the major African writers after Tertullian from Cyprian to Cyril the Great. Cyprian, who said he studied Tertullian's writings every day, was well aware of the bewildering incursions of Sabellian teaching in his own neighboring city of Carthage. Ingeniously Cyprian doubted that those baptized in the name of the Son only had rightly received the remission of sin (*To Jubianus*, Letter 72.18).[4] Such a sacramental blunder would imply the absence of the Father and the Spirit in the empowerment of the Christian life. It would be obvious to any astute lay person.

Long after Tertullian and Cyprian came the objections of Dionysius of Alexandria, Eusebius of Caesarea and Athanasius to a more complex form of Sabellianism. In due time Sabellianism would be almost completely rejected as unscriptural by the ecumenical consensus. That consensus was first defined in Africa before it would receive world-scale consent. Note again how African conciliar thought led the way for the world consensus.

## SAINT WASILLA (BASILIDES) OF THE PENTAPOLIS

The name of St. Basilides as recalled in the Russian tradition was spelled Wasilides, or Vasili (Vassili, Vasil, Bazyli, Basileios, Basiliedes),

---

[4]ANF 5:383.

or more recognizably Wasilla, which centuries later would become the name of a tiny but famous town in Alaska. It is ironic that the Western world knows the name Wasilla—the great Libyan martyr Basilides—only in a veiled and indirect way as a tiny town in Alaska that was once a Russian fishing village.

Eusebius had a written document that placed Wasilla/Basilides in the Pentapolis at the time of Dionysius, not as a myth but an active bishop:

> Many other epistles of Dionysius are extant, as those against Sabellius, addressed to Ammon, bishop of the church of Bernice. . . . Moreover, in a letter to Basilides [Wasilla], bishop of the parishes in Pentapolis, he says that he had written an exposition of the beginning of Ecclesiastes. (Eusebius, *CH* 7.26.1-3)

But who was Wasilla?

First, we are not here referring to the earlier notorious Gnostic writer Basilides of Alexandria (fl. A.D. 117–138). The Gnostic Basilides came *earlier* than the martyred Bishop Wasilla of Libya (d. 256). The earlier Gnostic heretic was censured sharply by the ecumenical consensus, according to Clement of Alexandria (*Stromata* 1.21, 2.6, 2.8, 2.20), Hippolytus (*Philosophumena* 7), and the treatise *Against All Heresies* (often ascribed to Tertullian), as well as Eusebius (*CH* 4.7). Wasilla/Basilides appeared a century *later*. He is a hero of early Libyan Christianity and one of its earliest martyr saints. In order to distinguish these two figures sharply, I will use the convention of employing the Russian spelling for the martyr saint: Wasilla.

Wasilla was more than a legend. He was a real figure in Libyan Christian history. Bishop Dionysius of Alexandria (fl. A.D. 248–265), wrote letters of counsel to the bishops of Libya. Among these letters were those he wrote to Wasilla (Basilides of the Pentapolis), and Ammonius of Hesperides (Benghazi/Berenike). Though Bishop Dionysius of Alexandria was the patriarch of the See of St. Mark, he himself was forced to spend a severe period of exile in the Libyan desert during the persecutions of Decius and Valerian. So he was well informed about Libyan Christianity. Though the letters of Wasilla to Dionysius are lost, some of the responses by Dionysius to Wasilla have survived in fragments.[5] All the Libyan bishops were serving under the jurisdiction of the bishop of Alexandria, in accountability to the revered apostolic tradition of Mark.

Wasilla, or Basilides, was then a famous but now little-known governor under Roman rule. The hazardous years of persecution before Constantine have made it difficult to uncover now lost documentation of his life and work, so I will rely on the Egyptian Coptic Synaxary to tell his story. It recalls the martyrdom of Saint Wasilla in this way (Feast Day Tout 11).

> Emperor Numerianus was the ruler, who was married to Basilides' sister, Patricia, and had a son called Yustus. Patricia was also the mother of Theodore El-Mishreke. Basilides had two sons: Awsabyos (Eusebyus/Eusebius) and Macarius.
>
> When the Persians waged war against Rome, Emperor Numerianus sent to them his son Yustus and Awsabyos, Basilides' son. Then he went to fight another enemy and was killed in that war. His kingdom was thus left vacant without a ruler. The people chose from among the soldiers a man called Agrippita. . . . One of the emperor's daughters . . . took him as her husband, . . . made him emperor and called him, "Diocletian." Shortly after, he forsook the Lord God of Heaven and worshiped idols. When Wasilla heard this, he was sorrowful, and he did not return to the service of the new emperor.
>
> Meanwhile, Yustus, the son of Numerianus, and Awsabyos (Eusebius), the son of Basilides, returned from the war with triumphant victory. When they saw that the emperor had renounced the faith, they were exceedingly sorry and drew their swords and wanted to slay Diocletian, the infidel emperor, and to return the kingdom to its rightful owner Yustus, Numerianus' son. But Basilides prevented them from doing this. Then he gathered his army and [servants/slaves] and informed them that he wished to lay down his life for the sake of Christ's Name. They all answered saying, "We also will die with you." They stood before Diocletian who feared them tremendously, for they were the rightful owners of the kingdom. So Romanus, Victor's father, advised him to banish them to Egypt to be tortured there. Diocletian sent them each to a different province: Abadir (Apater) and Eraee (Herai)

---

[5]William Cave, *Scriptorum ecclesiasticorum historia litteraria* (London, 1688), 1:69.

his sister, Awsabyos (Eusebius), Macarius, Claudius, and Victor. Theodore El-Mishreke was nailed to a tree.

He sent Basilides to Masrus, the governor of the Five Western Cities (Pentapolis). When Masrus saw him, he wondered why he had left his kingdom and his glory. Our Lord Christ sent His Angel and lifted Basilides up by the Holy Spirit to heaven, and showed him the spiritual dwellings, and his soul was comforted. As for his slaves, some were set free and some were martyred with him. St. Basilides endured severe tortures, on a squeezing machine (Hinbazeen) at times and at others his body was combed with iron combs. He was lifted onto a spiral device with a saw then thrust . . . on a red hot iron bed. Masrus, the governor, did not leave out any means of torturing him. When he saw that Basilides remained steadfast in his faith, Masrus ordered to cut off Basilides holy head, thus he received the crown of martyrdom in the kingdom of heaven in return for the earthly kingdom which he had forsaken. (*Coptic Synaxarium* for Tout 11)[6]

Thus Wasilla "obtained the crown of martyrdom; and so likewise a great number were martyred." Now many Russian boys are named Vasili.

## JULIUS AFRICANUS THE WORLD HISTORY CHRONOGRAPHER

Sextus Julius Africanus was the father of Christian chronography, the first to attempt to order all known events in universal history into a cohesive sequence of dates. He was writing at the time of Tertullian and Clement in the late second and early third century A.D. His full name in Greek was Sextos Ioulios Aphrikanos. Suidas reports that he was a "Libyan philosopher."[7]

His name itself suggests that he was an African. Those who argue that he was not African have to propose some plausible reason why he was called African. Among those who place him in Africa by birth, he is thought likely to be from Cyrene or Leptis. Little of his life can be

---

[6]"The Martyrdom of Saint Basilides (Wasilides)," *Coptic Orthodox Church Network*, <http://copticchurch.net/synaxarium/1_11.html>.

[7]Heinrich Gelzer, *Sextus Julius Africanus und die byzantinische Chronographie* (Leipzig: Teubner, 1880), pp. 4-5.

documented. Dates are conjectural. Only fragments remain of his writings. But his influence was unquestioned, especially as a source for Eusebius and for the ensuing tradition of chronographers and philosophers of universal history. He is crucial to our story of Libyan Christianity because of his influence on Eusebius, and through Eusebius upon many later writers of church history among the Fathers, and upon the whole Greek tradition of chronography.

He likely received his early education in leading centers of learning in Athens and Rome. Later he was drawn like a magnet toward study in Alexandria, according to Heinrich Gelzer, attracted by the fame of its catechetical school, possibly about the year 215.[8] He spoke and wrote in Greek, and knew Latin and Hebrew. Before his catechesis he had been a soldier. All his works were written as a Christian.

He appears to be well-connected and well-traveled. One tradition places him in the period of the Emperor Severus Alexander (222–235), and another under Gordianus III (238–244). It is less likely but arguable that he may have known Abgar VIII, the Christian King of Edessa (176–213). There is reason to think that he may have served under Septimius Severus against the Osrhoenians in 195, which would link him with Leptis Magna in Libya at the time of its greatest influence. He undertook an embassy to Emperor Severus Alexander, also of Leptis, to plead for the restoration of Emmaus (near Jerusalem), which had fallen into ruins. This mission succeeded. Emmaus became known as Nicopolis. The tradition that he later became bishop of Emmaus did not appear until the fourth century. Though born in Africa, he considered Emmaus his home later in his life. That is where the risen Lord appeared in the breaking of bread (Lk 24:13-35).

His history of the world (*Chronographiae*) began with creation and continued to the year A.D. 221. In his chronology Julius show his dependence on the *Stromata* of Clement of Alexandria.[9] It was the first Christian attempt at a universal history. As an African he preceded numerous later attempts at universal history, many of the most important by African Christian writers: Lactantius, Arnobius, Augus-

---

[8]Gelzer, *Sextus Julius Africanus*, p. 11; cf. Eusebius, *CH* 6.31.
[9]Gelzer, *Sextus Julius Africanus*, pp. 19-24.

tine and Victor of Vita among them. Why was universal history so intriguing to the earliest African Christian writers? One hypothesis: the African historians were looking at Mediterranean history from world historical perspective due to their tertiary status among the known continents.

He had a critical mind. He disputed the authenticity of the story of Susanna. He corresponded with Origen (two letters have survived). His critical spirit and broad grasp of history have won him praise among modern historians. In his letter to Aristides he explained the seeming inconsistency of the two pedigrees of Jesus reported by Matthew and Luke (Mt 1:2-17; Lk 3:23-38). His other works of commentary on the New Testament have disappeared. A fragment of his Kestoi (encyclopedia or "embroidery") treating innumerable subjects was found in the Oxyrhynchus papyri.[10] It is an encyclopedia of science showing the wide range of his mind. He is rightly regarded as among the most ingenious minds of early African Christianity.

## THEODORE OF CYRENE

Another Libyan confessor who appears in the Russian Synaxary is Hieromartyr St. Theodore (also known as Theuderius). Before his becoming bishop of Cyrene, he was known as a scribe or monk who quietly copied sacred Scriptures for public reading. Theodore was ordained by the Patriarch Theonas of Alexandria (fl. 282–300), as bishop in Libya.

Many Libyans suffered as confessors during the Roman persecutions, especially if they were public readers of Scripture. Theodore served the Pentapolis during the reigns of Theonas and Peter. Theodore was arrested in Libya, probably during the Diocletian persecution of A.D. 302–305, or as early as 292 by some accounts (*SEC*, Synaxarium for July 4).

This was a hazardous time to be a bishop, charged with the care of the Holy Scriptures.

Theodore was ordered to deliver up his copies of the sacred texts and to bring with him before the court all who read in public the testimony of the

---

[10]Martin Wallraff and Laura Mecella, eds., *Die Kestoi des Julius Africanus und ihre Überlieferung* (Berlin: de Gruyter, 2009).

apostles. The Dominican Martyrology (July 4) reports the outcome solemnly: "At Cyrene in Libya, St. Theodore, [was] bishop. In the persecution of Diocletian, under the governor Dignian, he was beaten with leaden tipped whips, and his tongue was cut out" (Dominican Martyrology, July 4). Though he survived, he was a confessor without a tongue.

On this same day the Libyan church remembers the deacon who served under Theodore, whose name was Irenaeus, and two lectors, or public readers, named Serapion and Ammonius. They also had their tongues cut out for reading Scripture in common worship. Also executed at this time were the holy women of Libya: Cyprilla, Lucia and Aroa (Russian Feast Day July 3 or 4). The Antiochene Orthodox Synaxary recounts that those killed with Theodore in Libya were all who were known to have been baptized by the holy bishop (Synaxary, Antiochene Orthodox Church of America). So the torture and death of the coworkers of St. Theodore has been solemnly recalled annually in the Coptic calendar. They died defending the Christian Scriptures. On this evidence it is reasonable to speak of a steady Christian witness (*martyria*) in the city of Cyrene from an early date no later than the 250s A.D. to about 303. This indicates that many in Libya were willing to die rather than yield the sacred Scriptures to the persecuting authorities.

The documented time frame of substantial Christian presence in Libya is no later than the 250s and continuing to the 650s. But the actual time frame could have begun much earlier, if we take into account the stories of the saints of Libya from Mark to Theodore of Cyrene. The celebrated city of Cyrene was not just an ancillary footnote to early African intellectual history. It bears evidences of a vital spiritual presence that extends over a half millennium. Christians were participants in this tradition. This willingness to die for the faith among Libyan Christians may have reached back to the Cyrenians at Pentecost and the life of Mark all the way to the holy women Cyprilla, Lucia and Aroa.

## LIBYAN PARTICIPATION IN CHRISTIAN NEOPLATONISM: MARIUS VICTORINUS

The Neoplatonic journey of Synesius toward Christianity (explored in chap. 6) may best be viewed in relation to that of two preceding

African intellectuals: Marius Victorinus the Afer and Augustine, then in Milan.

The fact that Marius Victorinus was also called Victorinus Afer suggests his place of birth. The term *Afer* refers to Africa, or the Afri peoples, after which the continent of Africa is named. Like Julius Africanus, this is an indelible clue to their identity origin.

Marius Victorinus was born, likely in Libya, about fifty years before Synesius, probably around A.D. 300 in the Pentapolis. He flourished in Rome in the 360s. Augustine was a youth in Tagaste when Synesius was born (365–370). Both Marius Victorinus and Augustine were Africans who took the high-flying trip through Neoplatonism. Both were following in the footsteps of the Alexandrian exegetes, Clement and Origen. All became significant contributors to ancient Christian teaching.

By the time of Victorinus, an emerging form of diffuse Neoplatonic prototrinitarianism was beginning to emerge. Synesius was likely reading Marius Victorinus in the 390s. This prompts the speculative hypothesis that Marius Victorinus Afer was likely from the Pentapolis of Libya, perhaps emerging out of the same Cyrenaic ethos as that of Synesius. Cyrenian Christianity was very experimental and oriented to a sophisticated philosophical culture. Thus it was found at first on the far edges of orthodoxy, later to be partially accommodated.

Victorinus migrated as a teacher of rhetoric to Rome, much like Augustine would do later. There he became sufficiently famous that in 353 a statue was erected in his honor in the Forum of Trajan (Jerome, *Chron.*, 2370). A prolific author, he was also a translator of many works, among them Porphyry's *Isagoge*. Three works written before his conversion have survived. They are on Cicero, grammar and the logic of definition. His conversion around A.D. 361 occurred through his study of the Bible. Victorinus was reluctant to become a confessing Christian, but when he did his profession of faith became well-known, public and conspicuous. The edict of Julian in 362 brought his teaching career to an end. All we know of him thereafter must be inferred from his writings against Arius, some hymns, and his commentaries on the epistles to the Galatians, Ephesians and Philippians.

It was out of Libya that the first great Christian Neoplatonic hymns were written by Victorinus and Synesius. In Libya, Christianity entered into its most decisive debates on the durable values of Hellenistic culture and Neoplatonic philosophy that would echo throughout the pages of all subsequent Christian history.

## MONASTICISM IN THE LIBYAN DESERT

After the period of martyrdom came the period of monasticism in Libya. There were remote monastic communities in the mountains and desert that survived beyond the Arab victories. They were following in the path of the crucified Lord and of the martyrs of the Roman persecution. Monasticism flourished in the Pentapolis and later in the northern parts of Latin Libya.

Palladius wrote of monks of the Libyan desert whom he had met personally. One of them, unnamed, was reputed to have been a monk since A.D. 291. If so, that was a very early date in the history of monasticism—he would have been a contemporary of St. Anthony of the Desert and St. Macarius of Scetis—among the earliest prototypes of the monastic life. Palladius mentions another Libyan monk named Stephen who was very old and who also had personally met Anthony. Bishop Synesius tells us that early Libyan bishops were largely chosen from among the holy monks of the diocese.

To assess the extent of monasticism in the Libyan desert, it is necessary to define the Libyan desert, which itself presents a puzzle. The term "great Libyan desert," as employed in late antiquity, was used variably to refer to the vast regions that now lie south of the coastal populations of Tripolitania and Cyrenaica. But it also encompasses some territories that would be politically identified today as the western desert of Egypt. This immense Libyan desert included the desolate tracts from Tripolitania on the border of present Tunisia all the way to the sparsely populated deserts of western Egypt. Vast areas of these Egyptian-Libyan desert regions were inaccessible to all but the hardiest of monks and desert nomads.

The desert areas of Libya also include (1) the territories of the Latin west, which were in late antiquity called Gaetulia, (2) Phazania, (3) the southern desert area of Tripolitania called Aethopia, (4) Macae, (5) Laguata, (6) Garamantes, (7) the great southern desert of Syrtica, and (8) the deserts of the Austurianti and Nasamodes. In Eastern Libya there stretched the vast desert areas south of Marmarica and Hammoniacus, and the vast area called Libya Inferior all the way to Zeszes or Oasis Parva.[11] It is not until the regions far to the east of the present Libyan-Egyptian border—east of Mareotes—that one would come to parts of the great Libyan Desert that fall politically into present-day Egypt. This would include the uplands of the Libykon Oros, and the lowlands of the North Arsinoites and the Krokodielopolites. At various times these have been under direct Egyptian control, and at other times quite independent of Egyptian control.

Why is the definition of "the Libyan desert" pertinent to the question of the extent of monasticism in Libya? It is likely that the earliest forms of monasticism spread from the Nile in both easterly and westerly directions, in both cases to the desert regions. They have been hardly touched archaeologically in Libya. Many have not even been properly identified by place names. In Tripolitania, the best source remains the work of Isabella Sjöström (*TT*). After archaeological work has matured in these vast areas, we will know more about Libyan monasticism. For now this remains an embryonic discipline.

## LIBYAN PARTICIPATION IN CONSENSUS FORMATION AFTER THE DIOCLETIAN PERSECUTION

Assuming many records were destroyed during the persecutions and wars, the extant records reveal only a small portion of the leaders of the Libyan church. Following the Diocletian persecution, some of their names are stored in church records. This we know because the names of bishops representing dioceses in Libya appear regularly in the annals of the ecumenical and regional councils. Though this evidence—the mere reporting of names—is sparse, it is a part of the buried story of early Libyan Christianity. It is all we have that has been preserved from a time of the intentional obliteration of an entire cultural memory. The following are some of the surviving fragments.

---

[11]For visual presentation of these territories in late Roman times, see Barrington Atlas, p. 73.

Zopyrus of Barca (sometimes referenced as Zephyrius or Zephirus) and Dathes were two Libyan bishops who were among the delegation to the First Council of Nicaea (*HEO* 2:578). Barca (Barke, Barka, modern el-Merg/el Marj) was inland from Ptolemais. Boreum (Boreion, modern Bu Grada) was near the southernmost point of the Gulf of Sirte. It was represented at Nicaea by Bishop Sentianus.[12] Later, Zenobius, bishop of Berenike (modern-day Benghazi), attended the Ecumenical Council of Ephesus in 431. Among others known to be present at Ephesus were bishops from the Libyan cities of Oea, Diasthis, Barca and Taucheira (Tauchira). Among the subscribers at Ephesus was another named Sosipater, bishop of Septimiace, a city otherwise unknown, which appears to have been situated in Libya (Mansi, 4:1128, 1221). Attending the Robber Synod of Ephesus (449) was one Theodulus, presumed to be bishop of Ticelia in Libya (Mansi, 6:610), though the location of Ticelia, or Sicelis, remains uncertain.

The point: Libyan leaders were at these councils, participating in the formation of the most influential forms of ecumenical consensus. They played a significant part in the earliest stages of consensus formation, sometimes by challenging, sometimes by confirming the catholic consensus. Partly through issues arising out of Libya, controversies over Scripture were brought to orderly agreement. Especially the problems presented by Sabellius and Arius required urgent and explicit attention. Consensual orthodox teaching continued in Libya, even under the strained conditions of the Arian, Vandal and Muslim periods. Libya challenged the church consensus with some of its smartest heretics. In this way Libya contributed indirectly to the earliest forms of emergent ecumenical consensus. Among the earliest layers of conciliar decision making were the African Councils of Carthage and Alexandria. There deliberate attention was given to analysis of Scripture texts pertinent to the issues at hand, always with prayer for unity of spirit.

This leads us to the most painful conflict of Libyan Christianity: Arianism. With the few exceptions of insurgents like Arius, the ordinary believing Christians of Libya were blessed to feel cared for by the

---

[12]Giorgio Fedalto, *Hierarchia ecclesiastica orientalis*, 2 vols. (Padua: Messaggero, 1988), 2:658.

benevolent See of St. Mark, the leader of the wider African diocese of Mark. But Arius had a knack for creating strife.

## THE TROUBLE WITH ARIUS

Arius proved to be an even more challenging and intrusive force than Sabellius. Both of them thundered out of the Libyan Pentapolis to echo throughout the Christian world. The most durable issue was spearheaded by this shrewd, speculative Christian teacher from Cyrene, Arius. His quasi-scriptural teaching would ultimately be declared completely out of bounds from classic consensual Christian teaching. But that took a long time.

Some might dispute the Libyan origin of Arius, but the weight of evidence for it is stated by Rowan Williams, formerly of Oxford, now of Canterbury: "Epiphanius tells us that Arius was born in Libya: and a number of other small pieces of evidence tend to bear this out" (*Arius*, 29). Arius (250–336) was born during the Decian persecution. He had a long life. Late in life in A.D. 317 he appeared in Alexandria actively teaching his disturbing views.

Arius is portrayed by Epiphanius (*Heresies* 69.3) as uncommonly tall, thin, ascetical and severe. His moral character was never challenged, only his exegetical innovations and their consequences for catechesis. He was a cultured and popular preacher, handsome, earnestly religious and eloquent in his arguments, though he gave the impression of being a bit arrogant. He lived at a time when consensual teaching was becoming severely challenged and divided due to disputes over whether or in what sense Christ was truly God as proclaimed in Paul's letters and the four Gospels.

Arius's key assertion was simple: There was a time when the Son was not. The Son is not eternal in the same sense as the Father is eternal. His intent was to protect the unity and immutability of God. But the unplanned result was to devalue the Son from the eternal relation with the Father as set forth in John's Gospel. This was a controversy that Arius of Cyrene intentionally initiated in the churches of Alexandria. It would spill blood for years to come. Simply put, it taught that Christ is not eternally divine but rather a creature, since there was a time when he was not.

Only a few documents credited to Arius have survived: his letter to Alexander of Alexandria (as preserved by Athanasius, *On the Councils of Arminum and Seleucia* 16; Epiphanius, *Heresies* 69.7; and Hilary, *On the Trinity* 4.12), his letter to Eusebius of Nicomedia (as recorded by Epiphanius, *Heresies* 69.6, and Theodoret, *CH* 1.5), and his confession (as recorded in Socrates Scholasticus, *CH* 1.26.2 and Sozomen, *CH* 2.27.6-10). Most of what we know about him we must learn from his detractors. He was declared an archheretic due to the breadth of his influence. The controversy he started and insisted on prosecuting to the very end did in fact stimulate the clarification of basic points of classic Christian consensual teaching.

Arius studied under Lucian of Antioch, who died a martyr. When Arius returned to the African continent, his headstrong temperament became a vexing problem for four successive Alexandrian bishops: Peter (300–311), Achillas (312), Alexander (312–328) and Athanasius (328–372). In 306 Arius aligned himself with Meletius of Lycopolis and thus against Peter, bishop of Alexandria. A feeble reconciliation followed in which Peter received Arius as deacon. But the disputes on Christology and ordination continued unabated.

Arius was at last excommunicated by Bishop Peter in 311 for his controversial exegesis and for his disruptive collusions with Meletius. Note the geopolitical aspect of the controversy: Some of the Libyan bishops, under the spell of Arian ideas, found it useful to side with Bishop Meletius, the defiant leader of the Middle Nile dioceses, against the leadership of the See of St. Mark.

Under Peter's successor Achillas, Arius was readmitted to Communion and in 313 made presbyter of the distinguished Baucalis district in Alexandria, the place where Mark was reportedly martyred and where an ancient congregation was located. This prestigious office gave Arius a platform for expounding the Scriptures publicly. He exercised increasing influence until in 318 his irreconcilable differences with Bishop Alexander became a matter of public conflict.

Bishop Alexander, mentor of Athanasius, defended the received apostolic consensus that taught that the Son is fully and truly God. Defying his bishop, Arius maintained that the Son was not consubstantial or coeternal with God the Father, but that there was a time when the Son was not, that before he was begotten, he did not exist. The confession of the preexistence of Christ, as apostolically taught in Colossians 1 and Philippians 2, was dumped.

A synod of nearly one hundred bishops was assembled in 321 in Alexandria from all regions of both Libya and Egypt. All arguments were carefully weighed. This was four years before Nicaea. Arius was condemned for his novel and disruptive form of exegesis. Arius, however, was not willing to yield to the consensus. He went roaring through Palestine to fuel conflict among other Eastern bishops, organizing a vast opposition movement. Many of these were former students of Lucian of Antioch. As the debate continued and enlarged, it became enflamed, with various councils either condemning or endorsing the views of Arius.

Constantine was so disturbed by the disunity of the church caused by Arius that he convened the First Ecumenical Council at Nicaea in 325 to safeguard the unity of both the empire and the church. The council fathers declared the Son to be of one substance (*homoousios*, or consubstantial) with the Father, equal to the Father in eternity. They confessed the apostolic teaching that Christ is "God from God, true God from true God, begotten not created, of the same essence as the Father." To make this confession is necessarily to deny Arius. The Council condemned Arius's teaching and exiled him to Illyricum.

Three Libyan leaders were decisively condemned of Arianism at Nicaea, all three from the Cyrenaic coast. One was the priest Arius, and the other two were Bishop Secundus of Ptolemais and Bishop Theonas of Marmarica. Nicaea was a victory of the prestigious Markan See of Alexandrian patriarchs over Libyan dissidents whose influence had extended throughout the region. The Pentapolis had nurtured an experimental intellectual culture that prized independent reflection above apostolic unity.

Though Arius was rejected, the debate continued throughout the empire. The Arian-prone Synod of Tyre deposed Athanasius on feigned charges in 335 of which he was later acquitted. Long after Nicaea, the Arians, along with their middle-Nile Meletian allies, continued to roil the See of St. Mark. Eusebius persuaded Constantine to recall the exiled Athanasius in 328 to reconcile his views with the Arians. Athanasius stood fast. Athanasius was exiled five times in this lengthy, excruciating conflict, often due to changes of authority in Constantinople. During the years of maximum Arian influence, the orthodox were severely punished. Athanasius won the doctrinal battle, not only in Nicaea but in its aftermath, but only after an extended struggle through which he endured almost alone, *contra mundum*. Arius would spend his later years trying to be readmitted to Communion in Alexandria. But just as Arius was as a very old man about to be readmitted to Communion in Constantinople in 336, he died suddenly from unknown causes.

## THE METASTASIS

Libya was the amphitheater where the integrity of the original apostolic teaching was most sorely tested. But the ordeal that was first tested in Libya had to be tested elsewhere—almost everywhere—in order to corroborate the unity of apostolic teaching. These ideas that began in Libya were exported everywhere. The Arian controversy would not be settled for decades after Nicaea in the East and three more centuries in the West. Like his fellow Libyan Sabellius, Arius had ignited a flame that spread far beyond Libya.

Ultimately the controversy sharpened the attentiveness of the church to the careful exegesis of scriptural passages on the relation of Father and Son. The Nicene formula on the eternal Son was gradually received more universally and precisely than ever before. This was the ironic "contribution" of the Pentapolis to apostolic and catholic reasoning. Observed from the long view of providence, this is a story of grace, not merely of conflict. It is a story of growth through rigorous exegetical and intellectual exertion, not merely a meaningless struggle. After Nicaea, those who persisted in denying that the Son is truly eternal God would be viewed as defectors from the apostolic consensus. The holdouts would be given only a limited time to repent or be disallowed the sacrament of the table. On the contrary the Holy Spirit was celebrated as having plenty of time to redeem and nurture back the fallen.

This controversy of course might have arisen somewhere besides

Libya. But it did in fact first appear in Libya. This datum resonates with my previous South to North thesis in *How Africa Shaped the Christian Mind*: The exegetical speculation began in Africa and was resolved conceptually in Africa by Athanasius and the great exegetes following him. By the time it was being rigorously debated in Europe, the wave of Arians had subsided in Libya and Egypt. It would continue to be fought through in every diocese in the eastern Mediterranean and later in the western Mediterranean. But in the long run, the patterns of apologetics developed in Africa were reappropriated throughout the *oikoumenē*. To sharpen the point for our purposes: the greatest challenge to apostolic Christology was contested and settled in North Africa, beginning in Libya, long before it was in fact settled in the rest of the Christian world.

The irony: After circling the known world, the Arianism that began in Libya and spread widely finally came full circle back into Libya for its final act. This is the most poignant aspect of the history of Libyan Christianity.

With your finger trace it around the Mediterranean. The Arian perspective moves from Libya to Egypt to Constantinople and then north and west into the lands of the Bulgars. Then it shifts west upstream around the Danube beyond Hungary to Gothic and Frankish and Visigothic tribes. At one time the whole span of the Danube was largely Arian. The Arian Visigoths eventually swept over northern Europe. That momentum took them down through the Rhine and Rhone valleys and finally into Spain. It dominated Christian controversy during the fourth century amid the crucial years of the formation of doctrinal dogmatic definitions of the eternality of God the Son and the triune definition. What began in Libya would after a long journey end in Libya.

## THE FINAL ASSAULT OF ARIANISM IN VANDAL LIBYA

In the 430s Arianism finally returned to Africa in the form of the Gothic Vandals' tribal conglomerate. Again they dominated the controversies of the fifth century and sixth centuries in North Africa all the way back to Libya, where they finally petered out.

Classic Christian teaching combated Arianism all the way from the Pentapolis to Alexandria to Nicaea, all the way, on every river and hill, through every village and city, moving in Roman Asia from south to north and from Europe east to west. Think of the hands of a clock moving counterclockwise from Libya to Egypt to Palestine to Anatolia to the Danube valley to France to Spain and back to Gibraltar.

The final assault of Arianism came with its second arrival in North Africa ending with its denouement once again in Libya. It arrived with a fury in the North Africa where it had been born. From Spain it swept across the straights of Gibraltar to coastal North Africa through Mauritania, through modern Algeria and Tunisia, and finally back to Libya. It had gone full circle around the great middle sea. Thus two centuries after Arianism began in Cyrene in the 280s, after a long journey through Europe, Arianism returned to Africa in corrupt Vandal garb, overtaking Carthage in A.D. 439.

The flourishing city of Sabratha, west of Tripoli, was the first Libyan town to be pillaged by the Vandals in A.D. 455. Gaiseric (Geiseric or Genseric) "tore down the walls of all the cities of Libya" and "robbed the rest of the Libyans of their estates." Some "men of note and conspicuous for their wealth" were sent away as slaves. Those who survived were unmercifully taxed (Procopius, *Wars* 3.5.8). By A.D. 533 Libya would be reconquered by General Belisarius under Emperor Justinian, and reoccupied by the Byzantines who fortified and developed it until the Arab sweep in A.D. 643.

The depopulation of Christian Libya was the consequence. The economy fell with the political order. The oppressors were Arians enslaving Libyan Byzantine Christians in a quasi-religious form of "ethnic cleansing" by Gothic interlopers. The fifth-century orthodox Christians of Libya would suffer from the windblown seeds of Arianism that would all but destroy Christian Libya.

This weakening set the stage for the Byzantine military initiatives under the Emperor Leo in 470 (led by Heracleius) and Justinian's reconquest of 532–534. These bloodlettings shaped the conditions for the Arab conquest in A.D. 643.

The tombs of the cemeteries of the Christian cities of en Ngila and Ain Zara show Germanized (Gothic) names along with the African and Latin names (*TT,* 37). So the Arian virus that spread from Libya circled the Mediterranean and finally landed on its feet again in Libya, but this time with a sword. This is the sad story of Arianism—beginning in Libya in the 200s, in time it would circulate through Asia and Europe, and finally then come back to decimate Libya again from the west until 643. The final irony: Arianism would burn like a prairie fire for four centuries (260s-643) before being extinguished in Africa, not by Christian orthodoxy but by Islam. By the time it came back into view in Libya two centuries after it was born there, Arianism was spiritually a spent force. By that time orthodox Christology had become more firmly reestablished in Cyrenaica and Tripolitania than in the lands the Vandals had conquered. Islam prevented the Arian Vandals ever again from exercising dominant influence.

Although Arian teaching arose in Libya and extended throughout the Christian world, it did not ever gain durable hegemony in Libya itself, especially during the Byzantine period of Libyan Christianity (fourth through seventh centuries). After Athanasius Libyan theology was largely orthodox, and only marginally Arian.

Few modern historians have sought to connect the narratives of the early Cyrenaic Christians of the New Testament, the Arians, the Vandals or Islam, or with the theological struggle of Nicaea. It remains a hypothesis for further theological inquiry as to how they correlate. But these interpenetrations became the matrix of the greatest crisis of Christian providential teaching since the Roman persecutions. This story is told by Victor of Vita.[13] He was watching the denouement unfold in Libya's neighbor, now Tunisia but then called Byzacena and Proconsularis. He joined the previous great African Christian teachers on the ironies of providence: Arnobius, Lactantius and Augustine. This draws us toward theological reflection on the issues of the astute African doctrinal reflections on providence, another gift of Africa to Europe and Asia.

---

[13]*Victor of Vita: History of the Vandal Persecution,* trans. John Moorhead, Translated Texts for Historians 10 (Liverpool: Liverpool University Press, 1992).

## THE ENSUING CRISIS FOR THEODICY

Arian teaching recounts a strange providence that became a pressing problem for Christian teaching—theodicy, that is, What is God's purpose in allowing evil? Why did God allow this form of wayward Christianity to survive through the Vandal invasion through a course of history that would kill, imprison and harass so many orthodox Christians, and weaken them for the onslaught of Islam? This prompted the orthodox after the Vandal conquest to reflect deeply on the mystery of God's permission of wrong thinking and the hard cost of soft exegesis. Arians had to be overcome and were overcome by consensual orthodoxy, but never so completely as to be forever vanquished. Arianism is still a force and an embittered, hidden minority voice within world Christianity.

The Roman hegemony in Libya lasted from 75 B.C. to A.D. 429 with the coming of the Vandals under Gaiseric. By 455 Rome itself was sacked, and most of the former Roman cities were under the thumb of tribal Vandal chieftains. In 533 as Belisarius was preparing for an expedition, Tripolitania revolted against the Vandal dominion and joined forces with the emperor Justinian.

From 533 to 643 the Byzantine hegemony was largely secure. Under the emperor Maurice (582–602), Tripolitania was more decisively separated politically from Proconsular Africa and attached to Egypt. The Arab invasion came to Cyrenaica in 642 and to Tripolitania in 643. The ethnic culture remained Berber. Many Libyans under duress became Muslims but hardly Arabs. The Tuareg were melded into an interior tribe that included populations from as far away as Mali, Niger and Mauretania.

The outpouring of North African reflection on the philosophy of universal history is a special feature of early African Christianity and intellectual life. Some of the most important early reflections on universal history came out of North Africa: those of Lactantius, Julius Africanus, Augustine, Victor of Vita and Cyril the Great are among the best. These brilliant North African views of universal history would likely have continued beyond the Vandal experience if it had not been for the virtual extinction of Christian presence in North

Africa. The continuity of African orthodoxy continued in Coptic
Egypt and Ethiopia. This providential reflection would again appear
in Arabic in the work of Bishop Sawirus Ibn al-Mukaffa' on the history of the patriarchs.[14]

## WHY THE ARIAN CHALLENGE TO ORTHODOXY BEGAN IN LIBYA

At the heart of these providential musings must be the question of why
Arian challenges to orthodoxy began in Libya and not somewhere else.
Here are five tentative conjectures:

1. Libyan Christianity was nurtured in a hothouse environment. It was
   perennially in a competitive sibling relationship with Alexandria—
   the younger brother overtaking the older brother. This existed long
   before Christianity. Cyrene was the older city, founded in 631 B.C.
   Alexandria was the younger, founded three hundred years later. But
   Alexandria overshadowed the Cyrenaic experiment, especially at the
   time of the formation of early Libyan Christianity.

2. The experimental and innovative intellectual tradition of Cyrene preceded that of Alexandria. Cyrene had been more deeply traumatized
   and radicalized by the Jewish Revolts of A.D. 66 and 115. This intensified the ever-smoldering latent rivalry between Alexandria and
   Cyrene. With this background it should not be surprising that Cyrenaic Christians would find reasons to challenge Alexandrian Christian leadership on the most decisive questions of Christology and triune teaching. The Meletian schism would reinforce this perennial
   rivalry, challenging the Nile Delta from both the south and the west.

3. A prevailing philosophical skepticism lingered in Cyrenaic culture.
   Contrarian thinking had become the native temperament of Libya.
   Arianism arose out of the critical skepticism of the philosophical
   schools of Cyrene, and the temperament of sophist critical inquiry,
   to become one of Christianity's most persistent theological debates.

4. There was less stringent surveillance of orthodox doctrine in Cyrene

---

[14]See Thomas C. Oden, *The African Memory of Mark* (Downers Grove, Ill.: IVP Academic,
2011), chap. 4, on literary sources.

than in Alexandria where the patriarchate was located. Hence these heretical imbalances had space and time to be planted, nurtured and to grow before they were finally exhausted.

5. This elicited a far-reaching theological reflection on the general course of history. This thought could only emerge out of minds thoroughly immersed in Hebraic prophecy. Jeremiah and Isaiah were the prophets most quoted in African Christianity. Prophetic reasoning cried out: God's just judgment was chastising the misjudgments of the faithless and purifying the witness of the faithful. The Libyan culture was in the tender stages of Christianization following centuries of polytheism. The ruinous path of Arianism was viewed as a just sentence of God. Those who succumbed to its temptations had to live with the consequences of their lapses. The incomparably just God gave permission for the disease to run its course. Like all other events in history, the emergence of Arianism out of Libya offered a case in point where social suffering arose out of bad faith. Arianism became a blight on not only its Libyan origins but the surrounding cultures.

The truth being tested in such reasoning is the truth embodied in the larger pattern of history—as far as the eye could see. It is known only by perceiving the course of history from a very long perspective. In the case of Judeo-Christian historical consciousness that length is no less than fifteen hundred years, but more accurately from creation to consummation. It is the beholding of a vision of the meaning of the total scope of human history. That scope is the premise of prophetic thinking about divine revelation which conditioned Christian eschatology.

Many modern historians have difficulty grasping this reasoning. It is complex. It is strange. It is a language alien to their tongue. It requires premises completely foreign to the modern construction of reality. It is grounded in a history of revelation and juxtaposed with an intense awareness of the wretched history of human fallenness.

## APOSTOLICITY, AFRICANEITY AND CATHOLICITY

Orthodox consensual Christian teaching holds that God is sovereign over human history, following Hebraic and apostolic teachings. Yet as we have seen, the history of heresy is an evident component of early Libyan Christianity. The conflicts that began in Libya have echoed throughout the world Christian community.

My passion as a historical theologian is focused on how the world Christian consensus was first formed and through diverse times sustained. This consensus is what is often called classic Christianity, the orthodox faith or early ecumenical teaching. In the minds of most ancient African Christian writers, the apostolic testimony was delivered to the church as a seamless, unified witness. The idea of profound doctrinal diversity among the apostles is strictly a modern myth. While each of the apostolic witnesses retained their own personal voices and idiomatic thought patterns, all did so under the unitive guidance of God the Spirit, according to classic Christian teaching. The apostles did not differ substantially among themselves on those teachings essential for salvation. When they did diverge temporarily, they resolved those differences through the Spirit with prayer and fasting, and conciliar consensus following rigorous exegetical debate.

There is a specific theological explanation that stands as a sufficient reason for this unity. It is not a sociological or political reason. It is, in dogmatic terms, the work of the Spirit. God the Spirit has chosen to steadily and surely shape this internal consistency in the believing community. Only the Spirit sustains unity in Christ. This explanation massively prevailed in patristic Christianity. Early African Christians had been well taught by the apostles that the Holy Spirit is constantly creating and recreating this cohesion, despite human recalcitrance.

The best of early African exegetes wanted their Scripture studies to reflect accurately the actual cohesion the Spirit was creating and sustaining. Hence they were profoundly committed to embodying the consensus that the Holy Spirit was engendering and establishing. They sought agreement on what the apostles taught, and trusted that this choice would correspond with fact-based, healthy reasoning and good conscience. This agreement could only come by comparing Scripture with Scripture by the analogy of faith where seeming differences were reconciled by the larger cause of the revelation of truth.

The apostolic tradition of preaching sought to teach believers in widely *different* cultures a *single* internally consistent teaching on one God, one faith, one baptism, one God and Father of us all, who is revealed in his only Son Jesus Christ by the reconciling work of God the Spirit.[15]

This assumed primordial unity of apostolic testimony was challenged by counterclaims and nonapostolic innovations that elicited division in the unity of the body of Christ. Among the earliest and toughest of these innovation were those that occurred in Libya.

This quest to embody the unity of the body of Christ took place earlier and more deliberately on African soil than it did anywhere else, as shown by the decisive African imprint on conciliar history. This is why the movement toward church councils, seeking doctrinal definition by consultation based on exegetical precision, began more palpably and with more sophistication in Africa than elsewhere, as most fully embodied in Athanasius and Augustine. This consensus was gradually received in Rome, Antioch, Jerusalem and everywhere the apostolic work was carried.

## LIVING ON THE BOUNDARIES

The overlooked datum in the story is this: Libya was the unique crucible where the limits of early Christian unity were earliest and most rigorously tested. People preparing to be baptized were being catechized in the same apostolic faith, whatever the language or culture. They all felt the same need to discover and articulate the original unity of the apostolic witness couched in the idioms of their specific culture, just as believers today still do. Through carefully preserved sacred texts that were approved for reading in the churches, the apostolic teaching itself has not changed in the slightest, though cultural formations continue to change. Culture never stays the same. The apostolic witness never changes.

Although the African writers were preaching in diverse cultures, their citizenship was in the eternal city. They were seeking to present that same faith that had been delivered by the apostles to all these cultures without subjective distortions, in a way pertinent to varied cul-

---

[15]To get a fuller picture of my own thinking about this model of ecumenical reflection on history, see my previous studies on postmodern orthodoxy in *Agenda for Theology* (1979), *Systematic Theology* (3 vols., 1987-1992), the Ancient Christian Commentary on Scripture (General Introduction), and *Classic Christianity* (2009).

tural conditions and without losing the local heart language of believers. They were living the same Christian life in different places of the world—even its most remote localities (Irenaeus, *Ag. Her.* 1.10.1). They found that their unity in Christ bought them closer to their common humanity with all whose hearts yearn for God. It is a deep kinship. A decisive advantage of the early Christian mission over all its detractors was that it embodied a cohesive world-wide community of believers that soon spoke virtually all the world's known languages.

The acts of the martyrs of Scilli on July 17, A.D. 180, contains the first known court record of African Christian martyrdom. It records a trial before the proconsul Saturninus of Carthage concerning defendants that were brought in from a tiny village either in Numidia or Proconsular Africa. These saints indicate that they had "books and the epistles of Paul" which they refused to yield to the authorities. In unwavering fidelity to this apostolic teaching they offered their very lives.

We are here attempting to connect the dots between Irenaeus, Scilli, the continuity of apostolic testimony through time, the Arian heresy and its consequences. To the orthodox mind these are easily and evidently connected. They form a plausible gestalt. But to the modern mind the gestalt looks like miscellaneous dots.

To what extent was early Libyan Christianity consonant with catholic-orthodox-consensual-ecumenical Christianity? The geography of Libya places it on the border. It is on the border of the Roman ethos, on the border of the interface between Africa and Asia, and between Africa and Europe. It is on the border of the entire continent that split Latin and Greek-speaking Christianity. Arguably it remains today on the border of competing worldviews that were generated in late antiquity. Libya has been on the border of almost every key conflict of the last two millennia. Most issues of early Christian teaching were intensified in Libya. It was on the border of the Latin versus Greek liturgy and exegesis. It was on the border of Africaneity versus Roman colonialism. It was on the border of Arian versus Athanasian visions of the eternal lordship of Christ. It was on the border of Roman versus Byzantine hegemony. It was on the border of the Meletian versus the Alexandrian vision of church authority. Its perennial border status is symbolized in the fact that the division of Europe between the powers of the East and West was measured by a line pointing due north from the southernmost point of the Libyan Gulf of Sirte.

Today it remains on the border between Africa and the northern Mediterranean community of nations. It remains on the border between socialist and enterprise economies. It remains on the border between the technological revolution and traditional oriented Islam. It remains on the border between economic populism and political elitism. It remains on the border between modernization and sharia law. If so, that makes it unlikely that it could have been a historic epicenter for ecumenical consensus, yet the history of the conciliar movement indicates that it was the heart of that epicenter, especially in the early struggles with Sabellian and Arian teachings.

## THE WHOLE EARTH MAP OF LATE ANTIQUITY

The patristic geographers and early medieval cartographers of the known world divided the whole earth into three obvious parts:

- Africa
- Asia
- Europe

There was no fourth. Some of the earliest maps show Jerusalem at the center and three oval-shaped disks spinning away from the center: the African disk in the south, Asia in the east, and Europe in the north, like a three leaf clover with river systems primitively etched in.

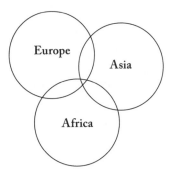

Whole-earth map of late antiquity

Triune teaching reinforced this unity and this diversity. Early African Christian exegetes, such as Origen and Lactantius, used these same word pictures to describe the whole known world. The term *catholic* or *catholikos* meant the whole inhabited world. It would become a defining term for all those Christians who shared the same doctrinal truth celebrated in the rest of known-world Christianity, as distinct from nonconsensual views such as Arianism, Sabellianism, Gnosticism and Manichaeism. From the outset the term *catholikos* embraced equally Africa, Asia and Europe. Africa was never a minor partner. On the contrary it was a defining partner on behalf of its unity.

By reasonable inference Africa included all other conceivable (even if yet undiscovered) parts of the contiguous world to the south. Africa was the entire vast range of tribes and nations that inhabited a single continent, even if mostly unknown. Africa meant whatever lies to the south of the Mediterranean, west from the Red Sea all the way to the Atlantic and south as far as (and farther than) anyone could imagine.

Early maps and their narrative equivalents show that Libya was thought to extend from Egypt to the Atlantic. There is no doubt that both Libya and Egypt were included in the earliest representations of Africa, despite the political differences between Roman Africa and Roman Egypt.

This is one among many reasons we cannot properly imagine that Egypt is separable from Africa. That denies both geography and Nilotic linguistic history. Those who wonder if the Nile is in Africa do well to first ask any cartographer about the boundaries of Africa. Admittedly the habit of separating Egypt as a political entity from Africa was common during the Roman period. But Egypt never belonged to a different continent than Libya in any ancient geography. That assertion would be easily dislodged by the records of the milestones of ancient roads west of the Nile into the great desert and south from the Mediterranean toward the heart of the continent.

In traveling from Libya to Egypt no one ever passed from one continent to another. The term *Libya* was sometimes identified with the whole of Africa, or the whole of North Africa, or that portion of Africa west of Egypt—to and beyond the Gulf of Sirte.

## EXCURSUS: WHY AFRICA IS ONE CONTINENT, NOT MANY

Since Libya is a part of Africa, it is pertinent to set forth clearly an uncomplicated geographical definition of Africa as a continent. By "Africa" the ancient world meant simply the entire massive continent, mostly unknown to written sources at the time, that lies to the south of the Mediterranean. Other definitions tend to increase ambiguities. Culturally, Africa is a vast blend of many diverse cultures and languages, but geographically Africa remains one single continent. It may take millions of years for the great Rift Valley to drift away completely from Africa, but until then Africa remains one continent, not many.

By "Libya" the ancient world meant the land area that is still called Libya: west of the Nile, south of the sea, deeper into the desert than anyone could imagine. Among historic cultures known in ancient Libya are many forms of early Nilotic, Pharaonic, Proto-Coptic, Berber, Libyan, Austurian, Garamantian and other indigenous peoples dating back to prehistoric times. Both ancient and modern Libya have drawn together a vast blend of diverse cultures and languages. Among major written sources for ancient Libyan geography and history are Herodotus, Pliny the Elder, Ptolemy, Procopius and Corippus.

The indigenous tribes of Roman Libya living mostly inland are as follows (we are moving from west to east Libya): (1) the Garamantes of inland western Tripolitania (south of the Ater Mountains, see Barrington Atlas, 35), (2) the coastal Macae, (3) the piedmont Laguatan of Syrtica south of Leptis Magna and south to Wadi Caam and Wadi Soffegin, (4) the Nasamones (east of Tripolitania and south of Berenike/Benghazi), (5) the Nafusa and Phazanii of Gebel Nafusa, (6) the seminomadic Austuriani with their camels in the desert, and (7) in the far eastern part of Libya bordering Egypt were the Marmaricans. All of these locations are, over the centuries of Roman rule, approximate and variable. Most of these are likely prehistoric. The Hawara and Zenata Berbers of Byzantine times may have come from prehistoric Palestine (Sjöström, *TT,* 24-26; Norris, 34). The Nefusa from the Gebel near Sabratha had a tradition of holy men and scholarship prior to the Arab conquest, which continued through the thirteenth century (Norris, 71-91, 227).

We know from Punic-Libyan-Latin-Berber tombstones and inscriptions that the predominant ethnic identities in inland villages of Libya were not Roman as such but a bilingual mix of linguistic cultures. (For a visual picture of the interlapping cultures, consult Barrington Atlas, 33-37, 72.) Some who today live in Libya and Egypt have plausible reasons for stressing their Nilotic or Berber or Middle East identity rather than their African identity, understandably preferring to be identified ethnically as Libyans or Egyptians or Ethiopians or Tuareg. Yet scientists, demographers and people of many religions, races and languages most commonly agree on the name of this one discrete continent: Africa. The same root word is variously transliterated as *Afriquia, Ifrika, Afrique*, after an indigenous ethnic tribe in the far north of the central Maghreb, when the earliest written histories of the continent were written. Most do not search desperately for a hyphenated word to describe the whole. So this study joins the majority in using it unapologetically as a geographical description of a single continent, aware that there remain many qualifiers, tensions, incongruities and useful footnotes within that single designation.

# 6

# SYNESIUS OF CYRENE

■■■

Synesius is the most important philosophical mind from early Christian times in Libya. His writings offer the best literary depiction of Libyan Christianity around A.D. 400. Among Libyan intellectuals we have more substantial documentary evidence for him than any other. This is why his life and thought justify more extensive investigation than any other figure in this study.

Synesius of Cyrene (c. 365–413) served as bishop of Ptolemais and metropolitan of the Pentapolis in Libya from A.D. 410 to 413. As the overseeing ecclesiastical leader of the vast territory of Cyrenaica, reaching from the Mediterranean far into the African desert, he supervised all aspects of Libyan Christianity—its religious, liturgical and civic functions.

## AN AFRICAN WISE MAN

This African intellectual was the author of letters, hymns and poems, as well as scientific and philosophical treatises, all highly readable. His writings put on bold display the earnestness of Libyan Christian spiritual formation in the early Byzantine period. He remains a model for those young Christians in Africa today who have a deep commitment to truth telling and the life of the mind, and to their own local cultural traditions.

His life presents a lively case study of what happens when a leading African philosopher is asked to become the leading bishop of the worshiping community of his nation. He was steeped in the forms of cultural formation characteristic of the coastal Maghreb of North Africa in late antiquity. He was especially indebted to African Neoplatonic philosophy. He exercised crucial leadership at a time when the underpinnings of philosophy were shaky. Emergent Christianity had produced a crisis of authenticity within his intellectual world. The great stream of African philosophy that had preceded him had become weakened and corrupted. Its weaknesses were exposed by the glare of the integrity of emergent Christianity.

The African coast of the Mediterranean was like a kitchen for the mixing and cooking of intellectual energies over much the known world of that time. Africa was producing intellectual ideas for all points north and east. The great southern giant was the place where the combinations and recipes were first tasted. This intellectual creativity existed in an arena of political instability. Synesius lived through a critical time of cultural confusion: a time of rapid deterioration of the economy and constant military challenges. The security of citizens was difficult to maintain. It was an anarchic and hazardous period, and he was a man devoted to cultural tradition and civic peace.

Synesius found ways of combining old and new cultural formations. He helped move his country's classic Libyo-Punic Hellenism toward an intellectually renewing form of classic Christianity. As a young man he found it hard to decide about the truth of Christianity. As an older man, he was challenged to apply that truth to historical circumstances.[1]

Nobly born, Synesius stemmed from a wealthy family of royal stock. His highly respected family was thought to go back to the very beginnings of Cyrene—no other than the descendants of Eurysthenes, of the family of Heraclides, who led the Dorians to Sparta. His father was named Hesychius, as was Synesius's oldest son (*B&P*, 16-17). Synesius was born a half century after Constantine's edict tolerating Christianity. This was at a time of the rapid early growth of orthodox Christianity in Libya and Egypt. Synesius was born and raised in a family tradition that was considered by Christians to be basically heathen, that is,

---

[1]Denis Roques, "Synésios, évêque et philosophe," *Revue des études grecques* 95 (1982): 461-67.

oriented toward traditional polytheistic gods. It was a sophisticated heathenism of a very genteel and urbane variety. It would take him a long struggle to come gradually to Christianity.

## THE AFRICAN WELLSPRING OF NEOPLATONISM

The Libyo-Punic African environment of the young Synesius was quite different from the more Romanized Africa of his contemporary, Augustine of Hippo (A.D. 354–430), who was born of a Berber Roman family in Numidia, in modern-day Eastern Algeria.

Synesius was born around 365, about a decade after Augustine and a decade before Cyril the Great. Augustine had a Christian mother and a Roman father. Synesius had pagan parents strongly attached to classic Afro-Hellenic sensibilities. Cyril was a brilliant product of the emerging Coptic Christian culture after the pattern of his uncle, the savvy Patriarch Theophilus. Though Augustine and Synesius never met, it is likely that young Cyril would have met and known Synesius during his times in Alexandria.

The earliest Neoplatonists—Ammonius Saccus and Plotinus—first taught in Africa. Only then after having become maturely formed in Alexandria, they subsequently went north to Europe, in both cases to Rome. This is not a trivial point: Both were first teaching and writing on the continent of Africa before their ideas appeared in Italy and Cappadocia. Contrary to common opinion, Neoplatonism had its beginnings far more in Africa than in Greece. This is an exemplary confirmation of the south to north movement of African intellectual creativity, which I discuss more fully in *How Africa Shaped the Christian Mind*. Augustine the Numidian and Synesius the Libyan both got their Neoplatonism from writers living on the African continent. Hence I will refer to them as African sources.

Other African Christians before Synesius had been shaped by Neoplatonism—among them Clement of Alexandria, Origen, Marius Victorinus and later Augustine. In Milan Augustine gathered a group of ascetics who were reading Neoplatonic sources and toying with the Porphyrian route of Neoplatonism.

After Synesius, these same themes would be developed further by

Christian philosophers like John Philoponus (490–570). The school would become largely depleted in energy following the work of Olympiodorus the younger (495–570). All of these were Africans.

## SYNESIUS'S EDUCATION

The considerable resources of Synesius's family enabled the older brother (Synesius) and the younger brother (Euoptius/Evoptius) to study abroad (*B&P*, 16-17). They received the best education available in the most lively intellectual centers of the continent of Africa— Cyrene and Alexandria. Synesius grew up among the intellectual and cultural elites. His extensive inherited family resources and landed properties enabled Synesius to travel to Athens (c. 392–393) and Constantinople (397–401). The sequence of his visits to Athens, Constantinople, Alexandria and back to Cyrene is still disputed.

In his *Letter* 136 he described his visit to Athens. He had gone there with high hopes, soon to be disappointed. Synesius had idyllic fantasies of talking with philosophers, intellects and priests, especially about his primary interest in the meaning of dreams. He later wrote jokingly that after this first visit he would no longer feel the need for revering people just because they had been to Athens. He had brushed shoulders with the elites of Athens and found them wanting. His time in Athens proved to be a disenchantment. It would never compare in importance with his Neoplatonist education in Alexandria with Hypatia. He described his soul as he left Athens as seared "like a victim burned in a sacrificial fire" (*Letter* 136), with nothing remaining but dead skin. He may have been first initiated to Eleusinian mysteries while in Athens. But he recognized that these mystery rites represented an intellectual ethos that was already wasting away.

In the mid 390s he returned to Cyrene for the quiet life of an intellectual aristocrat. The family lived as gentleman farmers with a sprawling estate near Cyrene. It was large enough to provide him a place where he could hunt and escape the world's responsibilities—at least until the marauders struck. He enjoyed the benefits of living among simple, rural people without pretenses. Many of them thought of his family as if they were true-life descendents of Agamemnon.

He lived an elite life destined for leadership, much like the Christian families of Basil and Gregory of Nazianzus, who were only a few years his elders. He always looked forward to returning to his rural estate to live in serenity close to the land. But Patriarch Theophilus (Theophilos) called and persuaded Synesius to serve as the leading bishop of the Pentapolis.

His writings reveal him as a man of easy wit and good humor. One of his earliest written pieces was in praise of baldness, showing why baldness is more revealing than hair. Dion Chrysostomus had previously written in praise of hair (*Letter* 1). The lighter side of Synesius is seen in this early essay: Why is baldness superior to having hair? Because the bald head is more round. And round is the symbol of perfection. That is the most perfect shape for the head, viewed in relation to human reasoning. Thus a bald head would be more akin to reason in a platonic universe. There would be no unruly hair on it. It is a sphere, with all points related equally to the center.

## Synesius in Alexandria with Hypatia

Synesius proceeded to Alexandria to look for a philosophical mentor who could teach him the way of true philosophy. He had a great love of truth that could be fully embodied in daily behavior. He arrived in Alexandria not long after the edict of Theodosius I, closing pagan temples and outlawing all sacrifices in 390.

Synesius is said to have received his instruction at Alexandria in both the Catechetical School and the Museion, and he entertained a great deal of reverence and affection for Hypatia, one of the last pagan Neoplatonists. He found in Hypatia his lifelong mentor, friend and confidant. Already she was a recognized leader in mathematics and philosophy. Hypatia introduced Synesius to the classic texts of mystical Neoplatonism (especially Porphyry and the Chaldean Oracles).

Hypatia was the brilliant daughter of the renowned scientist and mathematician Theon, who was probably from Cyrene. "Hypatia's closest, most loyal students were people who later held high imperial or ecclesiastical positions. Of even greater significance is evidence that agents of the imperial power arriving in Alexandria became close acquaintances of Hypatia and most likely attended her lectures." (*HOA*, 38; *B&P*, 49-59).

Synesius and Euoptius studied classic literature and rhetoric as well as science and philosophy in Alexandria under Hypatia. Years later Synesius would continue to correspond with her. This relationship would endure to the very last days of his life. He was devoted to her unstintingly. He learned from Hypatia that all things in nature are harmonious (*B&P*, 49-58). All parts of the universe are like a symphony. In each discrete thing there are intimations of all other things. Synesius learned by heart many of the dialogues of Plato. He quoted them from memory with approximate accuracy.

Within the close circle of Hypatia's disciples Synesius experienced his first and most long-lasting conversion. It was a deep commitment to the philosophic way of life. He discovered that "the eye of the soul" within him was prompting him to see the sacred depth of the universe in all things. He stood in awe of the One embedded in the many. He dedicated his mind to "mysteries without rites." He was devoted to close attention to the evidences of divinity within the human soul. These correspond with the divinity penetrating the cosmos.

Hypatia introduced her coterie to occult studies. She commented extensively on the literature referred to as Hermes Trismegistus, the alleged teacher of the magical system known as hermeticism that mixed alchemy, mystery and magic. She was the tutor to the Mediterranean elite. Though tolerant of the growing Christian movement, she remained unconvinced. She was a veritable model of the philosophical way of life. In time the mind of Synesius was flowing within a kaleidoscopic stream of scientific, philosophical and literary inquiries in Alexandria. There he became a convinced Neoplatonist.

Under Hypatia's tutelage the young Synesius viewed science and especially astronomy as a way of ascent toward God. Their circle wove together religious mysticism with nature. Hypatia was enthralled with occult studies and arcane ways of meditation. She was an experimentalist with paths leading to a higher life, the ascent of the soul. She was inspired by her father toward a complete devotion to the philosophical life. She herself was a model of the search for truth in daily life.

This led Hypatia to produce a commentary on the body of Hermetic literature attributed to Hermes Trismegistus (*B&P*, 290). "Clad in the modest mantle of the philosopher, [she] gathered around her a circle of young adepts living in a moral order circumscribed by philosophy, convinced that they were made of better clay than others" (*HOA*, 60-61). Although sympathetic with aspects of Christianity, she was temperamentally unable to join any popular religious movement, due to her independence and cultural elitism.

The young Synesius similarly had wide tolerance for differences of opinion, but with many affinities to Christianity. It is likely that Synesius had already had some significant exchanges with the Christian believers of Cyrene before he launched out on his own philosophical quest. It is unlikely, however, that he was baptized before his early thirties. Maria Dzielska in *Hypatia of Alexandria* writes:

> Thus, close association with Hypatia did not prevent Synesius from strengthening his ties with Christianity (both in Alexandria and in Cyrene); just as spiritual rapport with Theophilus, a Christian marriage, baptism, and a growing affirmation of his faith did not alter his attitude toward his woman teacher. . . . Neither do we notice that his close affiliation with Hypatia provoked any conflicts with Bishop Theophilus. (*HOA*, 46)

He reflected on the implications of the Eleusinian mysteries with the circle of Neoplatonists under Hypatia. As his lifelong teacher, she favored him with continued correspondence and counsel. Under her guidance, he learned not only philosophy but rhetoric, poetry and spiritual formation.

## THE AFRO-HELLENIC INTELLECTUAL ELITE OF LATER ROMAN ANTIQUITY

Synesius was grateful to be an insider within the closest circle of disciples of Hypatia, the most famous woman philosopher of her time. He struggled with the truth of Christianity, constantly examining its truth claims in relation to his own classic culture. Hypatia introduced Synesius, as she did many of the pagan elite, to a mystical strain of Neoplatonism significantly informed by the *Chaldean Oracles* (*B&P*, 50). Neoplatonism remained the prevailing movement in African philosophy of late antiquity throughout Egypt, Libya and Proconsular Africa, before it was transported to Rome and Athens.

The philosophical mind of Synesius was thoroughly steeped in the best traditions of African Neoplatonic philosophy. There in Alexandria he had met and struggled with the truth of Christianity at a time and place when paganism was collapsing. He lived amid and through the collapse. He loved and trusted the old Hellenic way (*B&P*, 62-83). He was ambivalent toward the new unknown Christian way. His heart remained a conflation of Libyan-Punic-Hellenic-Pagan themes. He defended the pre-Christian search for truth as long and well as he could, until the growing power of the new era became evident and undeniable. He had to decide one way or another: Christianity or Cyrenaic Hellenic paganism.[2] Synesius was learning critical thinking from Hypatia. Sadly her irenic spirit was set in a city in which at times it was dangerous to be either a pagan or a Christian or a Jew, depending on the mob.

## THE PHILOSOPHER'S WAY OF LIFE

What special treasure did Synesius contribute from African Neoplatonic Christianity to world Christianity? A philosophical idealism that sought to preserve the best values of his home culture within the newly emerging world of orthodox Christianity. He brought to Christianity an increased seriousness about preserving the viable virtues of his intellectually distinguished Afro-Hellenic culture, yet within the orbit of the basic teachings of Christianity and the practice of liturgy.

Synesius was a nobleman who wanted to perfect inward and outward virtue for the benefit of the civic order. But temperamentally he preferred the quiet country life of scientific and literary study. He became a Christian bishop in a multicultural world in which he sought to nurture a just order within his own society, preserve the best virtues of all competing ethnicities, tell the truth, serve the civic order and keep the

---

[2]Christian Locambrade, *Synésios de Cyréne: Helène et chrétien* (Paris: Les Belles lettres, 1951).

peace. He never left behind the virtues of the native philosophical idealism that nurtured his soul during the early years of his life.

As with Pantaenus, the teacher of Clement in Alexandria's school of catechetics, the search for truth to Synesius was an eclectic journey and an experiment. He gathered wisdom from everywhere. He sought the nectar of every flower along the way of his journey, as a bee from blossom to blossom, seeking to bring it into a rational integration in which Christianity might be one among many options for integrating the whole. Synesius was already captivated by the notions of providence, vocation and election from his early period (*Letter* 137).

His major contribution was in the building of bridges between his older African (Libyo-Punic-Greek) culture and the new religion of Christianity in Africa. His Libyo-African-Hellenic ancestors had greater impact on his early thinking than classic Christian doctrine. These two strains would become melded in his later period. His earlier grasp of Christianity was couched largely in terms of Hellenic ideals and literary models, but it would mature beyond these limits. He was trying to reclaim an intellectus that was imploding.

The whole world was becoming Christian, or appearing to become so. In Constantinople the Christian emperor exercised dynastic power. The best of ancient culture was being absorbed in Christianity. He was forced to choose the basis on which he would cast his lot in the future. He was trying to make a cultural assessment that could sustain a viable political outcome. He was hoping for some accommodation between these polarities.

In the company of persons who were united to each other by their commitment to a fierce sense of intellectual integrity, Synesius hoped to ascend in the philosophical life toward a life with God (*Letter* 137). Yet in this early phase he was not fully convinced of the truth of Christianity.

## THE POLITICAL STRUGGLE FOR LIBYA

As a conspicuous intellectual and political leader of Libya, Synesius was facing decisions that many African Christians would face in augmented forms in subsequent centuries: occupation by foreign powers, guerrilla actions, cultural disintegration, loss of social cohesion, absurd taxation and economic dislocation. He was experimental while remaining grounded in his indigenous cultural tradition. He understood both the old and new in African syncretism. He sought to unite what was divided.

He applied shrewd cultural analysis to the matrix of political accountability. He would ultimately offer a great gift to African Christianity: building bridges between his native African polyglot (Libyo-Punic-Greek) culture and Christian orthodoxy. He supervised the recycling of pagan temples, remaking them into Christian churches in Libya, honoring them by preserving and integrating them into the emerging Christian world. He came to notice at a time when the wide world was first becoming primitively Christian, when social and civic administration was being thrust upon bishops amid the vacuum of power left by the collapse of Rome.

In the decade of the 390s Alaric and the Goths were ravaging Thrace and Greece, threatening Constantinople, and thwarting the armies of the emperor. About this same time the writings of Augustine reveal how deeply he was shaken by the advancing Goths, a thunderstorm that would lead to the sack of Rome in A.D. 410. Imagine the similar angst of his contemporary Synesius. It prompted imaginings about the final conclusion of history, the time of judgment and decision.

Synesius gradually realized that the best of ancient culture could be absorbed positively into robust Christianity. He took captive the mysteries of pagan religion and welcomed them where possible into the Christian ethos. This has remained to this day a problematic theme of African Christianity. In the ongoing current debates in African Christianity on traditional African religion, ancestry and inculturation, Synesius may provide a significant classical African model of bridging.

## BIRTHING HIMSELF

Synesius's early letters show that he was trying to give birth to a new self—a self rationally directed, the nurture of the soul and civic responsibility. In its early stages it was a desperate act of independent willing. His sense of grace would come later. Early on he was trying to raise himself up in the philosophical life, to purify himself (*Letters* 137-140) and to become entirely devoted to the life of the mind (*Letter* 140). His was a daily life of struggle and purification.

The hope of an immediate and sustained uplifting to the perfect life is something like the spirit of the long tradition of immediate perfectionism from Clement of Alexandria to Phoebe Palmer: seeking complete consecration now. He had a temperament much like that of Clement of Alexandria, especially as expressed in the seventh book of the *Stromata*.

Synesius realized that the philosophical life would not be easily adaptable to mundane concerns. He would live a different life than those preoccupied with getting and spending and providing and defending. It was more for those few who were, like athletes, energetically and willingly advancing day by day in disciplined thinking. This required a rigorous sense of restraint and self-control. He sought to transcend the ambiguous levels of existence of the common crowd that so often sadly displays a sad history of being deceived.

Many aspects of the philosophical life had to be held in confidence, so as not to disturb the public order. It would be irresponsible for a pedagogue to reveal the truth to those not yet ready for it. The truth cannot be popularly or widely revealed to multitudes unprepared to grasp it. At times it is better to be silent than misunderstood. He thought that vulgar forms of cheap philosophy would tend to "awaken among men a great contempt for things divine" (*Letter* 143). Those who have found its riches do not reveal its truths thoughtlessly to those who are wholly unprepared for the richness of the whole truth. The truth prematurely revealed might do more harm than good.

In his hymns Synesius grasped the depth of the philosophical vocation as a quest for purity to which he continued to aspire as a Christian bishop.[3] He had a strong disposition toward the study of religion from the outset. But in his early years the form of religion was chiefly a philosophical version of pan-Hellenic study, meditation and reflection.

---

[3]Christian Lacombrade, "Perspectives nouvelles sur les hymnes de Synésios,"*Revue des études grecques* 74 (1961): 439.

## OF TIME AND THE SOUL'S ASCENT

Synesius wrote hymns about mysteries without rites and the linkage of the soul to all things in time. At first this linkage was not well-coordinated with similar Christian ideas, but later that coordination was grasped. The soul lives on the frontier between material space and changing time. Consciousness of time does not exist except for the soul. It is the soul that flows through time, marking changes and considering options. The journey of soul to God calls for going back to its uncreated source. The soul has fallen into the moving streams of matter and time. That world is not intrinsically evil, but it always is tempting the soul away from the path of ascent of reason, to digress from the path to God and true selfhood. Reason invites the soul to continue its path to God, to take the leap of the spirit toward the higher life (*Hymn* 1).

Synesius was looking for the radical conversion of the soul to God, not in explicit Christian terms, but rather in Neoplatonic terms. He was not yet engaged in the deep study of Scripture, as he would be later. In his early period he shows little knowledge of Hebrew Scripture. As God looks empathically upon the temporal world and then returns to himself, so does the way of philosophy look empathically upon the world and then turns to reroot itself in its own soul. In Egyptian and Libyan traditions, this is analogous to the sun returning on a daily cycle from death to life.

Before he became more deeply engaged with the study of Christianity, Synesius was already searching for some connection between Neoplatonic proto-incarnational and trinitarian ideas and what Christian teaching would name as a fleshly incarnation. But that was very embryonic as a concept. Later he would develop a clearer notion of the divine descent in the virgin birth and participation in the divine ascent in the resurrection. The ascent of the soul to the eternal is a deep-seated theme of pre-Christian Libyo-Punic religion and of pharaonic Egyptian religion. It was actively maintained in Synesius both in his youth and maturity. It would be a mistake to term this secret knowledge as Gnosticism. Gnosticism was by the late fourth century a deteriorating movement. Valentinus had left Alexandria for Rome much earlier, in the second century.

## SYNESIUS'S HUNGER FOR CONNECTEDNESS

Synesius was an Afro-Hellenic traditionalist thrust into a time when Christianity was becoming the bearer of an emerging international culture that would transcend national impediments. Christian faith became, for Synesius, one among many perspectives he sought to integrate into his earlier cultural worldview. He was seeking a philosophical life that would bring him into close contact with a circle of critical inquirers. He was happiest among those who were seeking to lift their souls above the worldly sphere through the exercise of intellect and ultimately toward God. As a young man he was already probing the depths and the perplexities of Christian issues such as vocation, providence and justice. He thought that the special gift and purpose of our humanity was to engage in right reasoning (*Letter* 137).

By the 390s he was able to speak already in trinitarian terms, but only by means of the Neoplatonic metaphors, as they were informed by the *Chaldean Oracles* with their prototrinitarian ideas. *Hymn* 1 exalts superiority of divine knowledge to earthly and mundane matters without demeaning the earthly, which is to be transcended by reason. It was an earnest search of a philosophical idealist to raise himself up from a history of fallenness. He was engaged in an earnest, highly idealistic search to raise himself up toward life with God.

Synesius was on the road to God by way of a disciplined ascent of the soul. He was world-affirming, not world-denying. In his early thought there is a noteworthy absence of distinctly Christian terms and scriptural language. There is not much evidence of Christian orthodox reasoning at this stage. The young Synesius offers a view noticeably different from mainstream of Christian exegesis, not trying to connect directly with Hebraic views of history as revelation. He was not trying to connect the soul with historical narratives of Scripture, but rather to connect the soul immediately to God.

Above all he did not want to be trapped in a thought world that would rob him of his philosophical vocation. It is not unusual for Christian seekers to be drawn toward philosophy before they grasp its religious ground.

While studying Porphyry in Hypatia's school, Synesius was attracted to a Neoplatonic view of the triune being that did not require either an incarnation or a resurrection. Whatever premature view he may have had of Christian triune teaching, it was largely without the classic Christian view of revelation in history. Though intriguing to readers of Hellenistic philosophy, his maturity at this stage was hardly an adequate preparation for Christian leadership, much less the liturgical and moral challenges of the episcopacy. His concern was not with Scripture or orthodoxy, but cultural continuity and inward truth.

Synesius was writing poetry as early as his twenties. One of his early convictions was that everything is connected with everything else, just as the circumference of a circle is connected at every point to its center. In this way all nature is joined to God (*Hymn* 1, *Letter* 137). The soul hungers for reconnections with the divine as its source. It yearns to return to its original condition of right reason.

## THE MISSION TO CONSTANTINOPLE

Take a rich inward life like that of Synesius and place it in an intense political environment. You can watch the struggle unfold. This is what happened when Synesius was thrust into the crucible of Christian politics in Byzantium.

Synesius's early reflections on Christianity were from the outset profoundly mixed with political motives. He was fascinated with Christianity as a means of political cohesion and integration, yet feared that it would destroy the remnants of Afro-Hellenism.

After some years as a student, he returned to Cyrenaica hoping for the quiet life of aristocrat. Despite his protests, he was soon persuaded to head a diplomatic mission to plead the case of the Pentapolis to the emperor in Constantinople for tax relief and fair representation (*B&P*, 40). Though he preferred his books and hunting, he answered the call to public service. He remained in Constantinople for about three and a half years (from September 397 to the spring of 401).

Though young he headed the mission to Constantinople whose formal purpose was to present a gold crown to the new emperor Arcadius and to seek the protection of the city and make an appeal for the reduction of taxes. The cities of the Pentapolis were impoverished by wars with tribal invaders from the south.

He was both awed and puzzled by the world he found there. Eventually it would lead to a kind of disillusionment. He faced the frustrations of the internal manipulations and stresses within the imperial court, and the individual self-interests that played into the balance of power between the East and the West. He enjoyed the libraries that were being developed in Constantinople, hoping to rival those in Alexandria. The university was in its beginning stages there in the very area in which it is presently located. Arcadia was the emperor. Both Latin and Greek were spoken in the court. Among major pagan intellectual leaders in Constantinople of this period were Libanius of Antioch, and Themistius, prototypes of the genteel pagan scholar living in Christian Constantinople.

Themistius (317–c. 387) was a statesman, rhetorician and philosopher, born in northern Anatolia and taught at Constantinople. He held that Plato and Aristotle were in substantial agreement that God has made men free to adopt the mode of worship they prefer, and that Christianity and Hellenism were merely two forms of the one universal religion. Though a pagan, he was admitted to the senate by Constantius II in 355. He was prefect of Constantinople in 384 on the nomination of Theodosius. He corresponded with Gregory of Nazianzus.

Christian orthodoxy had been further defined by the creed of 381 at the First Council of Constantinople. Into this milieu Synesius entered. Christianity began to be more intriguing to him. He realized that he could make an accommodation to Christian teaching, but only by translating its doctrines into Neoplatonic terms. It was at first an awkward enterprise and always remained difficult, but not impossible. He was not a heretic, and was never prone to Arian thinking. He was not tempted to becoming captivated with the varieties of heresies so prevalent in the late fourth century. But he sustained his relationships with his old pagan friends who witnessed the decline of Hellenistic religion following the reign of Julian the apostate. In the reign of Theodosius, who reinforced the military defense of Byzantium against the Goths, Christian orthodoxy was becoming more precisely defined. It was amid this context that he entered more clearly into dialogue with Christianity. All of these traditional Hellenists wanted to defend the empire against barbarian dilutions, of which Arianism was considered a lethal type (*B&P*, 19-28, 66-67).

While in Constantinople, Synesius was not yet baptized, but Christianity began to be more intriguing to him during the time when he was back in Alexandria and had been introduced by Theodosius to the woman who would become his wife, a believing Coptic Orthodox woman. Her name has remained unknown but her influence on him was lasting. As he entered into a Christian marriage with this devout Christian believer, he was discovering that he could make an accommodation with Christian faith without diminishing his philosophical vocation.

On his way in this pilgrimage Synesius became a traveling political advocate seeking to adapt Christianity to Neoplatonic culture. Paganism was dying, Christianity rising. He was moving slowly toward Christianity, but largely on behalf of cultural values, peace, historic continuity and the preservation of what is possible to recover. He was seeking a deep cultural synthesis between the peace of Rome and the stability of religion. He was enmeshed in the same tensions Augustine described in *The City of God*. He hoped for a fresh new expression of a higher culture rooted in the wisdom of the past.

## THE PAGAN INTELLECTUAL IN A CHRISTIAN ENVIRONMENT

Synesius was a younger contemporary of Gregory of Nazianzus and John Chrysostom, both of whom served in the Constantinopolitan patriarchal office at a time that it was highly competitive with the supremacy of the See of St. Mark in Alexandria. Synesius in Constantinople likely read the Cappadocian fathers—Basil of Caesarea, Gregory of Nazianzus and Gregory of Nyssa. He was in Constantinople at the time when John Chrysostom was the patriarch. How could he have possibly missed meeting him? These were the brilliant Christian theologians who prepared the way for Synesius to take Christianity with intellectual seriousness. The Cappadocians would later provide much of the liturgical center for the Libyan, Egyptian and Ethiopian worshiping communities.

Synesius was in Constantinople and Alexandria a few decades after the death of the emperor Julian (363), often called "the apostate," who had once been a fellow student of Basil of Caesarea and Gregory of Nazianzus in Athens, but became an advocate of a reactionary form of diehard pagan religion. This reaction was in due time overpowered by the orthodox Christian emperor Theodosius, who was struggling to reestablish a reliable military defense of the capital city against the onslaught of the Goths and Huns.

Synesius grew up as a pagan North African intellectual before becoming a Christian philosopher. The genteel lightness of Synesius expressed the tolerant spirit of the Hellenistic idealists. They were at first hoping for an early demise of Christianity, but later became resigned to a needful accommodation to it.

Synesius remained imbued with the high ideals of Neoplatonism. Even after becoming bishop he continued to express that philosophical commitment in Libya's leading dioceses in a way that exhibited full respect for both classic Christian teaching and the philosophical quest.

## INTERNATIONAL HELLENISM AND CHRISTIANITY

By the end of the fourth century Synesius was standing against disintegrating voices such as the Arians. His orthodoxy was more focused on cultural continuity and the social analysis of history than on scriptural doctrine per se. It was as bishop, when he was thrust into a liturgical role of baptizing and teaching, that he was drawn into deeper Christian reflection.

Gradually Synesius realized that Christianity might play a role in the defense of the cultural tradition to which he was deeply attached. If the new religion represented by Christianity might be the means of saving the old religion, it might also save the literary and philosophical culture of the worldview he ascribed to. He was also learning that the pagan barbarians were more a threat to the classic Afro-Hellenic philosophical ideals than were Christians, who were defending the old order against imminent devastation. Christian leaders were proposing policies that defended the classic empire.

At length it dawned on Synesius while in Constantinople that Christianity ironically had the power to reshape the more virtuous remnants of the old religion! But would he become a catechumen and be baptized as a Christian? No. Not yet. He had too much independence to lose. Nonetheless he sees providence as a pagan doctrine that was working itself out in social conflict. He could see this outworking firsthand in the conflict between the Arian barbarians and the orthodox Christians. He had many affinities with the Cappadocian fathers politically, but had not yet grasped the full significance of their Christology and triune reasoning.

Synesius wanted to help make the world safer for Afro-Hellenic values, but not yet on the basis of orthodox Christian belief as such. Rather he was trying to save Afro-Hellenistic traditions from a coarse and politically dangerous barbarism. Later he would be able to correlate this with rescuing orthodoxy from Eunomian Arianism. He was realizing that the barbarian Goths and the Arian dissidents were a greater threat to his previous classic world than the Christian believers were defending against idiosyncratic views contrary to the classic Christian consensus (*B&P*, 98-100, 335).

In the 390s Synesius appeared to be a unique sort of political mind who was seeking to adapt Christianity to the ideals of Neoplatonic philosophical culture. He was tentatively moving toward Christianity, but on behalf of cultural values and continuity, and against the world coming unglued in conflict.

Synesius sought a deep new cultural synthesis between the peace of Rome and the vision of the City of God. Augustine's masterpiece with this title was not completed until after the death of Synesius, but Synesius intuitively anticipated many of its accents. He hoped that Christianity would become a new form of expression of a higher culture. All this was in formation before he became either a baptized Christian or a bishop.

How did this integration develop?

## THE TEMPLES OF THRACE

While in Constantinople, Synesius made visits to many of the temples of Chalcedon on the other side of the Bosphorus and to Thrace. He was making pilgrimages both to formerly pagan places of worship and to Christian leaders and locations. The mysteries he notes may refer to either pagan or Christian mysteries. At this time pagan temples were being remade into Christian basilicas in both Libya and Thrace.

In *Hymn* 3 Synesius reveals the state of his soul:

> Lord, to all these [temples] I came prostrate, . . . drenching the ground with tears, that my pilgrimage should not have been fruitless. I supplicated the divine ministers, as many as occupy the fertile plain of Thrace, and those on the opposite shore, who oversee the Chalcedonian lands, your sacred ministers whom you have crowned with angelic rays. (translation, Bregman, 64)

What ministers were these? Christian or pagan or an evolving amalgamation? Since Theodosius had already closed the temples, Synesius was probably referring to Christian priests and basilicas. He likely met Christian laity and clergy who were living holy lives, but amid the remnants of pagan temples. He could not help asking: What makes Christianity so vital in the creation of a culture? How can the old order survive within the context of these new forces? Can they be integrated?

## THE ASTROLABE EXPERIMENT: A GLIMPSE OF A RENAISSANCE MIND

In 397 when Synesius arrived in Constantinople as the representative of Cyrene in requesting tax relief, he did not cease his vocation as a philosopher and scientist. In Constantinople he appeared as a kind of renaissance man. He sought out Paeonius with a gift and an essay on the gift (*De dono*). Paeonius was a military leader who had "great influence over the emperor" (*Letter* 154). Paeonius was familiar with the circle of Hypatia, and was interested in their philosophical and scientific investigations. The gift was a silver astrolabe that Synesius had been working on. He had made it in Alexandria. It appears to be a prototype of a location device. He was soliciting the interest of Paeonius in the device (*B&P*, 85). In the accompanying short essay Synesius commends scientific and philosophical studies to politicians and military advisers.

The Roman architect Vitruvius (c. 88-c. 26 B.C.) had earlier (in *De architectura*) described an anaphoric clock (probably a clepsydra, or water clock) that he had seen in Alexandria, featuring a rotating field of stars behind a wire frame indicating the hours of the day. No one knows exactly when the stereographic projection was actually turned into the instrument we know today as the astrolabe. Theon of Alexandria (c. 390—shortly before the time of Synesius's embassy to Constantinople) had written a treatise on the astrolabe that became the basis for much that would be later written on the subject by the Arab authors in the eighth century.

Prior to these Arabic scientists, Synesius had apparently constructed the prototype of an instrument that had the key attributes of a primitive astrolabe. In doing so he was acting in the tradition of Hypatia, Theon's daughter, who combined scientific inquiry with philosophical reflection. Synesius called the devise a planisphere. Other early pre-Islamic descriptions of actual astrolabe instruments were written a century later, one by the Alexandrian philosopher John Philoponus (Joannes Grammaticus) in the sixth century.

The renaissance-like range of Synesius's interests are on display in his writings and activities in Constantinople. Synesius made one of the earliest known references to a hydrometer in a letter to Hypatia. He was seeking to invent a device that measured the flow of water. Here we see the mind of a renaissance man at work.

Synesius was also actively interested in research into paranormal activity, what we would today call extrasensory perception, dreams, theurgic prayers and alchemy. He also wrote a treatise on dog breeding, which regrettably did not survive. His military prowess and exploits became crucial to the survival of Libya during the period of the nomadic marauders. He wrote numerous poems and letters. This richly fitted mind was destined finally to play a major role in ecclesiastical affairs.

## EARLY WRITINGS

### *De providentia* (On Providence)

During this period Synesius wrote three works: one on providence, one on kingship and one on dreams. These early writings provide an indication of how broad were his intellectual interests.

One of his main early works was *The Egyptian Tale*, or *On Providence*, written in A.D. 400. It was an allegory representing two key ministers under Arcadius the emperor. The two competing advisers were Aurelian and Gainus, who were struggling in a way that was adaptable to the myth of Osiris and Seth. For Synesius this symbolized the conflict between ambiguous assessments of good and evil. It raised an overarching issue that would increasingly concern Neoplatonist and Christian intellectuals: providence, or the meaning of history in the light of evil present in history (*B&P*, 283-88).

Synesius was thinking about providence as an ancient teaching working in and through social conflict, embracing barbarians and empires and believers of various kinds. His motive was not to conform to orthodox belief but to make his Afro-Hellenic world more secure and capable of tolerant generosity. He sought to save the old order from new irrational compulsions. For Synesius the deeper question was theodicy: Why is evil allowed to exist in a good world? Why does God permit evil? No matter how prevalent evil is in history, God is caring for his creation through providence. Glimpses of providence are seen in the beauty and order of the universe.

Synesius was keenly aware of the demonic motives and dynamics of ordinary human history. It is all too evident that evil plays a major part of the story of all human history. He knew there could be no full accounting of the realities of fallen human history without a realistic assessment of the demonic in human freedom, the demons from the fallen spiritual realm struggling against the better angels from higher realms (*De prov.* 1.10 [1229]). These two worlds were in a decisive struggle. There history and the soul meet. The soul is in the middle of the struggle (*De prov.* 1.10 [1232]). By its choices the soul is moving either in ascent to God or further descent into the demonic sphere. Though Synesius was an outsider looking in, he could see that Christianity offered wisdom for this struggle.

Synesius had a special interest as a philosopher in the conception of universal history and how it could relate to the rational and Christian teachings of providence. In the broadest perspective the events of now must be seen in relation to the whole human narrative.

Along with other early African Christian philosophers of history
(Lactantius, Augustine and Cyril) the cultured critics of Christianity
were asking: What is happening to the soul in this world of struggle.
This is another way of asking, What is the destiny of the human story?
How does the whole impact the part? In Christian terms: What is God
doing in this ambiguous world in the long course of history?

In such circumstances reasonable persons will try to lift themselves
out of the mire into a longer range perspective. Reason says, Do not
accommodate to the brokenness of the world (*De prov.* 1.10 [1229-33]).
Live as if you were surviving in an armed camp in enemy territory, attacked by demonic spiritual forces you cannot see. These forces will
become enraged if anyone maintains foreign laws and customs within
their borders (*De prov.* 1.11 [1234-36]). Employ all the prudence and
rationality you can muster. You have the powers given to a divine soul,
even among demonic forces in attack mode. The soul always exists
within the special conditions of a particular time and particular place.
It is always enmeshed with its embodiment in a history.

Synesius was not yet a Christian at this time of writing. The ascent
is not by grace and is without reference to the incarnation, but nonetheless an ascent from the dead. A slow conversion is going on between
390 and 402.

### *De regno* (On Kingly Rule)

When Theodosius died in A.D. 395, Arcadius succeeded him as emperor of the East at the age of eighteen. Meanwhile the brother of Arcadius, Honorius, became emperor of the Western empire. In Constantinople the eunuch Eutropius became the chief obstacle to Synesius for
a diplomatic hearing with the Eastern emperor Arcadius.

Synesius arrived in Constantinople in September of 397. Synesius
waited at length for an audience. In 398 he wrote *De regno*. It was tran-
scribed and later made available to a wider readership. Synesius was
interested in the balance of power being played out between the Roman
Empire and the barbarian hordes. More so he was seeking to defend
the vulnerable interests of his native country in Africa. He was in-

trigued by the relation of these political energies to the intellectual traditions that were forming the culture of the early Byzantine period.

Representing an impoverished war-torn nation, yet living temporarily within a luxurious court life, Synesius, like John Chrysostom, wrote caustically against luxury and corruption. He stood against elaborate oriental ostentation and ceremony. The just king will be ruled by the fear of ultimate divine judgment and retribution. The ruler does well to seek the counsel of wise people experienced and disciplined in seeking the truth.

Synesius was especially intent on resisting the intrusion of debasing influences and threats to the public order. He was worried about the growing influence of the Goths on the outskirts of Constantinople and within it. He warned against getting involved in foreign alliances with those who would dilute virtuous energies. The armies of Gainas had almost toppled the Byzantine state at the turn of the century. Synesius urged the political leaders to listen to the best minds, to those disinterested in private ambition. Listen not to sycophants but to informed minds who can help the governing authorities to resist abuses of power. The first priority of the wise ruler is to combat corruption relentlessly.

This was a time when Eutropius was an overbearing corrupting influence on the court politics. Synesius remained in Constantinople for more than three years trying to obtain an imperial audience on behalf of his destitute people. He found it a burdensome and difficult task, but conceded it was necessary. He read many sources of widely different opinions and sought to integrate them. The city widened his range of perceptions, especially in the direction of Christianity. He did not give up his interest in theurgic and philosophical Neoplatonism, but drew closer to Christian minds. At length Synesius obtained the patronage of the powerful praetorian prefect Aurelianus and was allowed to present his request to the Emperor Arcadius. The message of Synesius to Emperor Arcadius is contained in *De regno* (On Kingly Rule). He received the tax remission for the Pentapolis and the exemption from onerous obligations. But Aurelianus fell into disgrace, and it seemed the case had been lost. When Aurelianus was reinstated, the imperial favor was restored.

Soon after this long-awaited hearing, Synesius left Constantinople. On the day of his departure there was an earthquake (*Letter* 61). Synesius escaped harm, but was ready to head back to Africa (*B&P*, 92-102). He returned to Cyrene and spent most of the next ten years in his country estate, in the interior of the province.

### *De insomniis* (On Dreams)

Freud was not the first to think of the relation of dreams and the human psyche. Synesius saw dreams as a clue to the art of grasping the truth, as a vehicle of the soul. His treatise *De insomniis* (On Dreams), written around 405, is one of the most astute books of ancient times on the causes and meaning of dreams and imagination. He was writing on what we may learn in dreams from the current life of the soul. In this work Synesius teaches that dreams give humanity direct access to sacred knowledge. They are the sign language of the soul. They provide intimations of the future and indications of the meaning of one's personal past. For this reason it is wise to pay attention to dreams. They show that everything in one's life is connected with everything else. Dreams show that divine revelations can be understood by the wise. Understood wisely, they will assist to usher one into life beyond death.

To the extent that we understand our dreams, they may help correct falsehoods and cure misconceptions. Those who are able to enter into the life of dreams find there a harmony of opposites (later a crucial term for Carl Jung—the *coincidentia oppositorum*). Through dreams we glimpse the unity of the cosmos. Everything is happening simultaneously as if from the viewpoint of eternal consciousness. As in dreams, all things in time are going on at once. Through dreams, all things "become linked with the spheres, that is to say, carried up as if to its own natural state of being." Dreams provide access to the truth quite apart from organized religion or the pagan temples which had been officially closed by Theodosius since 392.

Speaking from experience, Synesius described how his dreams had been a guide to him in specific situations, in distinguishing friends from adversaries, good from evil, and hope from despair. They provided him with major clues in his writing and in his public leadership.

He thought that it was attentiveness to his dreams that prepared him to come into more effective connection with political options. His inward dream life helped him face the confusions of outward public life.

Synesius thought of dreams as personal messages from the soul. They are not to be ignored. They provide knowledge from within the soul of every human being. They are the wealth of the soul, regardless of one's status in life. No one lacks dreams. No tyrant can deprive human beings of their dreams. That would require banishing sleep from his realm. Since the meaning of the dream is found in the experience of the dream itself, there is no general or objective guide to their interpretation. Most are self-evidencing. It is not the dreams that deceive us, but by our lack of attentiveness to them we are deceived.

Synesius commended keeping a journal of dreams and their effects—a night journal and a day journal. Allow them to have their own effects. He prayed for guidance of the soul in the engendering of dreams. He urged intentionality in hopes of a fruitful dream.[4] Synesius thought that in dreams we would at times be able to anticipate aspects or glimpses of future events. He anticipated the study of paranormal phenomena. These themes have much in common with traditional African spirituality.

On various occasions Synesius reported that he was counseled through his dreams to avoid terrible demonic forces that were being launched against him in the political arena. Learning this helped him later in public administration and civic leadership, when he became a bishop. He had to brace himself against the demonic in history to engage in works of public service. This one source of wisdom gave him more confidence than any other factor.

The dream sends a direct communiqué from the soul, from the intelligible realm into the space-time world. It is a vehicle for the soul's truth. It is moving in the uncertain realm of physicality. It is as if the soul was riding in a boat on unstable waters in this space-time world. Under these conditions the body-soul union awakens the faculty of imagination, which works in dreams. It links the spiritual world with the realm of sense.

---

[4]Cf. Robert Moss, *The Secret History of Dreaming* (Novato, Calif.: New World Library, 2009).

## THE RETURN OF THE INTERNATIONAL DIPLOMAT— ENTER THEOPHILUS

Arcadius proved to be a weak emperor dominated by court politics. Eutropius was deposed in August 399. When Synesius left Constantinople, he was still far from deciding to commit himself to Christianity. But he could see that Christians were proposing policies that were redefining and defending many of the classic traditions of wisdom he embodied. He had learned hard lessons in Constantinople. It was preparation for his future role as mediator.

Synesius was poised to be groomed by a genius of political administration. Like it or not, he was on his way to becoming a Christian politician within a Christian empire. On his travels after Constantinople he returned to Alexandria.

Theophilus was most famously known for three unforgivables: his alleged participation in the destruction of the Serapeum in Alexandria, his seemingly arbitrary leveling of charges of heresy against Origenists of his time, and his resistance to the patriarch of Constantinople (notably the beloved John Chrysostom). These acts have elicited centuries of animus against him, so as to cause him to be remembered as a ruthless, power-hungry manipulator.

The association between Patriarch Theophilus and the philosopher Synesius is perplexing to those who can see little but evil in the patriarch and enduring innocence in Synesius. There are indications however that a deep bond between them formed. It may have been begun in the 390s, but surely was maturing and deepening by the early 400s, even while Synesius was maintaining a close relationship to Hypatia. It is clear, however, that at some point Synesius became closely bonded to the patriarch of Alexandria in a way that still puzzles historians.

If Theophilus seems to be an example of the worst of Christian leadership, it is in part because he has been taken out of context and excoriated by those who have no patience with the urgent and dangerous realities of his context. Theophilus is often portrayed as an embarrassment to Christianity. But recent studies show that Theophilus led the way in the decisive transition of Christian society in Egypt from polytheism to Christianity. In doing so, he left a decisive imprint on the church of Libya at a crucial time. Libya was under his jurisdiction. Theophilus was undoubtedly one of the most remarkable African Christian leaders of his time. He played a decisive role in the Christianization of liturgical space in both Egypt and Libya.

Those who insist on viewing Theophilus through the eyes of hostile contemporaries will do well to read a recent study of Theophilus by Norman Russell, who provides a sane reassessment of his contributions.[5] Against all expectations Theophilus is now being reevaluated and recognized as a thoughtful exegete, a careful theologian and the unexcelled expert on canon law and liturgical practice. Upon his election to the patriarchate of Alexandria (385), Theophilus showed himself a man of considerable intellectual and administrative gifts, but also extremely aggressive in the choice of his means.

Synesius was not deluded or manipulated by Theophilus. Synesius became his protégé, sent on a mission. The task was to lead Libya in the quest for a new Christian society that would integrate the best of cultural wisdom into a viable and defensible amalgam of postpolytheistic culture, piety and religious practice.

Both Theophilus and Synesius were seeking to move their societies beyond the immature popular pagan symbols still predominating in civic life. Theophilus worked by more overt means, Synesius by more subtle. Theophilus was seeking to Christianize an unruly society. Synesius was seeking to preserve the best values and virtues of the preceding classic moral tradition while leaving room for the worshiping communities of Christians to flourish.

## THE CHRISTIAN STRUGGLE AGAINST IDOLATRY

At this time the architectural landscape of both Libya and Egypt was still dominated by colossal polytheistic temples. On display was a world of smoke and mirrors, priestly tricks, and to Christian eyes the absurdities of outmoded gods. Many fraudulent practices were associated with these temples: prostitution, deceit, veneration of phallic objects, priestly enrichment and moral corruption.

---

[5]Norman Russell, *Theophilus of Alexandria* (London: Routledge, 2007).

Theophilus and Synesius faced the task of curbing these abuses and encouraging the formation of a public space that would more fully express the Christian hope for society. With the consent of the emperor Theodosius I in 390, Theophilus undertook to correct excessive abuses in some pagan temples of Alexandria where the offenses were considered most revolting (Socrates Scholasticus, *CH* 5.16).

Theophilus was the uncontested Coptic leader at the time of this bitter conflict going on between the newly ascendant Christians and the popular polytheistic recalcitrants in Alexandria. Some years before Synesius arrived in Alexandria, Theophilus had openly challenged the temple establishment by putting on public display some of the coarse and disgusting artifacts from a pagan temple for the public to see. This caused enormous offense to the populist polytheists. They attacked Christian activists who then counterattacked. When the polytheists had been forced to retreat to the Serapeum, Theophilus granted them pardon, but, according to a later source (Socrates Scholasticus, *CH* 5.16, whom some view as biased), he ordered the cleaning out of the phallic symbols of the Serapeum. In the environs of the Serapeum was a church that maintained a strong memory of St. Mark, who had been seized near that temple and dragged to his death in the late 60s A.D. The city was polarized in what approached the proportions of a civil war. Many on both sides died. With Theophilus presumably in charge, the Christians struck back by leveling the celebrated temple of Serapis.

Theophilus was the chief spokesperson for the See of St. Mark. It was here that "the images of their gods [were] molten into pots and other convenient utensils for the use of the Alexandrian church" (Socrates Scholasticus, *CH* 5.16). The destruction of the Serapeum was seen by many historians as emblematic of the harsh triumph of Christianity over other religions, rather than as viewed by Christians as the legitimate rejection of idolatry and a step toward the Christianization of public liturgical space in the interest of correcting chronic abuses. Like all virtues, toleration has its limit when taken to extremes.

The harsh stereotype of the destruction of the Serapeum is being challenged by Norman Russell, who offers a detailed fact-based reconstruction of the life, character and intentions of Theophilus. In his election to the patriarchate, as the leading voice of apostolic Christianity in Egypt, Theophilus was responsible for maintaining the authenticity of consensual Christian teaching throughout the See of St. Mark, including Libya.

For generations before Theophilus the bishops of Cyrenaica had looked to the patriarchate to give active leadership as guardian of apostolic teaching throughout the whole of the *oikoumenē*. It was the patriarch's duty, and not merely a personal or temperamental preference, to teach and lead the church. He supervised the large number of dioceses in both Egypt and Libya. It was not a *political* ploy for him to rule rigorously in the sphere of Christian doctrine, but rather a *liturgical* duty central to his role as one of the three most ancient patriarchates in Christianity.

These patriarchates in Antioch, Rome and Alexandria had exercised this responsibility for many years before A.D. 385. Theophilus did not create the expectations associated with his teaching office. Its importance had been long recognized before the times of Constantine, as seen in the leadership of Demetrius (189–232), Heraclas (232–248) and Dionysius (248–264), as well as Theonas (282–300), Peter I (300–311), and Alexander I (313–326), prior to Athanasius I (328–373). Theophilus was a savvy leader who exercised his impressive authority with firmness. He was fiercely protective of the interests of the church. He was recognized as one of the most important leaders of his time, not only in Alexandria but in the larger Christian world. By the end of his patriarchate the bishop of Alexandria was the leading primate in Eastern Christianity.

Contrary to the stereotype, Russell's study shows that Theophilus served as a mediator of conflict in numerous disputes. He convened and attended consensus-seeking councils. He led in the settling of long-standing quarrels based on exegesis of Scripture and attentiveness to consensual tradition. In 391 Theophilus was asked by the Synod of Capua to help end the schism at Antioch. When this attempt did not succeed, he joined with John Chrysostom in 398 to successfully reestablish ecclesiastical communion between Flavian and Rome. He faithfully represented the apostolic memory of the Egyptian church even when it was in conflict with the memory of other regions. Despite occasional intense rivalries between Alexandria and Constantinople, Theophilus, patriarch of Alexandria, consecrated John Chrysostom as bishop of Constantinople.

Theophilus was exceptionally well-informed on previous ecclesiastical customs and precedents. He was acting within those constraints when the destruction of the Serapeum occurred. His major concern was to exercise guardianship over the apostolic See of St. Mark in a way fitting to its historic role and weighty destiny. His actions on Origenism, Chrysostom and the Christianization of liturgical space all fit into this prevailing priority. Theophilus carefully applied exegetical reasoning in his role of preserving the unity and consensuality of Christian teaching. This was precisely the purpose for which he was called and consecrated by the church to patriarchal leadership. In the sad case of the conflict between Theophilus and Chrysostom, his interest was in resisting the encroachment of Constantinople's claims over the more venerable Alexandrian authority, making the case for the chronological and logical priority of the See of Alexandria to the later establishment of the See of Constantinople. His revered status in the Coptic tradition shows that his affirmations were not based on personal ambition but on precedents set long before him.

The extensive writings of Theophilus survive only in fragments, now found in Greek, Latin, Coptic, Armenian, Syriac and Arabic manuscripts. His *Festal Letters* were sent out each year at the beginning of Lent to announce the celebration of Easter and remind the congregations of the continuing mission of the crucified and risen Lord. Moreover, his homilies reveal Theophilus as a caring pastor and conscientious exegete. According to some scholars Theophilus may have written *On the Vision of Isaiah*, previously attributed to Jerome. The fragmentary nature of his surviving writings have made it more difficult for the stereotype to be corrected. Its correction will impinge greatly on subsequent perceptions of his choice of Synesius as metropolitan of the Pentapolis.

## THEOPHILUS AS MENTOR OF SYNESIUS

When Synesius came to Alexandria, he caught the eye of the larger-than-life Christian leader Theophilus, who served a lengthy term as patriarch (385–412), extending over the whole of the adult life of Synesius. Theophilus must have been exceedingly impressed by this young man from Libya. He saw in Synesius, a promising mind and heart, a person of high ethical sensibilities, and an experienced mediator capable of leading. He must have trusted that Synesius would be able to reenvision his Neoplatonic idealism and to recommission it for demanding Christian service in his own native country. What did this young man have that caught the eye of the strict orthodox Christian bishop Theophilus? We will let the story unfold.

Aware of the diplomatic mission of Synesius to Constantinople, Theophilus took a personal interest in Synesius. Just how he was wooed into the orbit of Christian leadership is not made clear in any documentation. But the outcome was clear. He was, over an undefined period of time, deliberately cultivated for Christian leadership. Synesius, who had first been mentored by Hypatia, was then substantially rementored by her temperamental opposite, the patriarch Theophilus.

Synesius was assiduously honest about his own limitations and feelings in his relation with Theophilus. Despite his friendship with people of influence, Synesius himself did not sit easily with the exercise of power unless it was accompanied by proper authority and good conscience.

In the spring of 401, Synesius left Alexandria for Cyrene. That year he was baptized, (*B&P*, xiv), the same year Alaric and the Goths invaded Italy. The grooming of Synesius for ecclesial leadership may have been occurring gradually during this whole decade. It is unlikely that Theophilus would have made an abrupt or impulsive decision about a matter of major importance. The chronology remains debated by historians. While the events of the political order are well established, the precise way Synesius fits into them is unclear.

## A CHRISTIAN MARRIAGE

Back in Alexandria, Synesius married a believing Christian woman under the patronage and blessing of Theophilus. Synesius may have undertaken serious catechetics in Alexandria about the time of his marriage. It is likely that *Hymns* 4 (*To the Supreme Being*) and *Hymn* 7 (*Christmas*) came from this period. He was united in marriage with a young woman whose name is not revealed in the record, but she was almost certainly from a leading Christian family in Alexandria, well known to and trusted by Patriarch Theophilus. It is clear from his letters that Synesius loved her ardently and remained devoted to her through thick and thin. His happiest times thereafter were with his family. Every indication is that she exercised a strong and welcome influence in the life of Synesius.

The ceremony of marriage between this young woman and this important diplomat was apparently presided over by Theophilus himself (*Letter* 105). Known for his strict adherence to Coptic Christian orthodoxy, Theophilus must have provided his good offices of ministry to the promising young couple in good conscience and with deliberate intent. The fact of his married status might have stood as an obstacle to Synesius taking high ecclesial office had it not been for his insistence on remaining faithful to his marriage and his unwillingness to treat it covertly. Whether his marriage to a Christian woman prompted him to become a more serious and thoughtful seeker of Christian truth, we do not know, but it is a likely hypothesis.

Eventually, Theophilus would not only find a wife for Synesius and join them in marriage, but also convince him—almost against his inclination—to become a bishop of one of his major appointments, as apostolic representative of the See of St. Mark for the traditional place of Mark's birth. Apart from his Egyptian dioceses, Theophilus had no more important venue of supervision than Libya.

In Synesius's internal debate of the vocation to priesthood, one thing was clear: There would be no question of setting aside his wife or family. On the verge of his accepting the demanding role of bishop, he felt that he must make it clear to Theophilus that he would have to be accepted as a married man. His wife was to him the gift of God blessed by the Patriarch. He left it to Theophilus to settle the question of whether a bishop can have a wife. For him it was nonnegotiable: "God himself, the law of the land, and the blessed hand of Theophilus himself, gave me a wife." This suggests that Theophilus himself performed the wedding of Synesius and his bride. He was determined to "not be separated from her." He would not consent to demean her in any way or to live with her secretly or surreptitiously. He hoped to have many children. He insisted that this be known to Theophilus. He would accept the episcopal office on the condition that he not be separated either from his wife or his library.

Synesius and his wife had three children. The lives of the children may have been taken in the wars with marauding nomadic tribes. He wrote one of his poems (*Hymn* 8) to his beloved wife. While Theophilus was Synesius's chief Christian mentor and sponsor, Synesius in turn became one of the most important protégés of Theophilus. Synesius was engaging in a deeper dialogue with those Christians who were remaking the world that for him was falling apart.

## THE STRUGGLE FOR LIBYA

Synesius and his wife returned to their quiet Cyrene country estate during the first decade of the fifth century. The happiest period of his life was spent with his bride in his country estate. Not yet a bishop, his life there was immersed in the concerns of marriage and family, along with books, dogs and his favorite sport—hunting the many forms of wild game in the mountainous areas of Libya. He describes his life as happily made up of books and the chase.

This place of relative solitude was his estate at Anchimachus, near Cyrene but far enough away to breathe quietly. There he studied "philosophy, mathematics, astronomy, everything; farming, hunting, having many a brush with hordes of pilfering Libyans; and every now and then uphold the cause of someone who had fallen into difficulties." He especially took to being a country gentleman in a serene place, writing poetry and hymns in Dorian Greek that praised the beauty of the universe. His life at times became torn between his chief passions: a quiet literary life on the estate (*Letter* 148, "The Good Life") versus his sense of noblesse oblige and civic duty in relation to his society and its people (*Letter* 95, "Even Enemies Have Their Uses").

During this period, his own villa was repeatedly attacked by unruly

nomadic mischief-makers. He had to act in defense of his own estate.
He took the lead in its defense, recruiting and levying volunteers (*Letter*
132, "War," A.D. 405), procuring arms, and leading troops. He financed
his own small army and commanded it—not unusual for a noble family
of his time. Late in the decade after his own estate was overrun (407),
he was forced to flee to the fortified city of Ptolemais, where he would
help in the military defense of that city against marauders. He had a
great love of his own homeland.[6] In the early Byzantine period the conflicts between ethnic identities were fluid: at times between Roman colonial citizen soldier and Berber tribes, at other times between generic
nomads and settlements. "This changes the way we see the *limes*, and
the conflict between Roman and native is metamorphosed into another
kind of conflict, that between nomad and settled" (*TT*, 34-35).

This dislocation and strife would prompt Synesius to write on the
theme of genocide, a tragic theme still haunting African diversity. We
meet his thoughts on genocide in the second section of his *Homily* 2. It
provides a glimpse into the brutal injustices being committed in wanton
killings. He compares these conflicts to the genocidal attack on another city of the Nile, Leontopolis. The anarchic scene pits brother
against brother, son against father, full of hatred, and "finally resorting
to the ancestral course of mutual extermination." Anyone who lives
near this scene of mutual destruction gets hurt. Combatants lacked the
gifts of living in the light of love and gentleness. All are tempted to
make false accusations. His fellow Cyrenians were not experienced in
courts of law. They knew the soil and planting and harvesting. They
were attacked by warrior people who possessed the dangerous skills of
mobility, callousness and resentment.

## THE CONVERSION OF SYNESIUS: SLOW AND RATIONAL

Theophilus was earnestly looking for reliable and intelligent civic and
religious leadership. Synesius had already proven himself in Constantinople, just as Ambrose had in Milan. Even though Synesius was in his
forties, he was not yet deeply rooted in Scripture studies (again like

---

[6]J. H. W. G. Liebeschuetz, "Synesius and Municipal Politics of Cyrenaica in the Fifth Century
A.D.," *Byzantion* 55 (1985): 146.

Ambrose). But his public gifts signaled that he could grow into the episcopacy. Synesius was not a Christian leader who came through a growing process to philosophy, but a philosopher who grew through a deepening process toward classic Christianity.[7]

This was a time when figures of formerly pagan but now converted Christian nobility were becoming Christian leaders. Among them were Basil of Caesarea, Ambrose and Gregory of Nazianzus. The church had an urgent need for leaders of excellent education, who were aware of diplomatic and legal affairs, and who could negotiate the rough waters of the early fifth century. The case has been made by Alan Cameron, Jacqueline Long and Lee Sherry, in *Barbarians and Politics at the Court of Arcadius*, that Synesius was raised in a culture that was becoming more oriented to Christian teaching. He was well prepared to deal with public life in the Christianizing Byzantine culture of the Maghreb (*B&P*, 19-28).

When Synesius returned to Alexandria after his baptism, he still had much to learn about classic Christianity. He was a quick learner. He was promptly drawn into the inner circle of the patriarch. He had an impeccable pedigree of nobility, a strong record of diplomatic experience, moral seriousness and a high commitment to the philosophical search for truth.

Synesius never displayed hostility to Christianity, but he had a strong sense of the truth of tradition, both Afro-Hellenic and Christian. He had a love for the unity of persons who in good conscience seek the truth. He yearned for peace in his world. It took him a decade to join together the two traditions of Christianity and its polytheistic antecedents without a denial of either, but displaying the best of both worlds.

## THE HYMNS AS WITNESS TO THE TRANSITION FROM NEOPLATONISM TO TRIUNE TEACHING

If further studies confirm the conjecture that Tertullian and Marius Victorinus were both Libyans, they would be (after St. Mark) the clear choices of the two greatest Christian teachers from Libya. That could

---

[7]H.-I. Marrou, "La 'conversion' de Synésios," *Revue des études grecques* 65 (1952): 474-84.

happen with diligent new research into epigraphic evidences, archaeology, ethnicity, name frequency and family studies. But lacking those corroborations, the leading intellect of Libyan Christianity remains Synesius.

The *Chaldean Oracles* stood in the background of the attempt of Synesius to make the transition from Neoplatonism to Christianity. Synesius had long been intrigued by the writings of Porphyry of Tyre (A.D. 234–305) and the *Chaldean Oracles*. They posited a cosmic conflict between a good world soul and an evil world soul. They would echo throughout his views of the incarnation, triune teaching and baptism. They were written in the 170s, combining Platonic and Persian streams of mystery teachings (Bregman, 68).

Synesius had long been intrigued by the potential analogies between these sources and classic Christian triune teaching. Synesius entered the decade of the 390s as a defender of classic Greco-Roman vestiges of paganism, and left the decade as a seeker after the Christian truths of incarnation, Trinity and baptism. After about 400 he is found plunging increasingly into the Christian-Neoplatonist interface, perhaps in the light of his Alexandrian catechesis. He felt that he had been poured out as an "ineffable parent," in order to beget a child (*Hymn* 3). These metaphors were already beginning to meld Neoplatonic mysteries with the mysteries of Christian teaching from incarnation to the second coming. Wisdom is being reborn into the postpagan world.

He discovered that in being poured out he did not cease to be himself. As the One God empties himself and becomes flesh, yet does not cease being true God: "Although you have been poured forth you remain in yourself" (*Hymn* 3, "To the Father and the Son"; translation, Bregman, 84).[8] The analogy with incarnation is apparent (Phil 2). Bregman notes that "this unity is a unity-in-trinity" (Bregman, 84). Synesius is ecstatic in song: "I sing to you monad. I sing to you triad. You are monad, while being a triad. You are triad, while being a monad" (*Hymn* 3; Bregman, 85).

The mystery of the incarnation is grasped in Neoplatonic form as a

---

[8]For an alternative online translation of Synesius by Augustine Fitzgerald, see <www.livius.org/su-sz/synesius/synesius_cyrene.html>.

holy childbirth: "Holy labor, ineffable childbirth, you are the limit of natures which generate and are generated." (*Hymn* 3; Bregman, 87). What is being begotten in flesh in the incarnation is already eternally generate. While these meditations were likely written in the middle years of 395–405, they showed that he was thinking in triune terms.

As true God, the Holy Spirit is the enabler of the relation between the Father and the Son, "herself mother . . . herself daughter" (*Hymn* 4; Bregman, 87). Note the bold use of feminine gender to express the third person of Trinity "who gave birth to the hidden root," that is, the Spirit who called forth and enabled the incarnate revelation. In doing so he warns against tritheism, subordinationism and emanation. The unity of the godhead is opposed to emanation, which does not permit distinct personae. "It is not lawful to speak of a second arising from you; it is not lawful to speak of a third arising from the first" (*Hymn* 3; Bregman, 88). All are coeternal, contra Sabellian modalism.

The Christian teaching of Synesius takes the premise seriously that the one God took on human flesh in God the Son, who suffered and died as the theandric Son, but did not suffer as God the Father or Holy Spirit. Theanthropos suffered in his humanity, not in his deity. This Athanasian teaching was passed on from Alexandrian catechesis through Theophilus to Synesius.

It is not until *Hymn* 5, lines 1-9, that we see deliberate historical references to Jesus Christ in hymns. At some point between *Hymn* 3 and *Hymn* 5 he has made a decisive shift to classic Christian teaching. Whether this was more grounded in Christian Scripture or the *Chaldean Oracles* remains subject to debate. In Milan the young Augustine was also wondering if the *Chaldean Oracles* might refract some echoes of Christian triune teaching.

As early as *Hymn* 3 Synesius was already affirming the Christian understanding of baptism as the seal of the Father's promise enabled by the Spirit: "Now let my suppliant soul bear the seal of the Father," a metaphor of baptism (*Hymn* 3; Bregman, 91), analogous to but not identical with the seal of initiation in the *Chaldean Oracles*.

In *Hymn* 6 he prays to the Sun, symbolic of the Son of God, who is born and incarnated to bring new order to the universe. The sun is not an object but a person. Synesius was expressing the paradox of the event of birth of God the Son, entering the life of humanity as Light and Word.

While Jesus of Nazareth is a historical human being, the mysteries of the *Chaldean Oracles* circled around the meditation of an idea, analogous to the pharaonic death-resurrection motifs of Isis and Osiris. That is quite different from an actual historical event. The history of Jesus is such an event. The preserved hymns of Synesius have strong embedded evidences of already being awake to classic Christian teaching.

*Hymn* 7 recalls a prior event, the incarnation, the naming of Jesus, the guiding star and the gifts offered to the Christ child. God the Father is revealing himself in the birth of the Son. His life is being poured out as a kenosis, but not diminished in duty or effaced in the incarnation. The Father gives himself wholly to the mission of the Son without ceasing to be the eternal Father. Synesius's hymns would have been singable in Christian worship. They are not exclusively for philosophical edification or aesthetic expression. His achievement was destined to be uniting his native cultural and family traditions with classic Christian teaching.

Did Synesius cynically officiate at Christian baptisms while being entirely ignorant of the Christian teaching of baptism? Implausible. Or serve the Eucharist without knowledge of the atonement, of the Lord's suffering on the cross on our behalf? That would be jarring, far-fetched and disingenuous of him, and inconsistent with all that we know of his moral character.

Yet the standard reading of the Synesius story often tells it that way: liturgist before he was baptized, bishop before he was catechist, metropolitan before he knew canon law. This version makes him out to be deceitful. The humanity and deity of the Mediator had already appeared in his writings before he was baptized.

Some commentators have preferred to picture Synesius as marginally Christian. Some imagine that his main virtue was his misunderstanding of orthodox Christianity. This lack of theological linkage is why they have remained puzzled by his relation with Theophilus. Synesius has been made into a pitiable and dishonest figure by the secularist interpretation of him, if we see him as lacking in basic knowledge of Christological and triune teaching. His was not just a political baptism, though it was politically aware. He sought to serve the actual civic order by hammering out a rapprochement between Cyrenaic philosophy and orthodox African Christianity.

*Hymn* 10 shows him seeking the grace of Jesus Christ, truly God, truly man. Synesius was following a persistent trajectory over fifteen years (since 395) in his steady journey from Neoplatonic Eleusinian mysteries to ecumenical Christian teaching. He comes back from Constantinople as a neonate Christian and would in due course be ready to be baptized, prepared to take leadership in the emerging church of Cyrene, to become its most outstanding mind.

In *Hymn* 9 we find adumbrations of the Christian narrative of the fall of humanity, the incarnation of the Mediator and his resurrection after his crucifixion and descent to hell. The metaphors of Synesius were grounded in indigenous Afro-Libyo-Punic pagan piety, but on the way toward Christian faith. He teaches that the soul shares in the divine image, as seen in the incarnate Mediator from the beginning (Col 1; Phil 2; 1 Pet 1). Faithful communicants participate through liturgy in the divine reality of life in Christ.

## The Challenge of the Vocation to Christian Leadership

It was around A.D. 409 that Synesius was seriously approached about becoming a bishop. He was still in his middle adult years when asked to consider becoming the bishop of Ptolemais, which at that time was the leading administrative city of the renowned five cities of the Pentapolis. Synesius was consecrated bishop of Ptolemais in 410.

Theophilus was willing to accept the stipulation that as bishop Synesius could continue his marital and family life, and that he would not be required to disavow his Neoplatonic interpretations of the soul and the resurrection. It is remarkable that Synesius was ever considered for the episcopal office, in the light of his deep Neoplatonic commitments, his nonnegotiable marriage relation and his open reservations about some commonly held Christian teachings.

Though the precise chronology is disputable, Synesius was moving gradually closer to a serious leadership role in orthodox Christianity. His voice would have authority in Libya. He would legitimate the acceptance of Christianity by those previously committed to Afro-Hellenic assumptions. His skills would lead Libya into the expanding world of emerging Christians who were ready to adhere to classic ecumenical teaching.

What motivated Theophilus? Synesius's record of diplomatic service? His political track record? His piety and orthodoxy? His practical wisdom? His integrity? Personal knowledge of his thinking and moral commitments? Probably all of these. Whatever it was, something in the steady character of Synesius appealed powerfully to the patriarch.

In appointing Synesius, Theophilus was not seeking to intrude upon Libyan prerogatives, but rather to maintain the apostolic order that had been observed since the time of Mark. Synesius was correctly viewed as one who could maintain this order with full respect for the independent spirit of the Cyrenians.

Theophilus had already observed the determination of Synesius to resist the Arians, Goths and Visigoths. He could see that some of them were already poised in Spain to spring into North Africa. The Arians were eager to make alliances with anyone who would further their interests. Soon after the death of Synesius, they would trample North Africa from Mauretania to Libya.

Theophilus needed an astute leader like Synesius to bring coherence to the dioceses of Africa under the See of St. Mark. The Pentapolis could be the decisive factor amid these vulnerabilities. Theophilus must have found in Synesius the most promising leader for this tough job. He would keep the Pentapolis in the bosom of orthodoxy.

## Resolving Doubts

Synesius went through a lengthy struggle. He had to settle his reservations before proceeding with the priestly task. He explained these reservations in a letter to his brother Euoptius. Several issues touched questions of conscience. If the decision to be a prelate should require any concessions of conscience, he would say no. He wrote openly of these to his brother (*Letter* 105):

1. Concerning the soul's creation, he would not consent to the opinion that the soul is of more recent origin than the body, or that the soul comes into being after the body. The soul is created with the body, consistent with classic ecumenical teaching, with a grace-given capacity to refract the image and likeness of God, however grossly fallen within history.

2. Concerning the nature of the resurrection, he regarded the resurrection as "a holy and ineffable mystery," contrary to some coarse populist and unorthodox explanations. He would stand steadfastly against those who hold a vulgar view of the resurrection. He wanted to make it clear that he was not unorthodox on any major doctrinal point.

3. Nor would he agree that the world will come to a complete end with the destruction of the material cosmos. Rather it may be destroyed in one form and renewed in a different form, as Scripture suggests in the teaching of a new creation. On the basis of scriptural declarations of the goodness of creation, he would not affirm that the cosmos will come to an ultimate destruction. Whatever is inconsistent with the justice of God will be destroyed. But not the material world as such—that would make light of God's creation.

4. There are common opinions held by ordinary lay Christians which he would not actively combat, but with which he would not fully agree. The populace would always have odd views he would not share.

Synesius set his own boundaries of conscience for the acceptance of the clerical office, to which Theophilus would have to consent if they were to proceed. At the heart of it were these conditions: "Philosophy is opposed to the opinions of the vulgar. I certainly shall not admit that the soul is posterior to the body . . . that the world and all its parts shall perish together. The resurrection . . . I consider something sacred and ineffable and am far from sharing the ideas of the multitude."[9] He knew that the visibility of the pastoral office might tempt him to lose the balance of the quest for excellence. His Christian ministry must be consistent with his philosophical pursuit of the truth. The false beliefs of

---

[9]*Letter* 105, as quoted in Francis Joseph Bacchus, "Synesius of Cyrene," *The Catholic Encyclopedia*, vol. 14 (New York: Robert Appleton, 1912), <www.newadvent.org/cathen/14386a.htm>.

many of the populace must be resisted if inconsistent with Christian teaching, but always with gentle respect.

For many of the populace, the light of truth itself is blinding. It appears to hurt their vision. Then falsehood appears to be functional to their adaptation. Fallen history requires that we live within the context of temporary and partial falsehood. But that falsehood is seen in the light of its end. To face reality would, for many, be an intolerable burden.

What the way of philosophy loves, but the mundane world resists, is the full radiance of truth. The truth is perceived as injurious to those not resolute enough "to gaze steadfastly on the radiance of real being" (*Letter* 105). Many are not ready for the radiance of the light. They are unprepared to receive it. When looking toward the full sun, they cannot see anything at all. They must be shepherded like blind sheep if they are not yet ready to have their eyes opened. To remain ignorant may be felt as a relief among those unprepared for seeing the light.

If he should become a shepherd of souls, he would be bound to take people where they are, tolerating private opinions and proximate delusions, as long as they do not disturb good order. He was braced for having to bear with the multitude who feel a need to be protected against that radiance of truth fitting to God. He was determined not to practice deceit. If unavoidable, he would tolerate others deceiving themselves, but he would not deceive himself before God. He would not consent to concealing his beliefs or affections. Truth is an attribute of God. The highest calling of the shepherd of souls is to tell the truth.

This is a struggle of integrity of soul in ministry. He would not allow his convictions to be at war with what his tongue says. If his flock should ask him to reveal the depths of his understanding, he would speak forthrightly and candidly, but would not try to correct every opinion of those unready to receive the fullness of truth. The calling to ministry required that he undertake an entirely different and higher level of responsibility. This he could not do if he looked only toward his own abilities. That strength would have to come from God.

He was pleased that the Christians of Ptolemais thought of his life as worthy of the episcopal office, an honor to which he had never aspired. There was no doubt in his mind of the importance of the office, but only of his capacity to fulfill it. He still was haunted by an old "fear of winning honor from men at the price of sinning against God" (*Letter* 105). Taking on the task would involve a difficult struggle, but less before men than God. For there could be no deception with God. He was aware that all the prayers of the church of the Pentapolis were already focused on him. Taking on priestly tasks would amount to removing him from one kind of life and thrusting him into another. If he were to take on this pastoral life, he would have to become inwardly convinced that God wills this.

The patriarch Theophilus would have to know all those weaknesses and reservations in advance. Synesius ends *Letter* 105 by asking his brother to make sure that these limitations are communicated to the patriarch and the people of Ptolemais.

## His Modest Self-Assessment

Synesius did not think of himself as having a political temperament. The episcopal office would require that he become a public figure, give up his private life, make himself available to all claimants. To serve as bishop would require that he teach the command of God in its fullness. To do that he would have to probe more deeply into the Scriptures than he yet had. He had little confidence that he was capable of administering ecclesiastical discipline. It would take a person of greater nobility of soul to bear the weight of so many cares. He feared losing his intellectual vitality. He wondered how he could keep the flame of the soul alive when so many outward duties would press upon him. He knew some prelates who did this well, and he admired their courage. He regarded them as truly "divine men whom intercourse with man's affairs does not separate them from God" (*Letter* 105).

But he knew himself too well. He knew the thoughts that dragged him down, the behaviors that covered him with "stains more than anybody can imagine . . . many personal defilements of old date." Echoing Psalm 51 he felt that "there is no health in me." He knew he could pray for greater grace, but knew that up to now he was "far from being able to bear the distress of my own conscience." The bishop "ought to be spotless" in all matters for which he is accountable for "the purification of others," and to whom he is attesting the forgiveness of sins. The struggle to accept the call to ministry is a struggle about whether one can rely on grace to cover his own sins.

All these comments were addressed to his brother, but he was well aware that others in Ptolemais would be aware of its contents, since it involved a matter of public concern and since they had honored him with their desire to have him as their bishop. "In addressing it to you, I wish to make it known to everyone what I feel" (*Letter* 105). In the spirit of full self-disclosure he wanted the church to know his limitations. He did not want to be accused before God or the worshiping community of deception.

His desire for full disclosure compelled him to make one further confession that he thought might stand as an inhibition to the priestly office: he loved his hounds, the hunt and the serene life of his country estate, withdrawn in order to enjoy books and to give himself readily to friends. He wrote in *Letter* 105: "I feel that I have a good deal of inclination for amusements." He then details what he meant. Hearing him tell it is endearing. He tells of his love for his horses. He trains them and obviously has a deep affection for them. With his strong military record and leadership in the defense of his country, his city and his own estate, he has taken special care with his arms, bows and arrows, and hunting paraphernalia. Especially he loves his hunting dogs and knows that they would miss the excitement of the hunt. He does not want to deprive them of that pleasure. He reveals himself as one who openly enjoys the good things of life, the joys of country living, the life of leisure and books.

He says he would resign himself to giving up these pleasures if seriously called to do so, but reluctantly. It was hard for him to say: I will do even this if I come to conviction that this is my vocation.

What did he especially dislike? Lawsuits and quarrels. But if that is required, heavy though it be, he would be willing to take on even these burdens. These limitations Theophilus had to know in advance. Those who would consider him for public or divine service needed to understand his soul. The internal struggle of Synesius about his own vocation was not unlike that of Gregory of Nazianzus in his *Flight to Pontus*.

## REFLECTIONS ON BECOMING BISHOP

Synesius was miserable as he attempted to work through his decision to accept or reject the priestly office. The closer he came to thinking about the priesthood, the more he resisted it, until some greater certainty appeared. Like Job, he felt assailed by God for disturbing his peace. He pondered gratefully that he had never tasted dishonor prior to his being pressed into the cauldron of the public-ecclesial arena. He interpreted his misery as stemming precisely from his effort to answer the call to do his public duty in the political order. This has left him roiled in conflict within and without.

Synesius's country was in peril. He was being called to leadership. Poignantly he remarked that he was learning how to submit both his honor and grief to God. This was shortly after a devastating barbarian attack on Ptolemais. This is what happens when those who have not found the path of reason acquire the power to destroy, but do not have the skill to build. They try to shatter heaven with their heads. He felt called to remain in his native country where God had placed him.

Synesius was acutely aware that his era was a very dangerous time to combine political actions with the priesthood, however necessary they might seem. He viewed these two spheres as intrinsically in tension and at times incompatible. When the resulting abuses emerge, all suffer. This was a time when competent public officials were becoming clerics, as in the analogous cases of Ambrose and Basil. This called for maintaining a steady equilibrium. But in the circumstances of his era, Synesius found it difficult to imagine how the priestly and governance offices could be combined.

The tranquil contemplative life of prayer should be the center of the priestly life. This is what Synesius would have preferred, but the times required public leadership from those in priestly tasks. He still was hoping for the day when religious and civic functions might be once again relatively separated. Temptations abound. Those who are not of good conscience are forced to deal with circumstances that are evil. When the moral man is living in an immoral society, his capacity to serve two masters is limited. Soon he finds that he would need a sea of water to be cleansed.

In struggling with his vocational choice to enter or reject the priesthood, Synesius himself must make the judgment as to whether for himself the "times and seasons are opportune." Though the times were hazardous, he confessed that he would be an imposter if he became absorbed in his own welfare and neglected a genuine calling.[10]

He knew that *Letter* 105 would be read by the leaders in Ptolemais, by Paul and Dionysius, and that they would communicate it to Theophilus, whom he wanted to understand fully what the people of Ptolemais already knew. If there should be any uncertainty about any of his reservations, he would have to know about it before proceeding another step. If all these matters were clear, he was poised to indicate his readiness to accept the invitation.

After seven months of temporizing and inner turmoil and delay, he yielded in A.D. 410. He undertook the uncongenial tasks of the episcopal office. He was consecrated metropolitan of Ptolemais. He made it clear: "I have no desire to be a popular bishop." He would not court applause (*Letter* 57). He would not make public lectures. He would "hold useful converse with one or two at a time." He would regard his life of communion with God as his first responsibility. He promised to try to be optimally useful at the right times as a priest with civic duties. He would measure his time carefully. He would not allow needless distractions from his priestly office (*Letter* 57).

## THE HOMILIES OF SYNESIUS

We have only two full homilies from the extant corpus of Synesius, though others were quoted in surviving fragments of subsequent sources. This is a small window for making judgments about his homiletic disposition. Since bishops must deliver many homilies, he must have spoken without record on many occasions during the years of his episcopacy.

In them he was dealing with Scripture, the Old and New Testaments, as the Word of God freely offered to all humanity. Where the literal words were ambiguous, he looked for the spiritual meanings of

---

[10]J. H. G. W. Liebeschuetz, "Why Did Synesius Become Bishop of Ptolemais?" *Byzantion* 56 (1986): 180-95.

these passages. He saw the New Testament as the fulfillment of the Old. Moses and Jesus must be seen in relation to each another, as promise is related to fulfillment. The contents of one cup must be poured into the other cup in order to taste the blending of the wisdom of both. For "one spirit inspired the prophet and the apostle." Each illumines the other. The promise prepares for its fulfillment. It illuminates the promise itself and makes its purpose more clear. The fine minds of the most consensual church fathers help illumine the ambiguities (*Homily* 1 on Ps 74 LXX; PG 66:1561-62). Synesius was especially drawn to the Psalms in his homilies. They give hymnic form to the history of sacrifice in the law and anticipate the Gospels.

The occasion of *Homily* 1 was a liturgical festival. He was pleading with his hearers to become worthy participants in the festival, to take seriously its implications, to be ready for its spiritual power. He called on them to offer themselves to God as a glorious cup of sobriety, not a confused state of moral drunkenness or laxity. The Christian festival is no time to misplace the faculty of reason. The Word of God remains the epitome of wisdom and truth. He alludes to Ps 2:11 (LXX): "Serve the Lord in fear and rejoice in him with trembling." When you come to the feast, be wholly attentive of God.

In *Homily* 2 he warned catechists against missing out on the gifts of baptism. The stain it washes out is total, unmitigated and without reserve. It is unrepeatable. If you have been faithful to your baptism your sins are all washed away. From that point on, your citizenship is in heaven (Phil 3:20). The faithful are being readied for eternity with God. But for those who sin after baptism, it is very hard to come back to the condition that prevailed at the time of baptism. Forgiveness is possible after baptism, but hard, and they must go through a rigorous penitential process. So do not throw away the gift of baptism cheaply.

The Light of the Holy is being made available to all seekers. It is a light that surpasses the sun, incomparable to any light on earth. It illumines the souls of the truly penitent. Light has come to those cursed by sin. The light is showing itself to whole world. The light is uncreated. It lights up the sun itself. It cleanses from pollution. By means of baptism, the Word has provided a means for this gift to spread throughout the world. The peace of Rome provided conditions in which birth of the world's Savior could be announced through those who are baptized.

During the Paschal season, the whole church is in the process of announcing to the world the meaning of the death and resurrection of the promised One. Each hearer is a messenger of the light of truth. What does the light ask of each? To behold and believe and be baptized. Those who behold it now will grasp it more fully in eternal life. The words of Scripture address each hearer personally. Those who are faithfully baptized dwell in the city in the Paschal season as sent messengers, as an apostolate, called to believe and attest their belief. This is the light that has come into the world.

## DOCTRINAL ISSUES

Though he wrote on Christology and the Trinity, notably in his hymns (see *Hymn* 9), Synesius was never focused on precise definitions of orthodox teaching, as if to present new proposals for the resolution of conflicts. He trusted the distinguished tradition of orthodox teachers preceding him.

It is uncertain whether Synesius was acquainted with Cyril, the brilliant nephew of Theophilus. But it is likely that the younger Cyril became a theological companion and exegetical mentor to the slightly older Synesius in Alexandria. The younger mind was more experienced in exegesis, doctrine and canon law than the middle-aged Synesius. In Cyril he would have had a magnificent partner in dialogue.

Though Synesius is sometimes portrayed as resistant to classic Christian teaching, the texts show that his core views were entirely within the range of orthodoxy. He refers to the Son of God as one who lived among us, thereby affirming the incarnation. He confessed the sinlessness of the Mediator, who though tempted was without sin. This mediator died for our sin. As truly human and truly God, Christ did for us what we could not do for ourselves, due to the weakness of our fallen nature. The Christological foundation is orthodox. The true God descended in the incarnation to become engaged in a fully human history, while "at same time remaining steadfast in his true nature" as the living God.

It is an unlikely hypothesis that Synesius could have accepted the episcopal office under the great orthodox patriarch who married him, taking it all lightly and without even understanding classic Christian teaching or Scripture, but only vaguely and symbolically grasping parts of it selectively. This is not a persuasive argument, and it is not reflected in his hymns or letters. This view underestimates his rigorous integrity.

Synesius was able to reassure Theophilus that "at least I will teach *no new doctrine*" (*Letter* 105; Bregman, 156, emphasis added). In accepting the episcopacy, he promised to guard against heresy and protect the good order of the worshiping community.

## THE QUESTIONED ORTHODOXY OF SYNESIUS EXAMINED

Bregman argues that Synesius "identified the innermost Chaldaean-Neoplatonic triad with the Persons of the Trinity: he equated the Chaldaean 'seal' of Nous with the Christian seal of baptism; he accepted the Incarnation and Resurrection allegorically and symbolically" (Bregman, 180). If this were so, a person of integrity would not have been able to take on the priestly office.

Synesius has sometimes been interpreted by modern philosophers as standing entirely outside the mainstream of classic Christian teaching. Philosophical academics have been prone to imagine that Synesius had hardly the slightest interest in core questions of orthodox Christian teaching such as incarnation and triunity, redemption, resurrection and final judgment. Since the orthodoxy of Synesius has been questioned or doubted, it is fitting to review these confusions. There is not a large body of literature from Synesius, but its quality is high. What has survived from a lifetime of literary activity are poems, hymns, letters, homilies, philosophical essays and political reflections.

Synesius did not often mention detailed doctrinal controversies, but he demonstrated his orthodoxy decisively through penitential disciplines at the Communion Table: by excommunicating heretics and barring Communion from tyrants. To anyone familiar with the metropolitan's liturgical role as supervisor of bishops, it is unthinkable that he could have in good conscience presided over services of Holy Week without reflecting on the crucifixion and resurrection. He could not have been an effectively received and beloved bishop and admired leader of the Christian community if he did not understand the baptisms he performed, or the Eucharistic services he administered.

Synesius joyfully received the core of classic orthodox Christian teaching. He did not feel any need to improve on it with his individual creativity. From this base he built outwardly to apply Christian truth to living human circumstances: social, political, literary and scientific.

The liturgy Synesius administered proclaims a real incarnation, a historic cross and a true bodily resurrection. This is the gospel story as told by the apostles in whose name he was consecrated as bishop. Whereas Dionysius suffered as a myth, Jesus suffered as a real human being, suffered unto death for the sins of others. There is no doubt from the texts of Synesius that this required sweat, blood and an actual death. To imagine a bishop who denies all these tenets and still remains a trusted and beloved bishop is implausible.

Synesius makes numerous references to both the humanity and deity of Christ the savior of humanity from the demonic power of sin. There is no credible teaching of the Christian doctrine of salvation that can ignore the theandric Mediator (truly God, truly human). Bregman's treatment of Synesius's view of the incarnation (pp. 93-124) shows a willingness to brush aside the meaty texts of classic Christian incarnational teaching from Athanasius to Cyril, quoting largely from a single secondary source (J. N. D. Kelley). It is foolish to assume that Synesius did not understand the baptism he administered, or that he did no more than give poetic expression to pagan views of the incarnation. If so, Theophilus would neither have appointed him nor allowed him to continue. The incarnation, for Synesius, was neither a myth nor an idea reducible to a pagan metaphor.

## SYNESIUS ON SCRIPTURE

Synesius is often found quoting Scriptures in a way that suggests that he was quoting them from memory. Where did he acquire this memory? Likely from catechesis. He had a special affection for Old Testament narratives and was especially drawn to the Psalms.

He was not known for resolving complex issues of canon law or Christian dogma, but neither did he lack a will for maintaining classic Christian teaching in his diocese. He sought a bridge with the best of Hellenic antiquity without denying classic Christian teaching. He lived in a time when paganism was declining and a Christian culture was emerging, however imperfectly. He was seeking to integrate the best of both in a way that would serve the old city of earth and the new city of God.

Early Christianity on the African continent has a magnificent textual tradition that reveals an intellectual depth that is grounded in the ecumenical consensus based on careful scriptural exegesis. Synesius provides a model directly out of early African history for the passionate pursuit of truth in harmony with the apostolic teaching. This is why he has become the major theologian of the later Libyan tradition. There is no Libyan voice of that time that compares with his influence. He became a busily engaged bishop. He served with all his heart as the chief Christian leader of the Pentapolis. We hear little more of his hounds or books or country estate.

## THE BISHOP AMID CONFLICT

He provided outstanding leadership not only to the academic and civic life of the city, but also to the Christian community during a period when the influence of the church was boldly emerging in civil affairs in Libya. His metaphysical views remained strongly shaped by Afro-Hellenic Platonism, but he melded them with doctrines received in classic Christian teaching.

The main challenge to the cities of Ptolemais and Cyrene in the time of Synesius was the defense of the cities from desert tribes, especially the Austuriani, from the mountains inland around Sirte. They had already succeeded in invading Tripoli. The military apparatus out of imperial Constantinople was weakening and virtually powerless by A.D. 410. Synesius was called on to protect and defend the Christian communities and cultural continuity of Christianity in Cyrenaica. This required the building of city walls and defensive structures, towers and fortresses. Synesius offered a poignant picture of the attacks, including the burning of crops, widespread destruction of property and the carrying off of children into slavery.

Synesius envisioned a role for the Christian leader in the civic order. He urged his congregations to "develop a character in sympathy with the common lot" (Bregman, 168). He came to the defense of those in his own city who had been plundered and displaced. He was willing to organize and support military means to protect the society from marauders and thieves. When his culture was almost overrun by marauding forces attacking by night, he was willing to take leadership to defend it with all means possible (*Letters* 125, 130, 132, 133). He designed and supervised the building of towers and berms and instruments of military defense. Synesius's term of episcopal leadership was full of troubles and challenges—from barbarian invasions and wars to economic disasters and slavery.

As the one called and required to preside over worship in the episcopal chair of Ptolemais, Synesius must have been regularly acting as catechist and liturgical leader in baptizing and offering the bread and wine of the new life. He was even prepared to cast away from the Lord's Table the recalcitrant impenitent who lives unworthy of the reception of the Eucharist.

The strongest evidences of his orthodoxy were Synesius's willingness to excommunicate blatant heretics, his readiness to debate seriously and resist the Eunomian form of Arianism, and his determination to carry out the sacramental offices of the episcopal office. These duties were apostolic teaching and preaching, baptism, Eucharist, and episcopal supervision of his large diocese. He mediated conflicts between the bishops under his jurisdiction in guidance under established canon law and consensual ecumenical reasoning.

## FOUR CASE STUDIES IN EPISCOPAL LEADERSHIP

*1. Dealing with the madness of war.* In 412–413, when Rome itself was under attack, Synesius was in his own cathedral city of Ptolemais, defending it against local tribal attacks. He was compelled as a bishop to take bold action. Synesius made a public appeal to the people of the city to save the Pentapolis. He feared that North African civilization would be overrun by plunderers. North Africa was in danger of losing its prize cities of intellectual culture and literary and scientific inquiry: the Pentapolis. In *Catastasis* he wept as he watched his own diocese respond to horrors of war. His tears had stopped his tongue. He was no longer able to speak. As ordained prelate of Ptolemais, he was witnessing a terrible fate (*Catastasis;* PG 66:1572). He repaired to the altar, he says, where he dampened its floor with his tears. His country was in danger of losing all that the people held sacred. What irony there is in this picture of the philosopher-bishop in his church at the altar weeping. He was the classical Hellenist who had turned to Christianity to pray for the survival of Afro-Hellenic culture.

   *2. Peacemaking between bishops.* Since Synesius was the leading bishop of the whole of Cyrenaica, he was obliged to settle conflicts that occurred between the bishops under his jurisdiction. One such conflict, which occurred during the period of the marauders, was between the bishops of Erythrum (Paul) and Darnis (Dioscuros). Synesius was called to mediate (*Letter* 67). Bishop Paul had unexpectedly consecrated a fortress on the border of his diocese with Darnis, and administered Holy Communion. Synesius had to decide whether it was a valid consecration. Synesius proved to be temperamentally a peacemaker. He loved peace, feared disorder and despaired over the destruction of civilization.

   *3. Resisting the Eunomians.* Synesius had been consecrated by the patriarch Theophilus with the imperative task of maintaining the unity and peace of the Libyan flock. Synesius was committed to resolving differences between diocesan leaders in accord with the apostolic consensus. The high ground of peacemaking had long been held by the orthodox Nicaeans. The disruptions were coming from the recurrent unwelcome episodes of Arianism. The determination of Synesius in such cases of discipline reveals his basic orthodoxy and aversion to the disruptions of heresy. By the time of Synesius in the early fifth century, most of the bishops were orthodox Nicaeans, but a few elders remained Arian well into the 410s.

   The influence of Arius had lingered longer in Libya than anywhere else in Africa. Synesius was bishop in the Pentapolis where Arianism first thrived. Long after Athanasius the Arians were still misreading the apostles' portrayal of the sonship of Jesus. It was the sworn task of Synesius to teach his people the truth. He had no choice but to resist its distortions as bishop through argument and if necessary ecclesiastical discipline.

The Arian assault at Nicaea had been led by Libyan bishops, among them Secundus of Ptolemais, along with Zopyrus (Zephyrius), Theonas and Dathes. All of these were from Libya and still had vocal remnants in the time of Synesius. The diehards among these Arians had been allowed to act without constraint in parts of Libya. Some were demanding a platform of legitimacy equal to ecumenical worldwide consent.

In *Letter* 5, Synesius warned against "those who have taken up the godless heresy of Eunomius." They were promoting the views of Quintianus, a shady character who was teaching the nonconsensual views of Eunomius of Cyzicus. Eunomius (d. c. 393) had altered the baptismal formula, baptizing, instead of in the name of the Trinity, in the name of the Creator and into the death of Christ. This was highly disruptive to the peace of the church and the unity of its liturgy. The followers of Eunomius were still holding outposts in the Pentapolis. They boasted of the "influence they themselves possess at court, to the end that they may again sully the Church." Some elders in his diocese were acting like "modern apostles of the devil and Quintianus. Beware lest they privily attack the flock you are shepherding." He warned, "Beware lest they privily sow tares amidst your wheat [Mt 13:25]. . . . You know well what estates harbor them. . . . Purse these brigands, nosing out their trail."

*4. Penitential discipline of a high civil official.* One clear case in which Synesius exercised decisive and courageous disciplinary rule was that of the cruel Prefect Andronicus. In his *Letters* 57 and 58, Synesius told of his barring Andronicus, then civil governor of the Pentapolis, from participation in the Holy Communion. Andronicus was excommunicated for interfering with the church's right of asylum. He had employed horrible forms of torture. Communion discipline was required. Despite the reputation of Synesius as an advocate of a culturally flexible Christianity, it is evident from this that when necessary he did not hesitate to exercise church discipline.

Andronicus was political governor of the Pentapolis; Synesius's legal superior had become a political tyrant "gourged with disasters, gloating over ruins of the city." His abuse of just power provided a place of vengeance, a court of execution causing many tears of ordinary citizens. He had left behind him a stream of atrocities. At last, there was no one to challenge him besides Synesius.

The offenses of Andronicus did not offer him time for gentle persuasion. It was a time to be resolute. Christ was stretched on the cross to provide forgiveness of sins, not to bless irresponsible actions. Having spent years nurturing a gentle spirit, Synesius now felt he was called to judge these abuses honestly. He had prayed on his knees to be relieved of such difficult judgments. He has asked God to guide him. At times he had "prayed for death rather than priesthood," due to his love of the philosophical way and the quiet life. But he had become inwardly convinced that he was called to undertake the priestly office and to do so seriously. In *Letter* 57 Synesius reflected poignantly on the malevolent forces lurking in human history. God can bring good out of our most evil acts. Meanwhile these are times that test the patience of those who trust in God's long range vision.

The Lord's Table is for sinners. There Synesius had learned to pray to be worthy to receive the mysteries of God. Those who come penitently to this Table, come with their own histories of their own unworthiness. Andronicus had shown no signs of repentance. It is not God who causes human calamities but human wills, one by one. Yet a ruler such as Andronicus has power to distort many wills. When a ruler causes vast calamities, he is unready for reconciliation with God, for Holy Communion, for admission to the Lord's Table. There are demonic temptations for tyrannical political leaders. The Adversary works through their leadership to affect many others. Andronicus had become like a pestilence for the whole region, his minions like locusts on the fruit, eating the crops back to the stalk, stripping the trees to the bark.

The Lord's Table is where God's hospitality is most surprisingly and wonderfully found. There is no whip on the Table. Exclusion of abusive communicants has the larger purpose of pointing toward the requirement of a deeper repentance to ready them for a fuller reconciliation

with the gentleness of God. Excommunication is a temporary chastise-
ment of those worthy of coming to the Table of hospitality. In situations of vast public injustice, such as those committed by rulers, God's
justice works in relation to whole communities, not only merely indi-
viduals. There remains much in providence that human perception
cannot understand. It was the bishop's duty to provide redemptive pastoral care for his parishioner. The only way to restoration is repentance.
Christian teaching sees remnants of moral purpose even in this process
of disciplining abuses.

In *Letter* 58, "The Excommunication of Andronicus," he sets forth
the charges. The reason for the condemnation of Andronicus was not
only that he

> methodically sought out the remaining victims of these disasters and
> introduced horrible kinds and fashions of punishment for the first time
> into the country (and would that I could say that he alone has made use
> of them). Not because of his instruments of torture to which I allude,
> that crush the fingers and feet, compress limbs, tweak the nose, and
> deform the ears and lips, of which things those who had forestalled the
> experience and the sight by perishing in the war, were adjudged happy
> by such as had by ill fate survived. The reason for this condemnation is
> that first among us, and alone of our number, he blasphemed Christ
> both in word and deed.
>
> In deed, for that he nailed upon the door of the church edicts of his
> own, in the which he denied to those whom he had ill-used the right of
> sanctuary at the inviolate table, threatening the priests of God. (Fitzger-
> ald trans.)

The excommunication of the governor Andronicus was dangerous
to Synesius. It could have ended his life. He stood firm as a confessor
in the face of abused authority. He upbraided and admonished Andronicus, and sent him away from the Communion Table for a long
season of deeper repentance. This courageous judgment regarding a
high public official is comparable to the action of Ambrose in 390,
who forced the penance of Theodosius I, who had recently given or-
ders which resulted in the massacre of seven thousand subjects of
Thessalonica out of vengeance.

Synesius admitted that the case of Andronicus had tempted him to despair over his own ability to act in the episcopal office, but ultimately it had made him all the more determined to continue. The matter of Andronicus had become for him a personal burden (*B&P*, 278).

Synesius recalled a telling incident in these times of testing. He had a noble friend, a treasurer of public funds, whose family name was engraved on the public monuments of the city. Andronicus had thrown this friend into a dungeon without food for five days. The jailers would not allow the bishop even to visit him to bring him bread. Picture the great bishop standing outside the prison, examining the thickness of the walls of the fortress, trying to find a way to enter, even in stealth, to rescue his friend. Synesius was willing to die to find a way out for his imprisoned friend, who could not even see out of his cell. He worried about the friend's displaced family. During these days Synesius felt ensnared in his ill-fated country with no viable options. He was touched by the intense irony of his feeling safe while his friend was being tortured.

## FULL PARTICIPATION IN LIFE IN CHRIST

Synesius struggled his whole life to nurture a gentle spirit untroubled by storms. He loved the quiet life. But he showed with Andronicus that he could act decisively. God had not made him useless. He had put Synesius in the priestly office for a reason: to persuade the faithful to desist in sin and return to the vows of their baptism.

The priestly office had elicited a total change in his life. "I listened to certain aged saints who averred that God was acting as my shepherd." He had met with those whom he regarded as saintly people in the Cyrenaic and Alexandrian worshiping communities. They had taught him of fullness of joy that was offered through life in Christ. He knew that the Holy Spirit was drawing him toward this life of fullness. In his political struggles Synesius had been sorely tempted to lose the sweetness of the Spirit in his prayers and to be personally devastated by anger and grief (*Letter* 57).

In the circle of scholars of the Alexandrian patriarchate and its catechumenate, Synesius likely had studied with or conversed with the younger priest Cyril, who would later become patriarch, Cyril the Great, the successor of his own mentor Theophilus. In that circle it was clearly held that in faithful baptism the Spirit was dispossessing the demonic in our souls, washing away our sins. This teaching held that the Spirit prays for us and with us and nurtures along the faithful toward unreserved commitment and full participation in Christ. If the demonic powers remain residually to cause trouble, we are not to think we are neglected by God but are being tested for stronger service. These testings are always humbling, but for good purpose.

## SYNESIUS'S LAST DAYS

Just as Synesius was having to face the bitterness of a city that had once welcomed him, he faced the inward loss of his own son. Every face of evil had moved in on him at once, like a tide, he moaned. The storm reached a crescendo when in A.D. 413, as we learn from *Letter* 70 to Proclus: "I have suffered many griefs in many ways this last year, and now this winter has snatched away from me that child who was all the joy that remained to me."

He reflected with Asclepiodotus,

> The third of my sons, the only one who remained to me, has gone. I still, however, hold to the view that good and evil cannot be predicated of that which is not in our power. Or rather, this lesson which I learned long ago has now become a belief of a soul schooled in experience; the blow was of course more violent than my own suffering from it. (*Letter* 126)

Synesius's grief was so deep that he wondered if he could even continue to live. His calm reasoning was overwhelmed by these harsh absurdities. He was unable to keep his mind on his previously healthy balance of soul and body amid these misfortunes. While his memories of stronger days sustained him, he was keenly aware of being deprived of everything at once (*Letters* 70, 81, 126).

Though Synesius followed the philosopher's way of life and resisted extreme forms of asceticism (*Letter* 147), he grew more sympathetic with the monks toward the end of his life. As a result he helped found a contemplative form of the monastic movement in Libya (*Letter* 126).

In pathos, he cast his glance out toward the contemplative lives that monks were privileged to lead. He would have wished for himself more of an opportunity to engage in spiritual ascent without distractions.

He wrote to Joannes, a philosopher friend who had become a monk, a "Congratulation to a Novice":

> I think you are a happy man beyond all power of expression, inasmuch as you have left us, poor wretches "wandering in the darkened meadow of Ate," tossed about as we are amidst earthly thoughts. While still alive you have raised yourself above these, and have entered into the happy life. . . . Ganus tells us then that you are living in a monastery, and that if you ever come into town, it is only to consult books, and so much of their contents as pertains to theology. (*Letter* 147)

Having worn the mantle of a philosopher, Synesius exchanged it for the mantle of man of constant prayer. He revealed his view of the high value of both vocations by supporting the monastic experiment.

Throughout his life Synesius sustained trusted friendships with people of high influence and a reputation of truth seeking. Such was the circle of Hypatia, whose influence had spread far wider than in earlier days in Alexandria. Synesius had consented to becoming a bishop in accord with the most rigorous self-examination, considering the task with all its difficulties. The classical world he valued so highly was in danger everywhere. It was crumbling around him. He continued to confide in Hypatia about these tragic circumstances.

No documented echoes of Synesius's writings are heard after 413. It is likely that he died about 413.

In these last years, Synesius continued to correspond with Hypatia. Her death would come much more brutally. In March of 415, rioting Alexandrian Christians would clash on the streets. Sadly, after the death of Synesius, Hypatia's life was brutally taken by the fanatic mob during the worst year of this ugly conflict.

# 7

# FIVE CENTURIES OF
# CHRISTIAN PRESENCE
# IN CYRENE

■■■

After this extended excursus on Libya's greatest philosophical theologian, we turn our focus back to the larger picture of the five-hundred-year tenure of Christianity in Cyrenaica.

Diaspora Jews were not late arrivals to Cyrenaica. They lived in Libya as a stably rooted indigenous ethnic constituent within Cyrene's pre-Christian culture. Some had been there since the Ptolemaic period, which began a new African history following the death of Alexander the Great.

## TRANSIT BETWEEN JERUSALEM AND CYRENE

It remains debated as to whether the first Christians in Libya came directly from Jerusalem or indirectly through Alexandria, Carthage or Rome. There are plausible reasons to hypothesize that they came from Jerusalem shortly after Pentecost. What is clear is that it was through messianic Jews that Christianity was transmitted into Libya.

Those who may still imagine that no Jews were indigenous to Africa may have not yet had a chance to read the histories of Ethiopia, Egypt, Algeria and Libya. They might have a look at the names in the cemetery memorials throughout the Maghreb.

When Jews came to Cyrene in the Ptolemaic period, they found a city congenial to their interests in trade, security, intellectual vitality and crosscultural variety. They settled in, reliant on its well-fortified defenses. They enjoyed its theater, baths and gymnasium. Many Jews were already deeply entrenched in Cyrene even before the Romans took over politically in 74 B.C., when they joined Cyrene to Crete as a Roman colonial province.

The part of the pre-Christian Cyrenaic population that we are here principally concerned with is the Jewish population, and particularly that part that was drawn to fervent messianic expectation. That subculture became the conduit through which the Christians began to emerge in the first century and all the more visibly by the middle of the second century.

To get from Palestine to Libya was a simple matter of leaving from the port city of Caesarea, hugging the coast all the way beyond Alexandria to Apollonia, and then going inland fifteen miles to Cyrene. These waters were frequently traversed by both merchants and military personnel.

Paleo-Christians could have followed by land along the same roads that their Jewish antecedents had followed. The Greek geographer Strabo was sent to Africa to help with the geographical survey of the lands and to determine which lands were public. Boundary markers were set up to show where travelers were along the roads. New roads were cut, and those used by the Ptolemaic Greeks were vastly improved by the Romans. These same roads were used later by the Byzantines and the Arabs.

Transit between Jerusalem and Cyrene could be by ship or by land, and if by land either by foot or by beast of burden. The route was well traveled.

## THE JEWISH-ROMAN WARS IN LIBYA

Even before the destruction of Jerusalem, Philo wrote that one million Jews were residents in Alexandria. Even if an exaggeration, this population was immense. Jews inhabited two of the five quarters of the city. To judge by the accounts of the wholesale massacres of A.D. 115, the number of Jewish residents in Cyrene must have been proportionally similar in size.

In A.D. 73 during the First Jewish-Roman War (A.D. 66–73), there was a revolt in Cyrene among Jews led by Jonathan the Weaver, who was killed by the Romans under the governor Catullus, along with many Jews living in Cyrene. The Jews had been coming into Libya long before the destruction of the Jerusalem temple in A.D. 70. After that the trickle became a flood. Synagogues were established in the coastal cities. There were Jewish communities in Benghazi, Apollonia, Leptis Magna and Sabratha, and chiefly in Cyrene.

The Libyan peace that followed was abruptly shattered four decades after the destruction of Jerusalem. The massive deportation of Jews from Palestine roiled the coastal cities of the Maghreb. In A.D. 115–117, while Trajan was the Roman emperor, the Diaspora Jews of Cyrene joined in a revolt against the Roman authorities, along with those of Cyprus and Egypt.[1] This widespread revolt in Egypt and Libya started in Cyrene.

In this revolt, Lukuas (also called Andreas) led many Jews in the destruction of the Cyrenaic temples of Apollo, Artemis, Hecate, Demeter, Isis and Pluto. The city was taken over by Jewish militias and there was an orgy of destruction wreaked upon these pagan monuments. Jewish rebels blockaded the road to Apollonia and holed up within the walls of Cyrene. Both Trajan and Hadrian confiscated Jewish property to pay for the reconstruction of the destroyed temples.

After A.D. 115 there was no real peace. Cassius Dio reported 220,000 casualties in Cyrenaica and 240,000 in Cyprus (*RH*, 68.32). Corpses were everywhere. It was a blood-soaked land. The revolt spread to other places—from Cyrene and Cyprus to Syria, Egypt and the Maghreb. Many displaced Cyrenians fled to Alexandria, the city with the largest accumulation of Jews in the world. There the Greco-Roman and Egyptian pagan mobs captured and slaughtered many Jews.

Why rehearse here the Jewish history in an account of early Libyan Christianity? Because these conflicts were occurring side by side with the earliest entry of paleo-Christians into Libya. The earliest Libyan Christians emerged out of the messianic Jewish communities of Cyrene and environs.

---

[1]Eusebius, *CH* 6.38. On the revolt of Lukuas, see Gedaliah Alon, *The Jews in Their Land in the Talmudic Age* (Cambridge, Mass.: Harvard University Press, 1980).

The Cyrenian revolt prompted thoughts of the end of world as seen in the Book of Elchasai.[2] Trajan ordered his Mauritanian auxiliaries to clear out the Jewish suspects from North African safe havens. The expulsion was led by Lusius Quietus, a Moor military officer. Many Diaspora Jews were killed, and Quietus was ironically promoted to become governor of Judea.[3] Cyrene was depopulated after the Jewish Wars of A.D. 115–117 and 132–135 under Trajan and Hadrian. Apocalyptic expectations were intensified.

For many early Christians the Roman destruction of Jerusalem and its temple signified the transition from the historic Israel to the "new Israel," the Christians.[4] "The destruction of Jerusalem, therefore, marks that momentous crisis at which the Christian church as a whole burst forth forever from the chrysalis of Judaism, awoke to a sense of its maturity, and in government and worship at once took its independent stand before the world" (Schaff, *HCC* 1.6.39; cf. Eusebius *CH* 3.5). This was viewed as a historical validation of the coming of the Messiah.

The stories of Christian confessors, martyrs and saints in Libya took place within this spectacular world-historical theater. I am now focusing primarily on the evidences of Christian presence in one city, Cyrene, but analogous events were happening throughout Tripolitania and Cyrenaica.

After these conflicts Libya was desolate, so desolate that it had to be recolonized (Eusebius, *Chronicle,* Armenian version, reporting the fourteenth year of Hadrian). It was also under Hadrian that reconstruction began. He brought new settlers in Cyrenaica, many of whom were Roman soldiers. The population was revitalized by about three thousand veterans and large construction projects. As late as A.D. 134 Hadrian was still taking personal interest in the revival of the city of Cyrene. It took many decades after the Jewish Wars of A.D. 115–117 and 132–135 for some of the temples of Cyrenaica to be repaired. By

[2]Gerard P. Luttikhuizen, *The Revelation of Elchasai* (Tübingen: J. C. B. Mohr, 1985).

[3]Shimon Appelbaum, "The Jewish Revolt in Cyrene in 115–117 and the Subsequent Recolonization," *Journal of Jewish Studies* 2 (1951): 177-86.

[4]Kathleen McVey, "Spirit Embodied," in *Architecture as Icon: Perception and Representation of Architecture in Byzantine Art,* ed. Slobodan Ćurčić and Evangelia Hadjitryphonos, Princeton University Art Museum Series (New Haven, Conn.: Yale University Press, 2010).

A.D. 200 many of the fallen columns of the pagan temples were again standing.

Diocletian redesigned the whole system of Roman administration and political boundaries in the entire Mediterranean region, but most particularly in the political-administrative division of the continent of Africa. After 297 under Diocletian, Cyrene was demoted and punished. It would no longer stand in the chief position among the cities of the Pentapolis. The city of Ptolemais became the politically favored capital of the Pentapolis. The persecution of Christians in North Africa reached its apex during the reign of Diocletian. The East-West division established by Diocletian would make permanent the already prevailing dominance of Greek language and culture in the East and Latin in the West.

Cyrene was in decline. This was the characteristic condition of the two Libyas at the time of Constantine. Christian population growth would not occur rapidly until some years after the battle of the Milvian bridge (312) and the Edict of Toleration (313). This allowed Christians to enter into the public forum with a sense of growing confidence. The inauguration of the new city of Constantinople (the New Rome at Byzantium) beginning in A.D. 324 would herald a new era of inclusion and legitimacy for Christian communities. Jewish populations would survive in coastal Libya well into the modern period in such cities as Tripoli, Khomes (Khums), Misrata, Tauchera and the oasis towns of Zoarua and Zanzor.

## ARCHITECTURAL FOOTPRINTS OF EARLY CHRISTIAN PRESENCE IN CYRENE

Most of the excavated areas displaying early Christian architecture are still to be found in the city between the ancient Temple of Zeus and the ancient agora. Walking along the ancient cobblestones of the valley road, with its broad sidewalks and splintered remains of public buildings, one can sense the physical environment in which early Christianity found its new identity in Libya.

On this road the earliest Libyan Christians would have seen a dramatic statue of the nymph Cyrene (Kurin) strangling a lion, with dedicatory inscriptions to the Roman emperors Commodus, Trajan and Hadrian. The statue epitomized the struggle of the city between the hazards of the sea and the inland wilds—a struggle that persisted in Byzantine times. Many of the buildings along this street collapsed or were destroyed either during the Jewish civil disturbances of 115 or in the earthquake of 365. A Christian church has been excavated in this area, with mosaics, a nave, an apse and the bases of colonnades.

Until recently many Christian pilgrims and travelers were unable to visit Cyrene. Even those permitted would not often see or hear mentioned any reminder that there were five centuries of Christian history embedded in its artifacts and building stones. For admirers of classical Greco-Roman architecture and art, Cyrene is indeed a spectacular feast.

The earliest Christian basilicas in Cyrene were not built from scratch out of new materials. They were rebuilt versions of older Roman temples that had been constructed in the period of the Roman emperor Hadrian around A.D. 120 and before the earthquake of 365. Under Constantine the main basilica was thoroughly redesigned and reshaped into the first Christian basilica of Cyrenaica. Roman period remnants of this great basilica may still be seen in the alcoves for votive statues typical of sanctuary niches in Roman temples.

The earthquake of A.D. 365 destroyed much of the original Hadrianic temple. The Christian believers of Cyrene then took materials from that enormous edifice and ingeniously reworked them into the first great Christian basilica of Cyrene. Its huge spaces were reconfigured to accord with the entirely different assumptions of Christian worship.

The cathedral had to be refitted for the purpose of its new mission and task: namely, the preaching of the Word and an active sacramental life. Even the pulpit, altar and baptistery were made out of salvaged materials. The new architectural function of the basilica was reformed under the need for Christians to meet in a place where the Word could be proclaimed and the sacraments administered. The house of God was for baptism and Communion, catechesis, conversion and mission. For fourth-century Christians, these conserving features of structural design fitted firmly into their understanding of stewardship of the created order.

This transformation into Christian sacred space has poignant architectural significance. The whole history of idolatry is being left behind for new life in the spirit. This is best viewed not just as an accidental or pragmatic use of easily reached materials. It was an intentional transformation of broken materials in a mighty effort to rebuild an entirely new way of life. These architectural innovations were gradually perfected in the service of Byzantine Christianity. It was saturated with liturgical functions. These uses differed entirely from the civic and religious functions of the Roman basilicas.

As Christianity retained the ancient Scriptures of the Hebrew people but viewed them in the light of the events surrounding Jesus of Nazareth, so did Christianity architecturally retain the rational order and beauty of Greco-Roman architecture, transformed in the light of the sacraments. They recast it in the presence of a living community of faith.

Classical scholars have often viewed this paleo-Christian stage of art and architecture as a dreary deterioration of a much greater earlier Roman tradition, a collapse of the glory of the classical period of Greek and Roman architecture. That is understandable among those whose aesthetic interests are limited to civic magnificence. But there is something deeper going on here in the reconstruction of liturgical space.

The history of early Libyan Christian architecture cannot be properly told if this purposeful architectural transformation is ignored. Our focus will be on buildings built or rebuilt by paleo-Christian communities and later redesigned by the Byzantine Christians during the zenith of early Byzantine architecture—from the fourth to the seventh centuries. Before the fourth century, Christian meeting places ("Houses of God") were humble and covert.

Churches built after Constantine in North Africa are best viewed in comparison with those of Rome, Jerusalem and Bethlehem of the same period. The pinnacle of this architectural style is often represented by a few extant, celebrated and well-preserved basilicas of this period around the Mediterranean such as the Church of the Holy Sepulcher in Jerusalem (early portions built in the fourth to seventh centuries) and the

Church of the Holy Nativity in Bethlehem (begun in the fourth century), and about the same time Santa Maria Maggiore in Rome (fourth through sixth centuries), and the great Hagia Sophia in Constantinople under Justinian. The ruins of Cyrene display the foundations of this new shaping of the Christian basilica. The abundance in Cyrene of Greco-Roman building materials and reusable designs made this transition natural and liturgically meaningful.

It is useful for the modern visitor to try to picture the challenge to the architects and artisans during the period of transition from Roman to post-Constantinian architecture. This transition occurred very rapidly during the early fourth century and continued to mature through the fifth, sixth and seventh centuries. The builders of fourth-century Cyrene had been born and raised and were living daily in a classical city of distinguished Greco-Roman monuments, while that city was being transformed into Christian habitation.

Though the damage done to Cyrene's monuments and buildings in the Jewish Revolt of 115 was great, it was not as great as the damage done by the earthquake of 365. It is reasonable to view the Christian architectural challenge as a recovery exercise, a recycling of materials, the remaking of sacred space. It was not a transition from total destruction to pristine reconstruction. The issue of architectural reconstruction became: How do we make use of great building designs and materials that are now partially damaged by wars and earthquakes when we are building a new society in North Africa shaped by classic Christian teaching, baptism, psalmody and Eucharistic life?

The European romantics such as Edward Gibbon downplayed the Christianity of late antiquity as a miserable moral and aesthetic deterioration. But this tendentious view is being revised by scholars who now better grasp the depth of the theological and liturgical transformation going on. The Christian artisans were redesigning Greco-Roman architectural tradition without abandoning its majestic lines. The architectural imagination sought the best possible use of precious stone and engineering in a new liturgical medium. In this spirit the Greco-Roman ruins were being radically recycled to distinctly Christian uses.

The location of the episcopal chair in which the bishop of Cyrene sat is still identifiable. It had its setting in a very large Byzantine basilica which has a broad nave paved in mosaics. The earlier version of this basilica (fifth century A.D.) was oriented with its apse toward the east, then later rebuilt with a new second apse to the west (sixth century). There were rooms for praying, robing, vestments and ecclesial functions connected with the east apse. The apse is a semicircular construction where the elders sat facing the altar in the center. The *synthronos* or seat of the bishop was located in the apse. The base of the altar table still survives in place in Cyrene. The church is located in the eastern sector of the city near the east gate of the Byzantine wall on the main valley road.

We get a glimpse of early Libyan liturgical life from themes portrayed in the mosaics of the main church. Among them we find pastoral scenes of lambs recalling the sacrifice of the body of Christ. When the church was reconstructed in the sixth century, new mosaics were set in the vestibule near the doorway showing peaceful grazing and natural scenes, with vine tendrils in geometric patterns as prototypes of Eucharistic elements. There is a mosaic with an inscription regarding Saint Menas of the pilgrim-healing monastery near Sketis. In the north aisle there is a dramatic mosaic portrayal of a fisherman catching fish in a net (Lk 5:1-11).

## A SACRED SPACE FOR BAPTISM

The profile and shape of the church baptistery are still visible, having survived fifteen hundred years since Byzantine days. It is now liberated from the sand by excavation. It speaks volumes about African Christian sacramental practice in the fifth century.

A flight of marble steps leads down to the basin where those to be baptized were brought into the Christian community. There they renounced the devil and were made ready to receive the sacrament of regenerated life. There they received the outpouring of the Holy Spirit. This began a new birth of life with God. This space encloses symbolically the place of decisive transition for all Christian believers. From there the faithful move out of the schooling phase to full participation in the worshiping community, with their confession of Jesus Christ as Lord and first Communion at the Lord's Table.

In every century since the apostles, baptism has been the pivotal rite and mark of the initiation into active participation in the body of Christ. In the context of fourth- and fifth-century Cyrene, it had extraordinary importance, due to the enormous change of loyalties it signified—a momentous transition from an old life identified with a pagan and polytheistic culture to a new life in Christ, intelligently confessing the triune faith of classic Christian teaching. There are few places in early Christianity where the construction of immersion baptisteries were more opulent and splendid than in North Africa.

The seeker did not come into baptism without a rigorous period of instruction in Scripture and church teaching and moral instruction called "catechetics." The seeker is a catechumen—one who has voluntarily decided to learn what is requisite to enter into life in Christ—dying to the old era and living to the new. Catechumens were not allowed into the mysteries of the service of Holy Communion until voluntary baptism, where the old life and its perverse authorities were irrevocably renounced. Following the period of persecution in North Africa, baptism was never considered just a routine or incidental transition. Baptism represented a fundamental conversion into a new life distinguished visibly and decisively from the old. It had international and crosscultural significance. It signified an entry into a new worldwide community of the redeemed, a community of shared truth and holy living.

The baptism that was performed in the baptistery at Cyrene was essentially the same as that practiced all over the Christian world—the same triune formula, the same blessing, the same prayer for the outpouring of the Spirit. Triune baptism was practiced wherever seekers came to be disciples. It brought into concise form the faith of the apostles. It dramatized an entry into a daily life of participation in the death and resurrection of Jesus Christ.

The initiatory act of baptism required immersion in water in the likeness of a burial. The water has cleansing and life-giving qualities. By participating in the death and resurrection of the Son, a death to the old way and a birth to the new way is enacted. The gift of the Spirit is received, a new life of faith and freedom through obedience. The rite that occurred in the baptistery signified a fundamental transition from an idolatrous and broken world into a forgiving community that is seeking to live in response to God's grace. For this reason a great deal of attention was given to an appropriate setting to receive this rite, in which the earnest prayers of the congregation for the gift of the Holy Spirit would be fittingly offered. In these waters the forgiveness that is manifested on the cross and resurrection would be reenacted and recapitulated. There the penitent dies to sin. The believer rises out of the waters of baptism into a new way of living, free from the burden of sin. The believer would step down into the water where the apostolic representative, the resident chief shepherd, would baptize in the triune name and pray for the gift of the Spirit to be received. The seeker goes into water as if a burial were taking place, down three times—in the name of the Father, the Son and the Holy Spirit, to death of the old life, renunciation of the demonic world, arising as a new person resurrected to a new life. Then the believer would move on up the steps to enter the resurrected life. This is a collective, visible and public liturgical occasion. Its meaning is not limited to or dependent on how the baptized person *feels*, but on what God is *doing* in the life of the believer through the Son by the power of the Spirit.

New life in Christ begins in repentance, faith and baptism. In Peter's first sermon in Acts when he was asked "What are we to do?" Peter replied simply: "Repent, and be baptized every one of you in the name of Jesus Christ so that your sins may be forgiven; and you will receive the gift of the Holy Spirit" (Acts 2:38). In modern Western cultures this transition is so routinized that we often have difficulty thinking of it as a fundamental life change. But in Cyrene and in all North Africa churches there was a long previous history of idolatry and persecution accompanied by many moral corruptions. Baptism enacted that decisive turnaround moment. That is what *repentance* meant: the turning around of one's life to respond to God's unmerited grace made known in the risen Lord.

The African baptistery itself was often built in a cruciform pattern, meaning that the baptistery basin itself was shaped in the form of a cross. The baptisteries in Cyrenaica were typically three to six feet in depth. The prayer of the gathered community was that the Spirit would come and give new life to the penitent, binding up the demonic powers that have distorted the old life, and enabling the believer to turn toward the incarnate grace manifested in the death and resurrection.

The architectural design of the baptistery itself rehearsed sacramentally the two most decisive events of the last days of the earthly ministry of Jesus—his death and his resurrection. When a person has been baptized by water and Spirit, he or she has actively participated in this dying and rising. This is seen by the worshiping community as having been in effect born again as a new person in the Spirit, who lives in Christ, sharing in his death and resurrection. Those who were "born again" in early Africa following the persecutions were those who were baptized.

In many Libyan Christian church remains, these steps into and out of the baptistery are still visible. In the sixth century these steps were often protected underneath a canopy supported by six columns, which symbolized the covering of the mercy of God over the sin of humanity. God's own sacrificial blood covers the sin of the penitent. In Cyrene the actual physical remains in the baptistery include materials from a marble sarcophagus in which pagan decor and symbolism were refashioned into an architecture of redemption.

## The Gift of Preservation

At the center of public life in Cyrene in the Ptolemaic era was a large judicial building that was later used in the Roman period for the administration of civil law. It was a Roman basilica in pre-Christian times, a civil building with columns with a semicircular apse, with a civic religious and memorial center in the apse.

In the Christian era of Cyrenaica this edifice was converted into a Christian place of worship. An altar was added, pagan images removed, and it was dedicated to the altogether different purpose of Christian preaching and teaching, nurturing the Christian community, catechizing, baptizing and serving Holy Communion.

In the mid-sixth century, during Byzantine times, a massive wall of defense was established to protect the ancient city against attacks either from the sea or inland raids. Inside this wall was the church, which was the ecclesiastical center of the Greek-speaking church in Cyrene. Prototype versions of the primitive liturgical services of St. Mark and St. Cyril that were being sung in Alexandria and Antioch were also chanted within the walls of these basilicas in Cyrene.

Nearby the Byzantine church there once stood a hippodrome—a circular racetrack. It covered a large area set aside for sporting activities and public ceremonies. These public events included the public ridicule of the enslaved Jews whom the Romans brought back from Palestine after the destruction of Jerusalem of A.D. 70. The Jews who took part in the Jewish revolt of Cyrene of A.D. 115 may have been chastised here, as well as Christian martyrs of the Diocletian period of A.D. 301–303.

Near the church are remains of vaulted cisterns that were supplied with water by an ingenious aqueduct coming from nearby mountain springs and streams. A portion of it can still be traced coming down from the escarpment. The water flow was directly connected with the church and its baptistery. An inscription indicates that the cisterns were constructed in A.D. 166 (under Hadrian), when the earliest Christians were appearing in increasing numbers along the Libyan coast.

The erosions and sands have quietly covered over most of the remains of Cyrene for over a thousand years. The medieval tribal leaders of the nearby Senussi people had for centuries avoided these strange haunts as ghostly and dangerous. The great city that had such notoriety for so long entirely disappeared from sight until the nineteenth century. It is an ironic fact of nature and history that the parched sands of Libya preserved the ancient water-flowing baptisteries, to be later rediscovered by modern archaeology.

An unexpected coastal thunderstorm in 1913 revealed by erosion one of the most spectacular early finds when heavy rains washed away the topsoil over the sanctuary of Apollo, revealing the statue of the Venus of Cyrene. During the Italian occupation in the 1930s, the agora and sanctuary of Apollo were gradually brought to light and the outlines of the city began to emerge from the irregular hillside. The first scientific excavations at Cyrene were carried out at the huge Necropolis, a vast cemetery with inscriptions dating over a period of ten centuries. These labors were interrupted by the war between Italy and Turkey. Some years after the battle for North Africa in World War II, excavations were resumed by the Libyan Department of Antiquities.

The archaeological site of Cyrene is vast. Its core is about 1,300 by 1,300 meters. Portions of some of these buildings have been reconstructed by archaeologists. Among these is the enormous temple of Zeus. Many of its huge columns had been destroyed by earthquake and civil disturbance. It was excavated and reassembled by Italian archaeologists after World War II. These materials were left in disordered fragments for many centuries.

Today we can see (like a puzzle being partially put together) the approximate way these columns of the temple looked when they belonged to a living city. These columns were a dominant feature of the visual world in which the earliest Libyan Christians lived. Most of the Christian architecture in Cyrene was built between the fourth and sixth centuries, when Cyrene was a prosperous commercial trading center with significant agricultural and mineral production. It then declined to rest in silent soil. The earliest levels of Christian presence in Cyrenaica have never been fully excavated or studied, or adequately understood.

I have reviewed archaeological reports on these fifth-, sixth- and seventh-century Byzantine churches because they provide the best physical evidence that we have for substantial long-term Christian occupation in Libya, at least from A.D. 250 to 650. These centuries of Christian evidence are the stated goal of our quest. The reason they are so difficult to uncover is that they have been hidden not only under strata of deposits but under layers of historical neglect, bias and ideological defensiveness.

The city of Cyrene sat on the northern slope of a once wild and fertile mountain from whose heights one can see magnificent and colorful views of the plains below stretching toward the sea. It nested in a spectacular hillside location on the two-thousand-foot high Jebel Akhdar ("The Green Mountain").

The visible ruins of Cyrene today combine a spectacular view of natural landscape with the huge scale of monumental architecture. There are many museum-stored artifacts. It is one of the best preserved sites in Africa. There are many broken shards, tesserae and remnants from once lofty but now destroyed materials strewn about the site.

The site has suffered far less modern damage than other oft-visited Christian pilgrimage sites such as Jerusalem, Carthage, Alexandria, Byzantium and Rome. In each of those cases, many layers of urbanization have been built up over the ancient foundations: streets, roads, buildings, walls, era upon era. In those cities the archaeological imagination must penetrate many heavy layers of modernity in order to envision the past.

But in Cyrene, those layers of occupation have been far less spoiled. Its remains have been far less intruded on over the last one and half millennia. Almost no hints of modernity or industrialization inhibit the current view of the ancient city. Even today the blight of urbanization is many miles away. Cyrene is contrasted with the heavily layered historic sites like Istanbul, Old Cairo and Benghazi, which on the surface look much like any modern city.

In Cyrene nothing looks modern. Nothing even looks medieval. By medieval times it slipped under the sediment and has remained so for centuries. It is a rare opportunity to see a noble, once lively ancient city that has survived through so many years of African history. Cyrene's monuments have endured since the seventh century A.D., and some as far back as the seventh century B.C. The remains of Cyrene are not markedly different from the way they were left in the period shortly after the Arab victory of A.D. 643.

# 8

# THE EARLY CHRISTIAN
# PRESENCE IN
# EASTERN LIBYA

∎∎∎

We have journeyed through five hundred years of Christian presence in Libya with a special focus on one city: Cyrene. In chapters eight and nine we will trek through the rest of Libya. Our goal is to get a glimpse of the whole span of Libyan Christianity over the five centuries of Christian existence in this vast and ancient country.

If the center of early Libyan Christianity was Cyrene, its circumference was the rest of Libya. We are not now describing the Christian present in the center, but more toward its circumference. More detail is required because it is least known. We will begin with Marmarica, the easternmost province. If we were content to focus largely on the Pentapolis, it might reinforce the misguided impression that Christianity in Libya was limited to only a few isolated locations. What follows will show the wide range of the Christian presence in villages and cities all over Libya. Wherever traders or travelers or soldiers plied the Mediterranean Sea on Libyan coasts, there would soon be Christian believers ready to spread the good news as far inland as the population extended.

The sequence of this discussion now moves from east to west along the sea, following the trails of sea and land passage from Paraetonium to Benghazi. By the first century A.D. there were well-established

Roman roads (coastal and inland) through the entire Cyrenaic region. They stretched from Alexandria to the five cities of the Pentapolis and then further west to three great ancient Punic cities of Tripolitania: Leptis Magna (Khomes/Khums), Tripoli (Oea) and Sabratha.

## FROM PARAETONIUM TO TOBRUK MARMARICA (EASTERN LIBYA)

On the coastal road from Alexandria east, the first city in Libya Inferior is Paraetonium (= Ammonia). A very early bishop's residence was located there, as early as 325. Bishop Titus of Paraetonium was sufficiently noteworthy to be in attendance at the Council of Nicaea. Paraetonium was the titular see of Libya Secunda or Inferior (i.e., Eastern Marmarica). Titus was followed by Bishop Siras, of Arian sympathies. His successor was the orthodox Bishop Gaius, who assisted the patriarch Alexander at the Council of Alexandria in 362.[1] Paraetonium was near the ancient border area between Libya and Egypt. At some times it was in Egypt, but in most time is was on the Libyan side of the border. Paraetonium is a port city on the road going toward Alexandria (Barrington Atlas, 73), and near Deir Abu Menas.

During the Valerian persecution, Dionysius, the bishop of Alexandria (fl. 248-265), student of Origen, later head of the Catechetical School, was exiled to Libya to an isolated spot three days journey inland from the port city of Paraetonium (Eusebius, *CH* 7.11.23). Through this region many Christian pilgrims traveled on the way to the inland shrines, including the fourth-century monastery of St. Mena in the Egyptian desert, a place of healing, miracle and retreat.

The coastal cities on the road between Paraetonium and Tobruk, from east to west, were Zygris and Tetraprygia (= Catabathmus Major). Though there were doubtless Christian churches in this area, the evidence is lost. Their bishops were accountable to the See of St. Mark. Fedalto reports that one Quintus succeeded Nikon as bishop of South-

---

[1]*Catholic Encyclopedia* (1913), vol. 11, s.v. Paraetonium; Jean-Raimond Pacho, *Relation d'un Voyage dans la Marmarique, la Cyrénaïque, et les oasis d'Audjelah et de Maradèh*, 2 vols. (Paris, 1827-29), 1:28; Michel Le Quien et al., ed. *Oriens Christianus, in quatuor patriarchatus digestus; quo exhibentur ecclesiae, patriarchae, caeteriquepraesules totius Orientis*, 3 vols. (Paris: Ex Typographia Regia, 1740), 2:631; *HEO*, 2:662-63.

ern Gareathis. This was an unidentified Marmarica location probably south of Darnis or west of Catabathmus Major (*HEO* 2:663). Clearer evidences of early Libyan Christianity in Marmarica are found in the ancient Greco-Roman port city of Antipyrgos (= modern Tobruk).[2] One of its prelates, Bishop Serapion, was in attendance at the First Ecumenical Council of Nicaea in 325.

This is the place where later the siege of Tobruk would take place in World War II. Tobruk became a household name due to the great battle between Rommel and Montgomery during that war. It has long been a strategic military port. Captured by the Italians in 1911 and taken by the Australians, it fell again to the Germans in 1942, but was recaptured by the British and Australians in the decisive desert offensive launched in Africa from Al-Alamayn all the way to Tunisia. The trim cemeteries of Tobruk are featured on the Libyan itineraries of many visitors.

## EVIDENCE OF CHRISTIAN CHURCHES AND MONASTERIES IN MARMARICA IN LATE ANTIQUITY

The first sign of monasticism in Libya was on its eastern edge, close to its Egyptian origins at Scetis, and those further east in the Libyan desert.

The oral tradition held that Mark went into hiding from the Roman army after the death of Jesus and fled to a remote desert location not far from his place of birth. Wadi Markos may have been a place to memorialize Mark's flight from Alexandria back to his home country to escape a pagan mob. The monastery of Wadi Markos was reportedly entered by a rope, a security measure necessary in desert monasteries vulnerable to plunder. There were several monasteries between Scetis and Carthage by A.D. 400. Only a few remote Libyan monasteries have been accurately mapped, and even fewer excavated.

Reliably documented information on Marmarican Christianity is limited largely to the names of exiles and of bishops and their dioceses.

---

[2]Barrington Atlas, p. 73; Sandro Stucchi, *Architettura cirenaica* (Rome: L'erma di Bretschneider, 1975), pp. 358-59; André Laronde, *Cyrène et la Libye hellénistique(= Libykai historiai): de l'époque républicaine au principat d'Auguste* (Paris: Editions du Centre de la Recherche Scientifique, 1987), p. 221.

Though these records are often limited to lists of names of bishops at councils, they are crucial in establishing the presence of sufficient numbers of believers in Marmarica in the third and fourth centuries to require the supervision of a bishop.

In his *Festal Letter* of A.D. 340, Athanasius included memorials to "bishops who had fallen asleep" and the names of those who had replaced them. One obscure reference said: "In Stathma, Arabion, and in Marmarica. In the eastern Garyathis, Andragathius in the place of Hierax. In the southern Garyathis [Gareathis], Quintus instead of Nicon. So that to these you may write, and from these receive the canonical Letters" (*Festal Letter* 12.2; *HEO* 2:662-663). Stathma appears to be in Marmarica, Eastern Libya, though its precise location is disputed. Eastern and Southern Garyathis may have been in Garamantes, in the area of Garama far into the Libyan desert (Barrington Atlas, 36). Among the bishops from Marmarica who attended the Council of Antioch in 363 were Pollux of Libya Inferior and Serapion of Antipyrgos in Libya Inferior, along with the previously mentioned Siras of Paraetonium. These documents present early evidences of Christian presence in far Eastern Libya at a considerable distance away from Cyrene. They provide indications of the vitality of paleo-Christianity in many small villages and otherwise forgotten locations of the vast region called Marmarica.

Further archaeological excavations and historical studies are required for establishing the *extent* of Christian activity in Roman and Byzantine Marmarica, but these references are sufficient to establish the *fact* of Christian presence there for hundreds of years before the Arab victory. There could have been no episcopal residences where there was a total absence of Christian believers. Wherever there is an episcopal residence, it is reasonable to conclude that some congregations were being served by that diocese.

## THE BYZANTINE MOSAICS OF QASR LIBYA (OLBIA)

We now proceed west out of Marmarica toward the eastern part of Cyrenaica. The major stops in this leg of our journey are (1) ancient Olbia (= Byzantine Theodorias after the empress), now called Qasr

Libya (Castle Libya), and (2) nearby L'atrun (variously, Erythrun, Al Athrun, L'anthroun).

Qasr Libya was the seat of a bishopric and had two churches. The artistic face of early Christian Libya is best displayed in this isolated location west of Al-Bayda at Qasr Libya (ancient Olbia/Olvea/Theodorias). The art of mosaic was magnificently expressed in ancient Olbia in a way that would anticipate the aesthetic magnificence of Byzantium. The zenith of mosaic art in Africa was perfected in this remote location.

The mosaics of two Byzantine churches were accidentally uncovered at Qasr Libya in 1952 by construction workers. They revealed fifty remarkable mosaic panels with numerous Byzantine inscriptions. An elaborate decorative inscription indicates that the priceless mosaics in the Eastern church at Qasr Libya were made in the era of Justinian (A.D. 529–540).

Qasr Libya was refortified after the Vandal period by Justinian, the emperor of New Rome in Constantinople, as a stronghold for resisting the Vandals during the fifth century, and later to defend the Christian population from tribal raids from the desert. The bishop of Olbia was present at the Council of Ephesus in A.D. 431, where the Marian doctrine of *Theotokos* (God-bearer) was contested and consensually confirmed. The church was dedicated to Saint Nekarios in the third year of bishop Macarius (A.D. 539), showing the continuity of the Christian tradition in a remote rural Libyan location.

The biblical content of the mosaics provides a clue to catechetical teaching in Byzantine Christianity. Here are the themes of eight of them:

1. One mosaic displays the four rivers of Genesis 2:10-14, which provides the Byzantine Christian imagination with a way of providing a biblical map of the world. The four rivers symbolized the world's greatest waterways: the Ganges (Pishon), which "flows in the direction of India" (Ambrose, *Paradise* 3.14), the Nile "which comes down from Ethiopia into Egypt" (John of Damascus, *OF* 2.9), and the Tigris and Euphrates. The Nile mosaic is luxuriously decorated with lotus flowers, images of deer, birds, horses, fish and waterfowl.

2. Another scene portrays a lighthouse, a symbol of light that saves from shipwreck. It is suggestive of the pattern of the great lighthouse of Alexandria, one of the Seven Wonders of the World—Pharos. This is where St. Mark, by tradition, first landed in Egypt. The symbol: the gospel provides light in darkness.

3. Another mosaic scene at Qasr Libya portrays a Justinian period Christian basilica, featuring four columns in the front, stairs leading up to the entry and a pitched roof with trees in the background. The tesserae are brilliantly colored with stones of blue, gray, white, black and brown. The inscriptions celebrate the lives of believers.

4. In one of the mosaic panels a gift is being offered to the church by the empress in Constantinople.

5. One of the mosaics is of a peacock in full color—a Christian symbol for immortality.

6. There is also a mosaic showing the fortresslike features of a city with a defensive staircase leading up into an entryway with soldiers on the top of the ramparts, symbolic of the safekeeping mercy of God toward the faithful.

7. Another panel shows two fishermen in a boat with a sail on a tempestuous sea. This may be a reference to the narrative of Jesus meeting the disciples in a storm on the sea.

8. Another portrays a soldier on a horse, reminiscent of the typical portrayals of the victory of St. George, whose martyrdom occurred in Cyrenaica.

These mosaics are now housed in the Qasr Libya Museum and are considered among the finest in early African mosaic art. The exquisite art of Qasr Libya challenges the opinion that the Byzantine period in Africa is hardly worth investigating aesthetically. It shows that Byzantine Christian artisans survived in remote rural Libya through many generations of social upheaval amid the decline and fall of Rome. They had miners, artists, builders and artisans capable of producing the highest quality of African mosaics.

These exemplary African mosaics seldom appear in the books that report the aesthetic achievements of this period or this continent. When they do, they appear only the sketchiest of terms. In much European literature this era is regarded as a declining period of the onset of "the Dark Ages," a time of late Roman cultural degeneration, economic depression and desperate efforts at military defense. Yet this was the period where the aesthetic arts reached a magnificent level even in such remote pastoral Libyan sites as Qasr. While Rome and Romanticism are gone, these mosaics have survived over fifteen centuries.

## THE CHURCHES OF L'ATRUN: THE VITALITY OF CHRISTIAN VILLAGE LIFE PORTRAYED

There are two churches in the village of L'atrun (Al Athrun). Though remote in location, they are renowned for their aesthetic artifacts, displaying beauty and quality. They are commonly referred to as the western basilica and the eastern basilica.

These basilicas show evidence of the vitality of the Christian tradition in the rural village of L'atrun around A.D. 550. This vitality is seen in the opulent furnishings of the western church sanctuary, whose altar area had marble panels with decorated crosses, with four large columns that provided a holy canopy for the sacred space of the altar.[3] There is also a cemetery with tombs carved in rock.

One L'atrun basilica has a panel that portrays crosses connected by a vine that surrounds the central cross, and an omega shaped geometric design. These visual symbols served a teaching function for both seekers and believers. They stood as a reminder of the crucifixion and its relationship with the Eucharist, and pointed toward the end-time with the alphabet's last letter.

Another L'atrun mosaic portrays a woman with incense, symbolizing the fragrance of the gentle and comforting work of the Holy Spirit. Another portrays a deer with antlers defeating a snake in combat, pointing to the defeat of demonic powers. Another portrays the donation of the basilica by the empress or some governess who is portrayed at the altar presenting loaves of bread as a lay representative. These

---

[3]For a brilliant overview of the architecture of this period, see Richard Krautheimer, *Early Christian and Byzantine Architecture* (New Haven, Conn.: Yale University Press, 1984).

provide glimpses of church life in Libya in the mid-sixth century.

When modern secular eyes gaze on ancient Libyan Christian art, they sometimes are at first only able to grasp a few curious geometric patterns with obscure crosses in it. But upon closer look it becomes evident that many Christian symbols are embedded in the geometric patterns—symbols of the creation, resurrection, Trinity, Eucharist and the outpouring of the Holy Spirit. These symbols provided a practical opportunity for visual catechetical teaching as well as a fitting context for the celebration of the Lord's Supper and preaching of the Word.

From L'atrun we journey west to describe four of the five cities of the Pentapolis, in addition to Cyrene, which we have already explored.

## THE EARLY CHRISTIANS OF APOLLONIA

Soon after Cyrene's founding in 631 B.C., four other cities were established in the area, which together with Cyrene were known as the Pentapolis (the Five Cities). Each became cities where Christian dioceses were formed in the third or fourth century.

The five Cyrenaic cities of the Pentapolis were (1) Apollonia (Susa or Sozusa), the port city for Cyrene, (2) Cyrene (Grenneh, now Shahat), (3) Tolmeita, or Ptolemais, and its nearby port of Barce (Barka, or Al Marj), (4) Euesperides (present-day Benghazi, also called Hesperis, Hesperides, Asperides or later Berenike); (5) Teuchira (later Arsine or Arsinoe, present-day Tauchera, Tukra, Taucheira or Tochera). In addition to these five, Darnis (Darna, Adriana) is sometimes reckoned as a sister city comparable to the cities of the Pentapolis.

The thriving coastal cities of the Pentapolis produced one of the greatest of early African cultures, sometimes called Afro-Hellenic. The five cities were founded long before Alexandria. Their establishment preceded Muslim cultures by about thirteen centuries. Since they have one of the oldest sustained indigenous cultures on the African continent with continuous occupation, there is no reason to mistakenly categorize these five cities as European. They have proven their notoriety as one of the world's high continuing civilizations by producing a literary tradition of intellectual excellence over more than a millennium. If you should ask inhabitants of the Pentapolis if they are Europeans, they would laugh.

Fifteen miles away from Cyrene was its port, Apollonia. It was stretched out along a mile of coastal area, with ancient port facilities. The city was surrounded by walls or ramparts between two ancient port sites, west and east. This port location has served continuously in some fashion for about two and a half thousand years. Where else on the great continent of Africa is that length of commercial activity and pre-Roman tenure to be found? Only a few. While the whole continent of Africa has every reason to honor and be proud of Apollonia, it has sometimes been viewed as lacking in the decisive features of Africaneity. This has had a destructive consequence for African self-esteem. Africa has suffered wrongly from the spurious charge that it lacks a distinguished written intellectual history and a record of entrepreneurial creativity. Apollonia had both. And two and a half millennia to show for it.

The port was first established early in the seventh or sixth century B.C. The previous coastline is now inundated with water. Some of the coastal land has settled several feet below the surface of the present-day water level. An abundance of archaeological evidence still remains unexplored due to this coastal shift. There are remnants of port storerooms between the eastern basilica and the theater near the ancient shoreline of the eastern port.

In the second century B.C., a defensive wall was built around the city to protect the harbor. In the early fourth century A.D., Apollonia served as the seat of the governors for the entire providence of Upper Libya.

## THE FIVE CHURCHES OF APOLLONIA

The special interest Apollonia holds for Christian historical awareness focuses on the remains of its five Christian basilicas, some of considerable size and importance for early Christian history. It is one of the best places to get a glimpse of the life and architecture of the church in a very early phase of Christian edifices, especially in the period of Justinian and Theodora, and at the height of Byzantine design before the appearance of Arab cavalry.

The Byzantine Christian monuments and edifices were built directly on top of the earlier layers of the port city. After the huge earthquake in A.D. 365, extensive repairs were required in the city walls, buildings, monuments and houses. Through the generosity of the Byzantine emperor Justinian the defenses of the city were completely rebuilt. Still extant are the remains of massive rectangular towers that show evidences of these structures. Wherever Mediterranean trading ships docked, they would eventually find their way to Apollonia.

The largest Byzantine buildings and monuments remaining were constructed shortly after the military reconquest led by Belasarius in A.D. 533. Today Apollonia is a city of spectacular ancient monuments, basilicas and towers. Though never a vast city, it has always been an important one. It served as the entryway to Cyrene and inland Cyrenaica.

Much of the Byzantine construction occurred by the refashioning of previous Punic, Greek or Roman structures and materials, or by means of mining the extensive rock quarries nearby. However colossal the fortifications, they did not hold long against the Arab strike in 643.

The remains of five churches built prior to A.D. 600 are found in Apollonia. These are usually designated by archaeologists as the western basilica, central basilica, eastern basilica, and the chapel in the Byzantine ducal palace.

The *western basilica* is just inside the wall of the ancient city near the western gate. It was a massive construction. Four green marble columns have survived, along with some of its large arches. Parts of this site may have been at one time a memorial, oratory or tomb for Christian martyrs. There is a baptistery in the northeastern corner and some remnants of mosaics on the floor. Older Greek materials and Roman marble columns were used to build the western basilica. The white columns are Byzantine style. The floors are marble.

Only a short distance away from the western basilica is the *central basilica,* featuring a marble floor and massive pillars decorated with Byzantine crosses, again with a separate baptistery. This central basilica lies very near the present-day shore. On the shore side of the basilica are the remains of Byzantine cisterns and water works. Evidence of the importance of the medicinal herb silphium is also evident in the décor of the central church.

Northeast of the palace is one of the largest Christian churches in Cyrenaica, usually referred to as the *eastern basilica*. It features a transept and is divided into three naves by tall columns of elegant cipolin marble. The cipolin comes from the Greek island of Paros. The granite is from Egypt. This great basilica in Apollonia is one of the finest monuments in the Pentapolis, with numerous mosaics that are on par with the high quality of those in Qasr Libya. There are remains of an altar and ciborium from the fifth or sixth century.

Near the apse is a trefoil baptistery designed to rest underneath a cupola. The baptistery is from the Justinian period. The original church foundation goes further back to the Constantinian period, making it one of the earliest in African Christian architecture. Another nearby ceremonial room is built in a cruciform pattern. A portico with arcades leads into the central nave. Fifth-century reconstructions featured Theodosian capitals. Several biblical mosaics were found in the area of the baptistery, one portraying Noah and the ark.

On the hill above the baths is a nobleman's palace, which was adapted as the *ducal palace* of Christian Byzantine rulers (c. 500s A.D.). It was a large residence with dozens of rooms, stone shelves for a library and an audience hall with an apse, a council chamber, a courtyard with porticos on three sides. There was a private chapel in the ducal residence.

An amphitheater was built nearby the old stone quarry close to the town. The amphitheater is unexcavated. Amphitheaters were places of gladiatorial combat and blood sport events. Documentary evidence is lacking as to whether Christian martyrdom took place in the amphitheater during Diocletian times, but it would not be surprising.

In the far eastern portion of the ancient city is a Greek theater and an ancient Acropolis.

The theater was in a spectacular location immediately outside the eastern wall facing the sea. East from the Acropolis there are ancient tombs of a large necropolis holding many epigraphic mysteries, but revealing multicultural ethnicities.

Excellent Byzantine mosaics and marble columns from Apollonia and Ras Al Hilal (30 km east of Apollonia) may be seen in the Apollonia Museum, along with some stunning mosaics that were excavated in L'atrun. Though the Museum of Apollonia is small, it contains mosaics important to Christian history of late antiquity. In the museum is a large sarcophagus featuring a hunting scene in bas-relief, as well as Hellenistic statues, funerary busts and artifacts from the ducal palace.

## THE CHURCHES OF PTOLEMAIS

The port and archdiocesan city of Ptolemais (Tolmeta, modern Dirsiya) was one of the cities of Libya where the earliest Sabellian teachings stimulated controversies as early as A.D. 257–260, as later attested by Bishop Dionysius of Alexandria (Eusebius, *CH* 7.6.1). It was the city where Synesius served as bishop from A.D. 410-413.

The continuity of episcopal succession in Ptolemais goes back at least to the early third century. This sequence includes both orthodox and Arian bishops at various times. Two of the third-century bishops of

Mosaic of an angel in the church of Ptolemais in the era of Synesius
[Museum of Ptolemais]

Ptolemais were Telesphorus and Basilides (Eusebius, *CH* 7.26.2). Other known bishops of the area surrounding Ptolemais were Euporus and Euphranor (Eusebius, *CH* 7.26.1-2). Bishop Secundus of Ptolemais was a delegate to the First Ecumenical Council of Nicaea (Philostorgius, *Ecclesiastical History* 1.9) to advocate the Arian view so much controverted in Libya at that time.

Under Diocletian in A.D. 279, Ptolemais became the capital of the Pentapolis, replacing the depopulated Cyrene. A generation later, upon the victory of Constantine, a magnificent archway (A.D. 311–312) was built soon thereafter and dedicated to Constantine, located on the main street of the city. After Constantine made Christianity a tolerated religion, the Christian presence in Ptolemais increased markedly. Athanasius elevated Bishop Siderius of Palaebisca to become bishop of Ptolemais (Synesius, *Letter* 67). Siderias later retired to a rural area near Palaebisca and Hydrax.

The western basilica of Ptolemais was built along the trefoil plan (the shape of a threefold leaf) with three naves, a chamber off the north side, and thick Byzantine walls. After being largely unnoticed for centuries, excavations began on ancient Greek Ptolemais in 1935 by Italian archaeologists. They found that the former Greek agora was redesigned and expanded to become a Roman forum. It continued to serve during the Byzantine period, when it became the center of ecclesiastic and political governance during the fifth century at the time of Synesius. The site is only partially excavated, yet extensive ruins have been discovered, many extending into the Byzantine period of Christian governance. They show that Ptolemais after Diocletian became an important administrative city, equal in influence to Cyrene, and remained so during the Christian period.

In the forum vicinity are large cisterns that were steadily fed by a Roman aqueduct. Still partially surviving are the remains of a Roman bridge that spans the Wadi. The availability of fresh, drinkable water was crucial to the cities in North Africa. The extraordinary hydrological expertise of the Romans is still on display in Ptolemais.

The University of Chicago Oriental Institute (1956–1958, under the direction of Carl Kraeling) excavated three buildings from the Roman and Byzantine periods: the Four Seasons villa (whose mosaics are on museum display), the Byzantine baths and a public building on the Street of the Monuments. Local Christians of five earlier centuries have strolled along this Street of the Monuments, lined with fountains, porticos, inscriptions, statues, the headquarters of the governor, a fortress which garrisoned Roman soldiers, and a basilica.

## THE EARLY CHRISTIANS OF ARSINOE (TAUCHERA)

The location of the ancient city of Arsinoe (modern Tauchera, Tokra, Tauchire, Teuchira, Tauorga) was a site first built upon by the Greeks in 510 B.C. Tauchera is a short drive north of the modern city of Benghazi. It stands on a striking vista overlooking the Mediterranean. During the Ptolemaic period it was named Arsinoe after Queen Arsinoe, the mother of Ptolemy III. After centuries of Greek occupation, Arsinoe became a Roman city in 96 B.C., and during the next two centuries it continued as a thriving port city. In the ancient quarry west of the city, there are remains of a large mausoleum that marks the burial place of the Ptolemaic governors of the Pentapolis. The site features a large necropolis with tombs from Greek, Roman and Byzantine periods, some carved out of rock. There is a western basilica and an eastern basilica. The latter is erected within the rebuilt Byzantine walls with an apse and a large baptistery for multiple baptisms.

The ancient city had many Greek and Roman columns, a gymnasium area, and heavy fortifications that were expanded from Greek to Roman to Byzantine reconstructions. The museum at Arsinoe contains large ceramic jars, pots, vases and terracotta items, and pottery lamps and funereal artifacts from all periods, including the Byzantine.

In the Byzantine Christian period the improved military defense of the city became a crucial means of resisting the assaults of the marauding factions of the people of Luata. Still visible in the remains of Arsinoe are a Byzantine fortress and a church that some claim to be the first Byzantine church in North Africa. For Christians this city was a diocesan center whose bishop supervised a wider area of Cyrenaica (*HEO* 2:661). During times of threat, Christians in Arsinoe withdrew into these heavy fortifications. There once were thirty towers built into Arsinoe's walls, yet all these defenses proved unable to resist the Arab onslaught.

## EARLY CHRISTIANITY IN BERENIKE
## (HESPERIDES, BENGHAZI)

West from Arsinoe are the coastal cities of Hadrianopolis and Berenike (Euesperides, Bengazi, Benghazi, Hesperides, Berenice or Bereniki). Benghazi or Berenike was the chief ancient Afro-Hellenic city in western Cyrenaica. It was called Hesperides in the Greek period, Berenike in the Ptolemaic period and today the Arabic Benghazi. Berenike was the wife of Ptolemy III.

The quays of the ancient city of Berenike were ingeniously reconstructed over the centuries to accommodate ever larger ships. This served particularly the trade in African elephants used for military and entertainment purposes. Throughout the empire, this port serviced a long history of trade in glass, grain, wine, gold, spices, pearls and textiles. It continued as a thriving commercial center from the period of Ptolemy II (275 B.C.) until the sixth century A.D. As early as the era of Cleopatra there were caravans plodding up from the south to Berenike from inland deserts to connect with world markets.

Ancient Berenike/Benghazi had two harbors. The heart of the ancient city throbbed between them as if it were a heart beating with the breath of two lungs. Always a cosmopolitan seaport, the city had a significant population of Jews from the time of the early first century. Many more would come after the Diaspora of A.D. 70. These Jewish communities became an important part of the story of early African Christian believers.

The active pursuit of advanced Christian learning probably occurred in the precise location in Benghazi of what is now one of Libya's major universities, Al-Jami' al-Libya. It is in the oldest part of the city near the shore of the north port. The ancient site of Euesperides near Benghazi goes back to sixth century B.C.

The vestiges of a sixth-century Byzantine basilica have barely survived. It had been refashioned out of materials from an older pagan temple. The new Byzantine fortress was built in the Justinian period. It survived until 643, when the Arabs arrived.

During the Sabellian controversy around A.D. 257–260, Bishop Ammon of Berenike was under the authority of Bishop Dionysius of

Alexandria (Eusebius, *CH* 7.26.1). The bishop of Berenike in A.D. 325 was Dakes, who attended the Council of Nicaea (*HEO* 2:658) and was viewed by Philostorgius as a sympathizer with Arius against the orthodox Athanasians.

The bustling modern city of Benghazi paves over most of the early ruins of Ptolemaic Berenike. Little remains of ancient Berenike, and even less of its Christian evidences. Only a few ruins have survived: warehouses, port substructures and a temple dedicated to Serapis, the protector of sailors and travelers. With a major airport, travel facilities and hotels, Benghazi is an excellent launching point for exploring the most important Christian monuments in northern and eastern Libya. It is the key modern city of the western part of the Jebel Akhdar (Green Mountain) range whose escarpments stretch throughout upper Cyrenaica not far from the coast. Western travelers in Libya will almost certainly transit through Benghazi, but often on the way to the other better preserved sites and monuments elsewhere in the Pentapolis, or to other nearby cities such as Misrata, Ghirza, Tauchera and Sirte.

Traveling with the sun east to west, at this point we have reached half way through the vast coastal area of Libya. Next we proceed to Tripolitania in the western part of Libya.

# 9

# EARLY CHRISTIAN
# PRESENCE IN
# TRIPOLITANIA

■■■

Tripolitania is that region of North Africa that now forms the north-western part of Libya. The massive body of water that dips into the coastline of North Africa is called the Gulf of Sirte (Sidra). The southern tip of the gulf is easily identified on a map as the southernmost point of the Mediterranean Sea.

This is the precise point that divided ancient Roman Tripolitania in the west from Greek-speaking Cyrenaica in the east. The part of coastal Libya called Syrtica is located on the coast of Tripolitania as the Gulf of Sirte is descending to its most southern point.

## The Dividing Line Between Cyrenaica and Tripolitania

Draw a straight line north from this southernmost point of the Gulf of Sirte and you will see that the border falls roughly between Eastern Europe and Western Europe. The line goes north toward the former Yugoslavia, and the rest is history. This line was drawn at the south end of the Gulf of Sirte, which since Punic times had been an obvious geographical marker. For nearly two hundred years this south-north line moving up from central Libya, established by the Emperor Diocletian, would divide eastern and western parts of the empire as it would later sharply divide Western Catholics from Eastern Orthodox.

The border between East and West was commemorated early in the myth of the Phileni brothers who raced between Carthage and Cyrene to establish their border at Fines Africae Cyrenorum near al-Sultan. The Arae Philenorum is the monolithic arch at the halfway point of the littoral road that ran the entire length of Libya's Mediterranean coastline. In mythology the Phileni brothers were Carthaginian citizens who ran eastward to meet two Cyrenaic runners to establish the border between the principalities.

This phantom boundary line in North Africa in late antiquity has had long-lasting consequences in the history of Europe and for all of early Christianity. After about A.D. 300, subsequent maps of Europe would be divided in the same way that Libya had been divided between east and west. In this way the rocky coastal terrain of Libya became the fate-laden marker of the interface between East and West, as reflected in the polarities capitalist/communist, Latin/Greek, Catholic/Orthodox, and Tripolitania/Cyrenaica.

This peculiar consequence is often missed by Eurocentric historians. It is ironic that the political history of divisions in Europe were decisively shaped by the physical shape of Africa. The effects of this frontier are still being felt especially in all those still-troubled European border states where the conflicts continue smoldering in the anguished Balkans: Bosnia, Croatia, Serbia, Romania, Albania and Macedonia. This is the fault line of European politics, the "clash of civilizations" and the source of much ongoing heartache.

The linguistic differences between Greek and Latin speakers were well established before Constantine. But it was with Diocletian that the geopolitical consequences were firmly set. Their intent was to unite the Roman West with the Greek East, but the outcome was division.

The bold new capital of Constantinople, the New Rome, was established precisely on the Asia-Europe continental nexus at the waters of the Bosphorus: Byzantium. But what was decided in Constantinople had to be applied in Libya. Constantine had hoped that the richer East and the poorer West would be united in a new world culture springing from the apostolic and political unity flowing from Constantinople. Christianity played a defining role in conceiving this ideal unity. But the forces of gravity would shift violently back and forth on this deep fissure during the long centuries between Constantine and the reconquest of Spain.

## THE LITERARY AND POLITICAL MIDPOINT

This line still marks enduring cultural differences within modern Libyan conflicts. The pre-Islamic literary tradition of Libya remains divided between the residual effects of the two ancient languages and their legal and ecclesiological systems: Latin-Greek, West-East. The pre-Arabic literary tradition of Libya is divided almost precisely into two equal parts, Latin-based and Greek-based law, language, economic traditions and social patterns.

While there is some overlapping, these cultural differences have remained resistant. As a consequence, for most of the five centuries (third through seventh centuries) of Libyan Christianity, texts of Tripolitania were in Latin, and texts of Cyrenaica were in Greek. This continued until both regions were overpowered by Arab armies from the desert east, which brought down the hegemonic claims of both languages. Surprisingly, Arabization brought greater unity to Libya than any previous force. But still the differences have remained long-lasting.

Even today, the further east you go in Libya from the Gulf of Sirte, the more you feel the Byzantine cultural echoes and architectural residues, whether in food tastes, personal encounters or political administration. The further west you go, the more you feel the effects of a Latin-Roman-Western legal, cultural and architectural history, later modified by Italian and French tones and textures.

The struggle between Christian orthodoxy and heresy was fought in two dissimilar linguistic arenas: the Greek East and the Latin West. Those early Christian teachers who were arguably born in Libya (St. Mark, Victor, Tertullian, Sabellius and Synesius) could speak both Latin and Greek with varying levels of competency. But later Libyan Christian leaders after Diocletian were largely forced to choose between Latin and Greek. It often made a great deal of difference as to whether they were quoting sacred texts, liturgies or patristic writers in Greek or Latin. This forced choice affected who their audience would become and how their Christian identity would form. Classical Christian teachings of the western part of Libya were faced with different challenges than those from the east of Libya. Orthodox Christians who were struggling against different nonconsensual (heretical) tendencies had to define Christianity with different language patterns and concepts. They were thinking and writing in the context of sharply divergent cultural histories and philosophical worldviews.

The most divisive forms of dissent in the East were Gnosticism, Sabellianism and Monophysitism. The most divisive irregularities in the West were Donatism, Pelagianism and Manichaeanism. Arianism plagued both. All of these heresies were confronted on both sides of the East-West divide, but with different social presuppositions, political accents, cultural tones and outcomes. All of these anomalies were challenged in a reasonably consistent fashion by the most inclusive thinkers of early Christianity: Augustine in Latin and Cyril the Great in Greek. Cyril could read Latin, and Augustine could handle elementary Greek.

According to late Roman political geography, western Libya was administratively integral to Roman Africa, whose political language was Latin and whose early Scripture translations were in Old Latin. The bishops of Tripoli attended consensus-seeking councils in Carthage and to the west. The bishops of the Pentapolis attended consensus-seeking councils in Alexandria and to the east. The eastern part of Libya was more closely connected culturally with Egypt, whose political language then was Ptolemaic Greek, whose Old Testament was the Septuagint, and whose New Testament was in Greek.

The earliest Latin theologians of the late second and early to mid-third century were African (notably Tertullian and Cyprian). Among the earliest African theologians writing in Greek were Clement, Origen and Athanasius.

The Latin form of early Christian literature began in Africa. The Bible was first translated to Latin in Africa. It is called the Old Latin version. It is counterintuitive for most Westerners to realize that the earliest forms of Latin Christian texts were written not in Europe but in Africa.

## EARLY CHRISTIANITY IN SYRTICA:
## GHIRZA AND MISRATA

In volatile times this border area of Syrtica changed hands many times. It was controlled variously by local Berber tribes or by various Punic, Egyptian, Greek, Roman, Vandal, Byzantine or later Arabic military, political and administrative caliphates.

Syrtica (Sirtica) is the center point of Libya and was at one time proposed (in a modern fantasy advocated by Qaddafi) as the future capital of all of Africa. Born in Sirte, Qaddafi's vision was to unite Africa under his own model of government and create something like an African Brasilia, a capital whose location was not natural but was determined by political circumstances and influences. While this idea never took root outside of Libya, it does again underscore the fundamental division of cultures in Libya in both ancient and contemporary times.

Our journey next takes us to major outposts of Latin Christianity west of the Syrtica/Cyrenaic border. We look first at Ghirza and Misrata, and then the magnificent Leptis Magna.

Ghirza was a frontier settlement south of Misrata (Misurata), in the contested area between Roman and nomadic tribal lands. Its tomb inscriptions provide a glimpse of the names and folkways of the earliest Christians in this area. The villages and farms around Ghirza were strongly fortified. They bear the scars of the perennial encounters between cultures that competed for influence in the area: indigenous Berber, later Roman and Byzantine Christian. This is a crucial period for understanding the times of early Christian presence in inland central Libya.

Ghirza is noted for its bas-reliefs from the Constantinian period. It provides a wealth of necrological and archaeological information about the transitional period between Roman and Byzantine times. The tombs date from the third to the fifth century, the early period of Christian presence in Syrtica. The southern necropolis south of the Wadi Ghirza has survived almost intact from ancient times. The northern necropolis has been partially restored.

The mausoleum and tomb inscriptions offer a glimpse into early

Christian funerary symbols. They portray a prosperous agricultural community producing grapes, corn, figs and dates. The tombs show visual images of a man feeding a camel, another carrying an amphora, and others hunting antelope and other wild life.

A large collection of coins from the period of Diocletian and Constantine was uncovered in 1981 in nearby Misrata, about 250 kilometers (about 150 miles) east of Tripoli. This treasury of some 100,000 coins dates largely from the fourth century A.D.—the period in which Libyan Christianity was in its early phase of development. These coins depict official government symbols and metaphors during the period when Christianity was first being planted and was growing exponentially. This is the time when Christians were struggling against Diocletian's persecution, yet growing rapidly against all odds and moving into the period of toleration that began with Constantine.

## THE GLORY OF LEPTIS MAGNA

For Christians, Leptis Magna was the titular see of Tripolitania, as Ptolemais was of Cyrenaica. The history of Leptis reaches back into Palestinian-Canaanitic roots. Residents from the Phoenician ports of Sidon and Tyre in the seventh century B.C. had early established a trading post on the natural harbor at Leptis. The watercourse there is variously spelled as either Leptis or Lepcis, but more commonly Leptis.

By the time of the Decian (249–251) and Valerian (253-260) persecutions there were martyrs in Libya. Antonio Di Vita writes: "In Tripolitania, the earliest traces of Catholic bishops refer to Lepcis and date from the end of the second century" (*LLC*, 162). This was at a time (190s A.D.) when Tertullian was a young man and Clement was completing his education under Pantaenus in the catechetical school of Alexandria, a generation before Cyprian's birth.

The preserved record of the first known and named bishop of Tripolitania is Dioga, A.D. 255, of Leptis Magna. Hence at least fifty-six years before the beginning of Constantine's rule (A.D. 311), Christians were known to be in residence in Leptis—contemporary with Cyprian in Carthage. If the evidence is found plausible, as set forth earlier, on the family roots of Pope Victor of Africa (gens Gaius) and Tertullian (gens Septimius) as likely citizens of Leptis Magna, then the date can be pushed back further to the 150s A.D. or earlier.

The earliest Christians in Leptis may have been slaves or servants, or had mercantile or artisan interests. But it is much more likely they were serving in the military or in state ministries, as was the father of Tertullian. All baptized believers were potentially evangelists.

Other bishops of Leptis whose names are known are Victorinus and Maximus in 393, Sylvanius, and later Calipedes during the Vandal period in 484. In addition there was a duplicate bishop in Leptis in 411—one a Donatist. Leptis, like all three of the Emporia cities of Tripolitania, was divided when the fourth-century dispute between Catholics and Donatists was at its height, with two bishops in the same city.

Since Leptis was one of the major Mediterranean ports that provided access to inland Saharan peoples, it was also undoubtedly a place where slaves were traded over a long period of time, a practice that continued well into the Arab period. It is likely that some were Christians.

By the time of the arrival of Christians in the first or second centuries, Leptis was growing into a stunningly impressive imperial city of great monuments. The most impressive constructions of the monumental period occurred under the leadership of the previously discussed Roman emperor Septimius Severus, who was born in Leptis of Tripolitania (A.D. 145) only a few years before Tertullian, who likely stemmed from the same distinguished family. Severus likely grew up in Leptis, and when he became emperor, transformed it into one of Africa's most spectacular cities. As an African, he rose in the equestrian military ranks, as did the father of Tertullian. Severus successfully led a major Roman army to victory in Pannonia. On the basis of his military prowess after the assassination of Commodus in A.D. 192, he began a dynasty of some of the greatest emperors of the late Roman Empire. Some say this was the time of the zenith of the imperial government of late Roman antiquity. The Syrian wife of Septimius (Julia Domna) had family members from Syria with sympathies toward Christians, one of whom was Origen, with whom she visited when he was living in Caesarea Palestina. It is likely that the bishop of Leptis before 189 was Victor, who became pope that year.

Christian missionary expansion occurred exponentially all over North Africa during the same time frame as the Severan dynasty. This is clear from legal edicts and records of intermittent Christian persecutions during the period from A.D. 180 to 203 and from literary sources such as Clement, Origen, Perpetua, Tertullian, Cyprian, Arnobius and later Eusebius.

The reign of Septimius lasted until 211, when he was killed in a battle in England. His reign came at a time when some of the most widespread and serious persecutions of Christians were occurring under local magistrates, despite his own more benign personal temperament. The reason for the persecution of Christians was not that they wished to be disloyal to the Roman civic order but that they refused to give up their Scriptures to the governing officials, and they refused to attribute the language of deity to the emperor. This occurred when a simple act of allegiance to Roman civic religion was required of them. But that signified an idolatry that would condemn them at the final judgment and bar them from eternal life with God. Although Septimius was not the most aggressive of the persecutors, some of the worst African local persecutions of Christians did occur under his authority.

Leptis Magna is one of the most magnificent archaeological sites in all of Africa. Its statues and monuments have been well preserved. They flood the eye on a huge scale in today's Leptis. The vast and most impressive Roman remains come from the period of Septimius Severus. This was during the time when Tertullian was writing. Tertullian unmistakably identifies himself as a member of the family Septimii, a famous noble family of Leptis, founders of the Severan dynasty.

The uniqueness of Leptis among early African Christian archaeological sites is its enormous scale and relatively unspoiled condition. Leptis is a case in point of a major Libyan city with five centuries of Christian presence. Yet seldom in the scholarly literature is there any hint of its Christian past. For this reason I will be focusing my attention chiefly on the early Christian sources, sites and artifacts of Leptis.

For more than a millennium this huge site was under sand. The sand performed two valuable functions: to hide the ancient city and to preserve its monuments in almost pristine condition, much as they were after the seventh-century Arab sweep over North Africa.

## THE UNIQUE VISUAL FIELD OF LEPTIS

Our interest is directed chiefly to the Christian period of Leptis history between about A.D. 180 and 643. The early generations of Christian believers in Leptis during Constantinian times (fourth century) would have lived out their daily lives trading and working in the midst of the great Severan monuments, walking daily through the forest of these immense granite columns, experiencing much the same visual field that can still be seen today for those who walk along the Via Colonnata—the Way, or Street of the Columns.

Where better than Leptis is it possible for modern Christians actually to behold a visual landscape that looks very much like it looked in paleo-Christian Libya? There are few competitors. Leptis provides a far more complete visual picture of an intact paleo-Christian city than the more familiar sites of Istanbul, Rome, Ephesus or Jerusalem. In all these places the civic buildings of the fourth and fifth centuries have been far more subject to destruction and ruin than Leptis.

The sand saved it. This is what makes Leptis of special interest to lovers of antiquity. For those who cannot visit Leptis, see if you can find a library where there is a copy of *Libya: The Lost Cities of the Roman Empire* by Antonio Di Vita, Ginette Di Vita-Evrard and Lidiano Bacchielli, with photos by Robert Polidori, which offers a stunning visual feast.

The modern entrance to the ancient site is accessed from the Tripoli-Zliten coastal road, a well-traveled Roman road leading east from Tripoli to Leptis, entering through a great Triumphal Way (via Trionfale, which was the old Roman cardo, the main street). On the beginning of the cardo there is a Roman milestone recalling the linkage of all Roman roads across North Africa from Gaza to Mauretania and all other points in the empire.

The great cardo stretches all the way from the Arch of Septimius to the old forum near the sea. It is a long, colonnaded thoroughfare (20 meters wide and 400 meters long) leading to the quays where ships from all over the Mediterranean once docked. They were coaxed into the port with the help of an enormous lighthouse about 35 meters in height, almost the same elevation as the famed lighthouse of Alexandria, one of the Seven Wonders of the World. The ships then moved into a safe, round harbor, one of the best in the Mediterranean. The ships would dock along the perimeter of the port and unload into warehouses on the quay. Among the major buildings on the south side of the quay was a large temple of Jupiter. The Wadi Lebda ran beside the old city.

Constructed in the glorious days of the Severan period, the colossal Arch of Septimius Severus celebrates the victories of Septimius, as seen in elaborate friezes and Corinthian columns and an archway of huge scale, comparable to the largest imperial Roman arches of the far-flung empire. This arch has been ingeniously reconstructed largely out of its original materials. As in the case of the Arch of Titus in Rome the carved, embedded statuary is still in a good state of preservation. The arch is one of the signature features of Leptis.

## CHRISTIANS AND THE MELDING OF CULTURES IN THE EMPORIA (LEPTIS, OEA, SABRATHA)

Libyan Christianity was quintessentially an African multicultural region from the outset. The three great cities of Latin Tripolitania were Leptis, Oea and Sabratha. Together they were known as the Emporia, the breadbasket of Rome, like a mall with everything. They were distinguished from the five cities of eastern Libya, the Pentapolis (Cyrene, Apollonia, Berenike, Tauchera and Barce) of Cyrenaica, where Greek language and culture were predominate. The people were independent, self-motivated, upwardly mobile and articulate. Think of self-assured, irascible Tertullian as a model.

Of all the cities around the Mediterranean, why did the early Christians elect to come to the Emporia, whose largest city was Leptis? For many reasons: (1) The Christians of Jewish descent were seeking refuge during the Diaspora after the fall of Jerusalem. (2) Some came with the motive of prosperity to a city where they had a good chance to be successful in their international enterprises or for local artisanship.

(3) Christians hungered for an international community closely connected with Rome, through which their aspirations could be embodied. (4) They were Great Commission Christian believers who had taken seriously the calling to go into all the world and proclaim the good news, teach its moral meaning, baptize and make disciples. These were reasons that made Leptis and the Emporia cities a natural place for Christian presence and witness.

The special status of Leptis was noted in numerous Greco-Roman literary sources: Pliny, Strabo, Scyllax and others. The city that had been called Neapolis under the Greeks became Leptis Magna under the Romans. Whether under Greek, Carthaginian, Roman, Vandal, Byzantine or Arabic authority, the Punic base of the seagoing culture remained deeply embedded in the city's traditions.

Linguistic competence was highly valued in Leptis. During the five centuries of Christian influence, Greek was normatively spoken along with Latin in this port city, as well as indigenous Nilotic, Libyan, Berber, Marmartian and Nasamones languages. Though not known as an academic center, Leptis was preferentially treated as an administrative capital city during the period of the early growth of Christianity.

All that survives of Punic remnants at Leptis are fragmentary ruins of walls, quays and harbor defenses. Archaeologist J. B. Ward-Perkins in 1948 searched for these earliest Punic layers with only modest visible results. He was able to show that the Punic portion of the ancient city was located precisely in the area where the Greek agora and later the old Roman forum were built. The abundant Greek and Roman layers were constructed on top of their remains.

During the time when Leptis was under the thumb of Carthage, a burdensome tribute of silver (nine tons per year) was required from Leptis by the Carthaginian rulers. So when the Roman General Scipio defeated the Carthaginians in the Battle of Zama, it was felt in Leptis as long-awaited tax relief. Carthage then fell to the Romans in 146 B.C. For a short time Leptis came under the authority of the Numidian kingdom (eastern Algeria). Soon it would reach its zenith as an official Roman colonial city led militarily by the family Septimius.

Roman colonial settlement did not increase significantly until 111

B.C., when an alliance was concluded and Roman military settlers began to arrive at Leptis. After that Leptis had a strong military tradition, brimming with sturdy old soldiers who had traveled around much of the known world.

Under Caesar Augustus (emperor from 27 B.C. to A.D. 14) Leptis first began to emerge as a leading city of Roman North Africa, with its own coinage, highly profitable trading, and the establishment of a Roman elite class that had vast resources to spend on spectacular civic monuments. By 193 the emperor of the Roman Empire would be an African general from Leptis Magna, and the bishop of Rome an African pope.

## AFTER CONSTANTINE: CHRISTIAN EDIFICES RESHAPE THE CITY'S LANDSCAPE

The previous Punic and Hellenistic trading center called the agora had been enlarged by the Romans in the first and second centuries A.D. with the addition of large temples and classical Roman civil basilicas, built by prominent local citizens in celebration of their prestigious status with Rome.

One of these families was the famous Septimii family, with which Tertullian proudly identified himself. The Leptis forum was paved with white limestone surrounded by porticos, a place where commerce flowed continuously and where much public business was transacted.

Procopius, the Byzantine historian, visited Leptis during the time of Justinian. At that time he reported that there were five Christian churches in Leptis. They were built out of materials available from previous constructions or direct adaptations of previous edifices. The curia (the senate house of the second century) was begun during the reign of Trajan (A.D. 98–117). The civil basilica was then reconstructed in the fourth century as a Constantinian church. Later it was converted into a larger scale Byzantine church in the sixth century.

The purpose of Christian worship was for the glorification of God, the training and baptizing of seekers (catechumens) by means of the hearing of the word, and the reception of the sacraments. The recycling of ancient Roman buildings had to take into account the new liturgical functions of Christian worship. The basic basilica architecture was adaptable to Christian worship with few modifications.

A cruciform—that is, cross-shaped—baptistery was built beside the church near the curia. The remains of one baptistery, once clad in alabaster, was found in the forum of the piazza near a Severan period exedra. There are evidences of many statuary niches around the circumference of the forum, which housed statues in alternating rectangular and curved recesses. This was the public square into which Christians daily entered, traded and prayed from the third to the seventh centuries.

## THE IRONY OF LEPTIS IN PROVIDENTIAL PERSPECTIVE

The irony of Leptis, seen in the light of classic early African Christian writings on providence in history (notably by Arnobius, Lactantius, Augustine and Victor of Vita), focuses on a single poignant fact: It was precisely during this enormous upbuilding of this great monumental city that believers before Constantine were required to make the hardest of all decisions—to stand up firmly as confessors of Christ in North Africa, refusing to submit to overt government-forced acts of idolatry. We do not know the names of those who paid with their lives for their witness. But their torture and death likely occurred in the amphitheater. There they were compelled to attest Roman emperors as divine gods. Refusing, their witness was called *martyria* (the Greek word for "witness" from which we derive the English word *martyrdom*).

During the era of Commodus, when Christians were gaining a small foothold in the culture and life both in Rome and Leptis, the Roman republic was gradually recasting itself into the perversion that the emperors were gods. This trend was taking on momentum just about the time of the entry of Christianity into Libya. It is precisely this era of architectural and monumental display that can be beheld today in Leptis. Its very mass and imperial majesty exhibit all the marks of the determination to identify the Roman emperor with divinity.

Paleo-Christian believers knew exactly how to read these signals. At this time this monumental architecture sought to make the precise point that the emperor is a god. The city itself was an embodied attempt to portray the grandeur of a deified emperor. Readers of the

Revelation to John are prompted to meditate on the causes of the distrust between early Christianity and the intimidating display of Roman power. One can go around the circumference of the Mediterranean and not find a better place than Leptis to reflect on this contrast. The irony of Leptis, providentially viewed, is that its imperial magnificence planted the seeds of corruption. This irony would take several generations to unfold.

The reign of the emperor Septimius Severus began in A.D. 193. Among his first priorities was the task of transforming his home city of Leptis into a magnificent imperial city. In an audacious act of city planning and nostalgia, he reconfigured the plan of the old city. The old forum built by the Greeks and the earlier Romans was relocated to a new area south of the old. A massive new complex was built—called the Severan Forum. It is in this area that the most important Christian buildings would be built or rebuilt in Leptis by the time of Constantine, who mercifully provided toleration for Christianity after many decades of bloody persecution.

Near the extensive port facilities and quay a new public space was created in a large scale for ports of that time. It was surrounded by colonnaded porticos with large columns of cipolin marble rising into archways. The décor of the archways were gorgon heads of which more than seventy have been recovered. The arches were made of limestone, and the heads were carved from marble with dedicatory inscriptions. The statuary of the forum featured Roman mythic figures, Medusa images, sea nymphs and symbolic representations of the goddess of victory. All this was designed to memorialize the military victories of Severus. The scale of the Severan Forum is colossal.

## THE CITIZENS OF HEAVEN IN THE SEVERAN FORUM

Walking through the Severan Forum today is like walking through a jungle of columns, capitals, broken marble, marble slabs and limestone fragments, stretching over an enormous scale. The colors are predominately white marble with earthy pinks and gold tintings set against a predominant background of red and sandy colors with various shades of grays and blues that change with the moving sun.

The earliest Christians to arrive in the port of Leptis would have seen these huge Roman temples and markets and theaters, many of which had just been completed in the first or second century. Hadrian (A.D. 117–138) had previously provided some of the early infrastructure for the development of commerce and luxury in the city, especially with respect to providing a reliable water supply. Exquisitely engineered aqueducts made possible one of the most spectacular edifices at Leptis still visible today: the Hadrianic Baths.

The region of Leptis was favored with excellent building materials nearby, including a highly resistant limestone. Marble facings began to be added to this basic construction material by the second century A.D. But all this conspicuous consumption did not dissuade Christian believers from the conviction that their city was heavenly, not earthly. Their journey was through time to eternity.

The next widespread persecution of Christians was in the Diocletian period intermittently from A.D. 284 to 305. Documentary evidence of persecutions in Leptis itself has not survived. Standing in the amphitheater ruins one can see the kind of setting in which many Christians were at that time being imprisoned, tortured and brutally killed all over northern Africa. During the reign of Diocletian, Leptis became the capital of Tripolitania, so Leptis Christians could hardly have been untouched by violence and intimidation during the widespread persecutions.

In the Christian period that began with Constantine in the early fourth century, Christianity was increasing in influence just at the time that classical Roman culture, myth, political power and military power were diminishing. The brisk growth of Christianity in Africa during Severian, Diocletian and Constantinian times occurred coordinately with the decline and almost complete collapse of Roman state-sponsored civic polytheism. The Diocletian period ended with Constantine, and the Christian religion in the Roman Empire became at first tolerable, then normative.

## THE CHRISTIAN TRANSFORMATION OF THE GREAT SEVERAN BASILICA

At the north end of the forum is the huge Severan basilica first built during the era of Septimius as a judicial building, a court of justice. It had two rounded apses at both ends with a nave and isles divided by red granite columns. This basilica was completed by Septimius's son Caracalla in A.D. 216.

Almost two hundred years later the basilica built for civic purposes was remodeled into a fourth-century Christian basilica. In this way these polytheistic edifices were being transmuted into places of worship of the one God. The basilica was transformed into a magnificent building for Christian preaching, sacramental life and education.

In Leptis we see the beginnings of the creativity of the earliest instincts of Christian architectural imagination. The Christian renovators were willing to receive the forms and aesthetic gifts and materials given to them through the Greco-Roman tradition, but radically converted that ethos into a place fit for the worship of the one God, the Father made known in the Son through the Holy Spirit. The vitality of Christian life in Leptis peaked in the sixth century. But the embryonic conversion of Roman architecture into Christian edifices began in the fourth century in the Constantinian era in places like Leptis. Here one can see the grandeur of Rome being both preserved and critiqued, and to some extent converted into the grandeur of Christian worship.

The walls of the Severan apse have been reconstructed by archaeologists. They rise to an amazing height. The Christian artisans showed conserving imagination in the use of original building materials in transforming buildings for Christian liturgical use. In the center of the apse are two columns crowned by a decorative capital that has been recently restored to its original location.

The great visual and tactile gift of the ruins of Leptis is that it gives modern people the privilege of walking through this huge maze of carved limestone and marble, fragments of sarcophagi, and steps, able to touch and experience this vast magnitude in a scale almost incomparable elsewhere in the ancient world. These beautiful materials once dedicated to idolatry were then for five centuries dedicated to the worship of the one God of Christianity. This renovated basilica became the site of an untold number of eucharistic services for many generations of Christian worship in Libya. Its carved columns climax with intricate portrayals of grapes, leaves, animals and music, all now reinterpreted in a liturgical context.

To this lofty Roman edifice was added in the Christian era a lowly altar for Holy Communion and a simple elevated platform for the teaching of Scripture and the preaching of the Word. The presbyters or elders were seated around the circumference of the semicircular apse with the congregation in the main space of the building, with the catechumens located in the far back, not yet ready to receive Holy Communion. Seekers were offered this practical means of learning about Christian teaching.

The grandeur of the worship of God was not diminished and certainly not demeaned or destroyed by the Christian adapters, but sustained and transformed for an entirely different use. Here a large congregation of Christians could educate seekers by bringing them into the place of worship where the baptized members could hear the Word and receive Holy Communion. The cover of this book provides a spectacular glimpse of the glory of Christian Leptis Magna.

## NEW SIGNS OF LIFE IN THE LEPTIS MARKET, AMPHITHEATER, CIRCUS AND BATHS

The central physical features of the market area were two round buildings which still in part remain visible: a south *tholos* and a north *tholos* clad in silver-gray limestone that has taken on a faint gold patina through weathering. This is the place where daily commercial exchanges occurred. There was extensive trade in fruits, vegetables, fish, fabrics, grains and olives. The foundations and marble pedestals for the market stalls from the second century A.D. may still be viewed in the inner portico of the market. There is a stone tablet that provides the official metric for goods, measuring the Punic cubit and the Alexandrian cubit with the Roman foot.

This was the trading center of Leptis. For all the years between Diocletian and the Arab victory (late second through mid-seventh centuries), there were Christians who traded here, among these booths and stalls. During these post-Constantinian and early Byzantine years, orthodox Christians were responsible not only for moral and religious instruction in this arena, but for the development of ordered justice in the civic sphere and economic life.

The construction of the great amphitheater of Leptis dates from A.D. 56—the beginning of Nero's reign, during the decade in which Peter, Paul and Mark had arrived in Rome. It has been partially reconstructed. It had seating for sixteen thousand people. It was quarried from a nearby hill with an elliptical crater. The early Christians of Leptis would likely have resisted the temptation to make the amphitheater theater a common part of their lives (as we see in Tertullian's *On the Spectacles* [*De spectaculis*]), but it surely was a dominant aspect of their physical environment. Christian preaching and piety of the time portrayed blood sport as a violent and corrupting place for baptized and committed Christians to avoid.

Here one of the main spectacles was the bloody experience of combat with wild animals and the punishment of offenders. At times there was also deadly combat between gladiators. Here is where prisoners were executed. A dramatic gladiatorial frieze was found in a mosaic at Zliten (Dar Buc Ammera, a nearby coastal village) portraying a gladiatorial battle to the death. It shows different figures in the frieze engaged in violent acts of combat—one with a net, another with a sword, and others with shields and axes (*LLC*, 85-86). Christians went through several intermittent periods of being regarded as pious but stubborn offenders against the Roman civic order. Some Jews and Christians may have been taken here for public humiliation or execution, but official records have not survived.

In the time of Marcus Aurelius, another large facility had been built in Leptis for chariot races on an enormous scale. It was one of the largest known circuses, almost comparable in length to the Circus Maximus in Rome. Races ran for 450 meters on the long portion and 100 meters in length in the circular ends, usually lasting seven laps. The circus was designed to accommodate about twenty-five thousand people. There were twelve starting gates for chariots. Portions of this circus are among the best preserved in antiquity. It had long rows of stone tiers, a stand for dignitaries, and monuments and pools in the central area. The Christian believers of the third century would have remembered this arena as an unsavory scene of idolatrous display.

Underneath the baths of the nearby Nymphaeum were furnaces to heat the water, channel it from room to room and supervise the whole system of water management. These blistering furnaces were serviced by slaves, as was typical of the Roman order of class stratification. It is likely that some of the slaves who heated and serviced the Nymphaeum of Leptis with its underground furnaces would have been Christian prisoners, who would have beheld at close quarters its pleasures and vanities, trapped in the absurdities of Roman politics. There was a circulation system (hypocaust) underneath the heated floor with ingenious and complex engineering construction so that the hot air could move in pipes under the floor and heat not only the floors but the walls through a system of terracotta flues. This complex was designed not simply as a bathing area but also as a social center, a place for citizens of Leptis to spend a great deal of time in a pleasant environment protected from the hot North African sun. One of the best preserved of the remains of the Nymphaeum are stone latrines. They are among the most photographed frames in the city today.

This huge complex was located at the end of the great colonnaded street with red granite and cipolin columns. The astute observer of quality marble can identify from their different textures and colors that they were produced from specific known quarries from places as far apart as Chemtou in Tunisia and Karystos in Euboea.

During the time of Hadrian large amounts of marble were made available to Leptis for use in construction of columns, capitals and walls. By these indicators the city was being elevated to a much higher position in the empire. Ships from all over the Mediterranean and from other African ports were docking in its spacious harbor. One of the advantages of the location of Leptis was its freshwater springs and its sufficient levels of rainfall, which could fill up large storage systems. Before Hadrian came, there were public baths in Leptis, but the conveyance of the water supply was limited. If the city were to increase in population so as to achieve the Roman lifestyle expected of it, it would need a much larger water supply. This water supply was built during the era of Hadrian with the help of two leading Leptis families:

the Servilli and Candidus families, whose names are preserved on inscriptions in the baths. A water conduit carried water from Cinyps Wadi, some twenty kilometers east of the town, to the city, discharging it into large reservoirs upstream from the city along the Wadi Lebdah, for which the city of Leptis is named. This water supply had many positive effects on the prestige of the city, its aesthetic appearance, and its quality of life.

During this period a new form of construction and décor was developed that is sometimes called the African style (*opus Africanum*). It combined limestone construction with marble facing, often with highly decorative mosaic flooring. The baths at Leptis provide the architectural historian with magnificent examples of significant developments in architectural construction. Even today it is easy to imagine the sequence of plunges through which the bathers would move from the hot rooms (*caldarium*), through promenaded corridors, through the *tepidarium* (warm water), to the *frigidarium* (cold water), and through changing rooms into an open-air swimming pool called the *natatio*. The floor was paved with marble mosaics, the roof was turquoise in color, and there were many statues and niches around the baths. Some forty of these statues still may be seen in the museums either in Leptis or Tripoli.

The beholder today is still moved by the scale and the magnificence of the Roman engineering and architecture of Leptis. Its huge magnitude and poignant beauty is now ruined splendor. In Christian historical memory there remains imprinted a direct correlation between God's judgment of human pride and the Roman emperors' insistence on the pretense of divinity. This would be a fitting reflection even if there had been no persecution of Christians. But it was made more poignant by the bloody African persecutions.

## EXCAVATION

In the period between 1686 and 1708, the French consul to Libya was Claude Le Maire, who had a hunch about the monumental importance of ancient Leptis. When Le Maire first arrived, Leptis was still almost completely buried under a mantle of sand several meters thick, and viewed as ghostly and inhospitable by the local populace. At that time only a few of the large monuments protruded barely above the sand. The French were particularly interested in the cipolin marble and attempted to remove some of the huge columns from the Hadrianic baths, getting them as far as the shore, but they were too heavy to load onto ships. Le Maire was responsible for moving a considerable number of artifacts from Leptis to the Versailles Palace in Paris and the Church of St. Germain des-Prés. Other Leptis artifacts became a part of the collection at Windsor in England.

During the Italian occupation, following the war between Italy and Turkey, major finds were made in Tripolitania. In the period between World Wars I and II, a major Italian excavation was undertaken at Leptis. Five hundred workers cleared tons of sediment and unearthed the remains that stunned the world. Beginning in the 1950s, the Libyan Department of Antiquities worked to develop important museums in Leptis, Sabratha, Tripoli, Benghazi and Cyrene. For readers interested, details of these scientific and archaeological investigations may be reviewed in several series of reports, notably *Libya Antiqua* and *Libyan Studies*.

## THE VANDALS COME WITH SWORDS AND FIRE

The fury of the Arian Vandals reached Leptis in the 450s. Both Catholic and Donatist Christians found themselves under a harsh Gothic political dictatorship viewed as heretical by most Christians. Clergy sought refuge in Sardinia, Sicily or monastic havens in the Mediterranean. The Vandals left a century of demoralization that turned out to be a prelude to the coming Arab armies. Leptis and other coastal cities were not only pillaged by the Vandals but also threatened by marauders from the Austuriani. There was a decline of population in the coastal towns during the Vandal period, except among the stable farming villages.

The Vandals were at last removed in the Byzantine reconquest in 533 under the General Belisarius, but the economy and polis were left depleted. The period that followed was most important for the renovation of Christian churches in Leptis. By the end of the sixth century there were at least four churches in the central area of Leptis that survived until the seventh century Arab invasion.

## OEA (TRIPOLI)

Most visitors to Libya today begin their excursions in the great city of modern Tripoli, capital of Libya, with its current population of over two million in western Tripolitania. Tripoli has a unique memory for Americans, since every schoolchild can sing of "the shores of Tripoli," recalling a crucial moment of American military history—the renowned birthplace of the American Marine Corps, who fought their first battle against Mediterranean piracy on these Libyan ramparts and quays, whose remnants still exist.

Historic map of Tripoli by Piri Reis

Founded as a port city by the Phoenicians, Tripoli has been continuously occupied since 500 B.C., from Punic through Greek, Roman, Vandal, Byzantine and Arab periods. Along with Carthage, Tripoli became a strategic perennial settlement. In time it melded with many other cultural influences, including Berber and Egyptian. The city prospered in Roman antiquity under the name of Oea.

When early Christians arrived in Roman Oea in the first three centuries, it was a lively trading center with one of the best harbors on the Mediterranean. It was the terminal point of a major trans-Saharan caravan route that connected Libya with Chad and Niger. Over this hazardous route came trade and commerce from central Africa to the rest of the known world.

The remnants of Roman Oea are lost under the busy streets of modern Tripoli but appear in ghostly forms in the vicinity of the Aurelian Arch and Museum. Near the arch in the medina is the seventeenth-century Church of Santa Maria degli Angeli Tripoli. Near that church there is a former prison. Many awaited ransom in that place, and not a few were Christians. Ransom of slaves was a business in Tripoli. The jail held seven hundred prisoners, cruel prizes of war and piracy. The church was in another kind of ransom effort: ransoming not only the fallen from their transgression but also the imprisoned from their captivity.

In the sixth century A.D. there was a fortified Byzantine wall around the city, with a governor in charge of the political order. It was designed to protect the city from sea-borne attacks. By medieval times there were reportedly thirty-eight mosques in the old city of Tripoli. It is not implausible to imagine that underneath some of these mosques are the ancient ruins of fifth-century Christian basilicas hidden under the silent pavements.

## EARLY CHRISTIANITY IN TRIPOLITANIA

The earliest church councils looked to African patterns for consultation in conflict. The besieged African churches had many conflicts to resolve. The earliest of these councils in Africa was held in Carthage, convened by Bishop Agrippius. It was composed of seventy bishops from Tripolitania, Numidia and Proconsular Africa. This was the first African Christian Council, and among the very earliest anywhere. It was seeking consensus based on exegesis and consensual historical memory of apostolic teaching. Its sessions were variously dated between A.D. 198 and 222.

The bishops of Libya were present in these councils that would form the pattern for subsequent consensual orthodox decision making in worldwide Christianity. Two Libyan bishops in A.D. 256 attended the seventh council of Carthage: Natalis of Oea and Pompey of Sabratha. (Dioga of Leptis Magna was referenced in the official record as absent.) We find in the conciliar records of bishops between 256 and 643 what appears to be an almost continuous list of successors of Bishop Natalis in Tripolitania. Thus a continual Christian presence in Tripoli can be assumed over the centuries from the time of Decius to the Arab Conquest.

The old city has been built over repeatedly into the great modern city of Tripoli. Like Alexandria, it has been covered over with many layers of construction and reconstruction. This has buried most of the sites pertinent to early Christianity in Oea. These sites were concentrated within the present medina area near the port and seacoast.

The Vandals overcame Tripoli in the fifth century. In 455 Bishop Cresconius was banished by the Vandal ruler Gaiseric, then returned, then was exiled again. During the Justinian period, Tripoli remained a heavily fortified city. By a century later it was militarily unprepared to resist the sweep of Arab armies in 643. Later Tripoli would be temporarily reoccupied by post-Viking Normans from 1146–1158. Tripoli has been best known over centuries as a hub of piracy activities toward the sea and slave trade from the south.

In the heart of the old city of Tripoli there remains the statue of the Roman emperor Marcus Aurelius (121-180), who died in A.D. 192. The citadel was built on the site of a Roman military installation and public bath from the second century A.D. Its defenses were extended in the sixteenth century following the Turkish occupation in 1551. These are the parapets referred to in the Marine Hymn. The castle is now an impressive museum and library housing the office of the Department of Antiquities.

Known as Tripoli Museum Jamahiriya (the National Museum) or Assaraya Alhamra (the Red Castle) Museum, this building displays some of the most significant ancient artifacts and art in North Africa. Many of these are important to the history of early Christianity in Libya. The most crucial finds come from Tarhuna, Leptis Magna and Sabratha. Two special galleries are devoted to artifacts of the Byzantine period. They feature glass mosaics, stone grave covers and tomb inscriptions, many from Tarhuna. It provides glimpses of the artifacts and décor of many Christian basilicas in the fifth and sixth centuries.

One dramatic mosaic portrays coliseum combat, with gladiators in various modes of struggle with different fighting instruments—one with a lance, another with a javelin being thrown toward an animal in the distance, and a fight between a bear and a bull. The blood sport celebrated in this sort of combat cannot but remind believers of the years of African persecution.

Among other large museum pieces from Leptis are the colossal statute of Ceres, God of the Harvest; sculptured figures from the Severan Forum; and the splendid Mosaic of the Four Seasons, which comes from the nearby late Roman Villa Darbukammera at Zliten.

The galleries deal also with Libyan prehistory (ceramics, tools, hand axes and rock art) from eight thousand years ago, and then with the ancient Garamantian empire. Items from the Greek period (fourth century B.C., galleries 7 and 8) include statues of Aphrodite, Persephone, Athena and Minerva with an owl on her arm and her spear and shield in her hands. Gallery 11 displays artifacts from the Severan period when Christianity was growing rapidly in Tripolitania. Students of the history of Christianity in Africa do well to consider the Tripoli Museum Jamahiriya a must-see venue.

## CHRISTIAN PRESENCE IN SABRATHA

The most serene and beautiful paleo-Christian site between Tunisia and Tripoli is Sabratha. It was a Punic trading post prior to the fourth century B.C. It owes its favored location to having a safe natural harbor able to accommodate the low draft of Punic ships. In the second century B.C. it became a Greek colony, and then in the second century A.D. a Roman colony, at a time when Christianity was spreading across North Africa. After the Vandal years it came under Byzantine authority, and finally fell to the Arabs.

As one of the three main cities of Tripolitania—along with Tripoli and Leptis—Sabratha was also a terminal point for caravan trade. Oil, grain and ivory were shipped to all points from Sabratha, as well as appalling trade in human flesh. After earthquakes destroyed parts of Sabratha, the emperor Marcus Aurelius undertook its reconstruction. Its amphitheater seated ten thousand.

The architectural jewel of Sabratha is its theater, one of the largest theaters in early Africa. It has been beautifully reconstructed out of its own original materials. The spectacular original Roman theater had numerous bas-reliefs in the stage proscenium, with floral mosaics and marble décor on a very large stage, with ample room for an audience of one thousand. All this has been brought back to prime condition with much of the original decoration recovered.

It was in Sabratha that the writer Apuleus of Madaura defended himself against unjust accusations of marital fraud in the Roman judicial basilica built in the first century A.D. The large court is surrounded by a portico. This building was originally used for Roman legal and commercial functions, but then its function was changed in the fifth century to a Byzantine Christian basilica with a nave and side aisles.

Christians survived successive transformations from Constantinian to Vandal to Byzantine to Arab rule. The period of maximum Christian presence was the Byzantine (A.D. 533–643). Christians in second-century Rome were meeting in catacombs. Similarly, "in Sabratha, catacombs of primary importance have also been found, dating from the second half of the third century" (*LLC*, 162).

Northwest of the theater are ruins of two Christian basilicas of the fourth through sixth centuries. The spacious scale of these basilicas gives evidence of a once large Christian population. Ruins also remain of a large Christian basilica built near the sea during the time of Justinian in the sixth century. The larger basilica has a baptistery connected with the church; the smaller basilica has a separate baptistery. We know that Sabratha was at one time a bishopric and that its bishops attended church councils. Christian architecture was entering its maturing form that would prevail for centuries to come. These beginnings and developments are found in the ruins of Sabratha, but one must look with a trained eye.

Sabratha was restored after earthquakes in the first and fourth centuries. The period after the Byzantine reconquest of 533 was an especially active time of rebuilding of both fortifications and churches. After building a secure fortress on the west side, Sabratha was an enclosed Byzantine city thought to be protected from attack. But even heavy fortifications did not survive the overwhelming force of the Arab advance.

Those who stroll through the streets of beautiful Sabratha will leave footprints among ruins that contain no less than five centuries of Christian life, governance and liturgical presence. These centuries of Christian presence are seldom mentioned in the guidebooks. Few have noticed them. The distinctively Christian features are easy to bypass and often hardly visible to the untrained eye. It is as though these centuries had fallen into a black hole of historical memory.

## CHRISTIANS IN THE FEZZAN DESERT REGIONS

The Fezzan is a wild region of mountains, predesert oases and desert. From the fifth century B.C. to the Arab conquest, much of it was under the Garamantian Empire. The Garamantes were desert dwellers who had control over the trans-Saharan trade routes between the Sahelian states of west and central Africa and the Mediterranean. As Isabella Sjöström has shown, there were numerous villages in the Fezzan where Christianity took root. This is evidenced by necropolis remains, ruins of churches and baptisteries, and archaeological artifacts with Christian symbols.

The map of Tripolitania and the Fezzan highlights the place names of locations in Tripolitania and the Fezzan. Symbols, ruins and residues have been found from the five centuries of Christian presence in the region. Some of these locations were known to be episcopal residences.

Among the most important of the oasis towns was ancient Cydamus (modern Ghadames). Other towns on the border of the *limes* were Zella, Gholaia, Banat, Tfelfel, Materes, Chawan, Dehibat and Tisavar (*TT*, 31). Some of the sites along the *limes* were Roman, but more often they display locally built defenses, farms, wells, dams and cisterns. Only

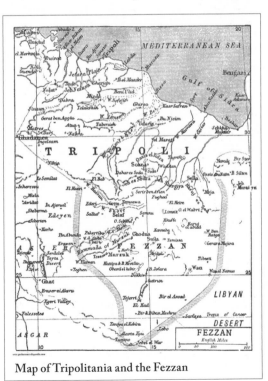

Map of Tripolitania and the Fezzan

a token military presence was there during Byzantine times.

The powerful Third Roman Legion was stationed in the Fezzan to maintain military authority in Tripolitania and throughout the inhabited areas. The legion established clear lines of Roman authority as far out into the desert as the southern borders of Tripolitania (a boundary called *limes Tripolitanus*). Permanent forts and Roman roads were established and defended in Gheria el-Gharbia and Ghadames, far away from the coast. All this pointed more to a self-sufficient, pioneering economy than a centrally based colonial economy. This was favorable to the spread of Christianity into the villages in some locations.

The high quality of olive oil from this region was legendary among the Romans. In 46 B.C. they levied an annual tribute from Tripolitania of one million liters of olive oil. There are still olive presses and amphorae (large jars for transporting grain, oils, food and goods) from this period that can be seen in Tripoli's Jamahiriya Museum. The trading wealth of the Fezzan came from cereals, ivory, metals and olives. The exotic wild animals that were featured in the Roman amphitheaters all over the empire came chiefly from Libya and Proconsular Africa. Leptis was at the north end of an important transdesert trading route from the southern Sahara and the river valleys of central Africa.

We have reviewed the centuries of Christian presence in Cyrenaica and Tripolitania, and marginally in the Fezzan, where more archaeological exploration is to be hoped for. This completes our east to west journey through the evidence of Christian presence in third- to seventh-century Libya. Why are these evidences important today?

# 10

# WHY LIBYA?

∎∎∎

Christianity in North Africa has an older history than its European and American expressions. It has set precedents for later Western Christian communities, such as ecumenical consensus formation. It has spawned enduring ideas and achievements. Christianity in North America has survived a scant five hundred years, since 1492. Some forms of Christianity in Libya are still alive after almost two millennia.

## THE IMPACT OF LIBYAN CHRISTIANITY

Libyan Christianity has played a durable role in the formation of Christian culture all over the continent of Africa. Libyan forms of Christianity have survived since the middle decades of the first century. It may seem as if Libyan Christianity has only barely survived, but a closer look indicates that its bare survival in its earlier venues still have meaning for the whole compass of world Christianity. Libya continues to instruct world Christianity on the art of survival, on the courage to persist and on the virtue of patience. But not just in Africa. Far more important is its impact on the whole of world Christianity. These echoes resound in every century since the apostles through the Cyrenaic influence on apostolic and ecumenical teaching.

Libyan Christianity begins with familiar names: the cross bearer Simon of Cyrene; the mother of Mark, who offered her home to the disciples at Passover; and above all the evangelist Mark, apostle to Egypt and Libya and symbolically to the whole of Africa. From modest beginnings, Libyan Christianity has touched the whole arena of world Christian believers over twenty centuries—from the earliest layers of exegetical, doctrinal, philosophical and cultural development to the present.

## THE PERENNIAL NEGLECT OF LIBYAN CHRISTIANITY IN WESTERN SCHOLARSHIP

The profound ways North African teachers have shaped world Christianity have never been adequately studied, except in the case of Origen, Augustine, Athanasius and a few others. Many have been hardly noticed, either in the northern or southern hemispheres. And if they were from Libya, it seems that that fact itself has made them all the more ignorable.

I have attempted to show that some of the most decisive intellectual achievements of Christianity were explored and understood first in Africa before they were recognized in Europe and the West. My intellectual passion in recent years has focused on this question: How did the African mind shape the Christian mind in the earliest centuries of Christianity? Libya is a case in point. It stands as the most dramatic example of persistent scholarly neglect. In this study I have selected that unique part of early African Christianity least studied by modern scholars. It is only now emerging in accessibility. Young scholars from the continent of Africa will take it much further. This vast and mystifying country has wisdom still to be disseminated.

The challenge that lies ahead for young Africans—both Muslim and Christian—is to rediscover the textual riches of ancient African moral and religious beliefs while preserving the recent values achieved in modern political independence and economic justice. This requires a generation of youthful African Muslim and Christian scholars to reevaluate modern prejudices that demean African intellectual history without inflaming Muslim-Christian points of neuralgia.

The challenge within the contemporary Muslim-Christian interface is not merely hurting each other physically but demeaning each others' genuine wisdom. Christians believe that the wisdom of their faith could benefit the Islamic way of life, while Muslims believe that the wisdom of their faith has been almost completely missed by Christians. These are inadequacies that can be remedied.

## Shared Christian-Muslim Interests

It is to the interest of Christian scholars to have a fair and accurate grasp of African Muslim contributions to world Islam. African writers on Islam from Cairo to Morocco have been among the most influential on the whole of Islam.

It is equally to the interest of Muslim scholars to have a fair and accurate grasp of African Christian contributions to world cultures. My conviction is that this is a *shared interest* between Muslims and Christians. This is the point at which the academic study of early Libyan Christianity begins to have unexpected practical consequences, promising some measure of reconciling growth for both viewpoints.

The picture of Muslims and Christians that is headlined constantly is polarized conflict. But that is not the whole story. There is no law or sacred text either in Christianity or Islam that rules out empathic listening to those who differ. Rather there is a mandate for listening in the moral teachings of both religions.

Orthodox Christians and Muslims have an unexamined shared interest: In both cases *the African layers of world intellectual and religious history have been neglected and debased.* If each could help the other to see how the world has not just suffered from but moreso benefited from both viewpoints, a new beginning might be possible.

The neglected datum: Neither Christianity nor Islam would have its present vitality in the world today without the intellectual riches and spiritual depth that developed in North Africa in what Christians call the first millennium and what Muslims called the formative centuries. The two systems of religion and law have emerged in an intertwining history. They shared the same continent for their primitive intellectual formation. Who can rightly assess current North African cultures without taking into account ancient North African religious teachings of both Christians and Muslims? Both have contributed mightily to world intellectual history, as well as science, literature, art, architecture and culture.

The research leading to this study has helped me see that there are many parallels and similarities between classic Christian and classic Muslim thought and religious practice, despite deep and obvious differences. I am convinced that the recognition of these parallels will serve as a healing balm for chronic points of conflict and pain.

## THE CHOICE TO BE ATTENTIVE

Those in Euro-American scholarship are called to participate in this inquiry, whether others do or not. We had best begin with the awareness that one of the most practiced European intellectual habits of the last five centuries is that of ignoring North African history. That perspective has been a choice, not a destiny. Being a choice, it is reversible.

This modern habit is contrasted with the ancient ecumenical habit of early Christianity. There the models of inquiry from Alexandria, Cyrene and Carthage were of high importance. The modern habit of dismissal would have seemed odd during most of the first thousand years of the common era, when the North African mind was being widely emulated throughout north Mediterranean cultures. It shaped Europe. A healthier inquiry would have been paying attention.

In these pages I have focused on showing that the classic mind of world Christian orthodoxy is significantly shaped by the North African imagination spawned indigenously on North African soil. The thought worlds following the genius of Origen, Augustine, Athanasius and Cyril bear the imprint of philosophical analyses, moral insights, discipline and scriptural interpretations that *bloomed first in Egypt, Libya, Proconsular Africa and Numidia before they were consensually grasped elsewhere*. The seeds then spread quietly from Africa to the north. This sweeping movement, so obvious to fourth-century believers, has remained largely unnoticed by subsequent Eurocentric and occidental historians.

I invite young Muslim historians to be attentive to *how Africa reshaped the Muslim mind*. The great intellectual centers of early African Islam—from Cairo to Kairouan to Rabat—have left a permanent stamp on the Muslim mind. Not everything now viewed as traditionally Islamic came from Arabia or Mesopotamia. The mutual study of classic African Islamic texts by Christians, and of early African Christian texts by Muslims, provides a foothold for an enriched conversation of both histories.

Under this frame of reference, classic Islam would seek to resist Western hedonism without confusing it with classic Christianity. Christians would find ways of beholding modern Islamic thought patterns without ignoring the irenic qualities of early North African commentaries on the Qur'an. The joint study of our different histories together promises to help us do both tasks without self-defeating consequences and without loss of intellectual integrity. The beginning point for this intellectual enterprise must be the history the exegesis of sacred texts in Africa, both Christian and Islamic.

The most promising scholarly arena for exploring the history of the interface between Muslims and Christians is in the African models of the history of exegesis of sacred texts. The study of early Christian exegesis is the textual and thought world in which I have spent my efforts in the last quarter century. It is a world full of delight, but it need not be limited by the recent fences that have been built between the two communities of faith. The study of methods of exegesis does not require doctrinal commitments. Rather it is the less controversial and more dispassionate arena of examining how authors of different traditions approach their sacred texts, and where are the analogies, diversities and complementary interests.

Although this comparative exegetical work is already underway embrionically among both Muslim and Christian scholars, it has been resisted by defensive voices in both blocs and has largely been conducted separately. This is not the occasion for a full review of this literature, but those who wish to find their way into the basic issues would do well not to miss at least some of these studies. Herbert Berg's *The Development of Exegesis in Early Islam: The Authenticity of Muslim Literature from the Formative Period* shows that there are differing theories about how Islam began, how its legal systems developed, and how they have been manifested within the modern period.[1]

---

[1]Herbert Berg, *The Development of Exegesis in Early Islam: The Authenticity of Muslim Literature from the Formative Period* (London: Curzon, 2000); see also his edited volume *Method and Theory in the Study of Islamic Origins* (Leiden: Brill, 2003).

The earliest Muslim exegetes are analyzed fairly and compared with Jewish and Christian exegetes in a book called *With Reverence for the Word*.[2] In her "Introduction to Medieval Interpretation of the Qur'an," Jane McAuliffe argues that

> commentary on the Qur'an, as both activity and achievement, has proven to be a remarkably stable enterprise over the long centuries of its production. In an academic world where intellectual fads rise and fall with ever-increasing frequency, the stability of this tradition runs counter to expectations that reward novelty and innovation. Yet stability does not mean a lack of vitality. (311)

It remains debatable as to whether the earliest African commentators on the Qur'an are even able to be compared with rabbinic and patristic exegesis. Let that inquiry begin in earnest.

All students in academic programs in Islamic studies engage in the study of Qur'anic exegesis. Some inquire into the intense disciplines of recitation and memorization. They study the Qur'an's specific language, analogies, narratives and legal implications. There are many unexplored analogies yet to be revealed between Jewish yeshivas and Christian seminaries, and advanced Muslim Qur'anic studies. Far too little has been written about the parallels and differences between them. The focus on Africa as the context of key exegetical developments may offer new perceptions for these discussions.

The defining phase of Christian exegesis in Africa is the third century. The defining phase of Islamic exegesis in Africa is arguably the thirteenth century. A conference on the comparison of Origen's exegesis to that of Malik of Kairouan would be an evident starting place.

## THE DEFINING AFRICAN PHASE OF CHRISTIAN AND ISLAMIC HISTORY

This is an unprecedented period of religious growth on the continent of Africa. The continuing exponential growth rate of Christianity on the

---

[2]Jane Dammen McAuliffe, Barry D. Walfish and Joseph W. Goering, eds., *With Reverence for the Word: Medieval Scriptural Exegesis in Judaism, Christianity, and Islam* (Oxford: Oxford University Press, 2003). See my *Agenda for Theology* (San Francisco: Harper & Row, 1979) for an argument anticipating this point in relation to patristic Christian exegesis.

continent of Africa is startling. Growth rates among Muslims have been equally amazing. This datum makes all the more urgent the understanding of the historical roots of both in Africa. Approaching these roots as comparative exegesis is better in the present climate than as comparative doctrines or revelations.

The population of Christians in Africa is steadily climbing toward the half billion mark. They will live out their lives on the same continent, we hope in peaceful and empathic dialogue, with more than a third of a billion Muslims. These African believers will constitute a significant proportion of global Christian believers in the generations to come. It is a demographic fact that the Christian communities are growing faster in Africa than in any other continent of world Christianity. It is toward this future that a deeper recognition is dawning.

The world Christian population is predominantly located in the southern hemisphere. This has been amply demonstrated by the careful demographic and sociological writings of David Barrett, Rodney Stark and Philip Jenkins. Europeans and North Americans are gradually getting the point: the future of faith lies far more to the southern parts of the globe than to the north. North American issues quickly begin to feel quite trivial when compared to the vast and decisive struggles going on in Africa.

Until recently, these growing numbers of Christians worldwide in the global South have had insufficient access to their own history. Further complicating is the fact that many young African scholars have studied in the universities of the North and West, dominated by Western values that began in Africa but are no longer recognized as such. They have learned much of their history from modern Euro-American secular elitists who have little or no interest in the distinguished intellectual tradition of early African patristic texts. The case is similar with Islamic intellectual history, which despite its intent has sometimes become captive to Euro-American secular elitists.

The remedy for the lack of historical awareness is improved historical research and textual analysis. Slipshod history or the ideological exaggerations of historical evidence intensify the problem.

## Retelling the Story of Exemplary Lives

The stories of the saints and great minds of early African Christianity are not being told and taught to the children of Christian families. This rediscovery has hardly begun among African Christian leaders, much less laity. It is a gentle and compassionate task for parents, educators and pastors.

The same process of reexamining the narratives of Muslim holy men and women awaits discovery. This is less a competition between Muslims and Christians than an exercise in reciprocal listening and learning. In both traditions it is a duty of teachers and parents to transmit their heritage and memory of God accurately and graciously to the next generation. It can be done on both sides without demeaning, much less killing each other. We see it gradually maturing as an educational agenda in Egypt, Ethiopia, Ghana, Nigeria, Kenya, Tunisia and parts of French West Africa.

The story of early Christianity in Africa deserves to be told in a simple and straightforward way. A global audience will be listening in. But it must ultimately reach the heart of the African child. From there it will blossom.

Early African Christian texts tell of narratives and stories of heroic proportions. They are filled with courageous characters and surprise endings. Here we are not talking about myths or paranormal events, but a real history. This history has been conveyed over a thousand years of indigenous African experience. These are the actual narratives of ordinary persons of faith and African believers facing tangible choices. Often they have called for life or death decisions. In a crucial middle African belt from northern Nigeria to Sudan, believers still are faced with life and death choices based on their faith.

The first thousand years of African Christianity occurred during times of political oppression, slavery, war, tyranny, hunger, social dislocation, displaced persons, forced migrations and economic hardships. Every one of these are issues we still face today in world Christianity. Similar narratives of exemplary lives abound in the early centuries of Islam.

It is timely today for African mothers and daughters, fathers and sons to relearn their own moving story. The opportune moment has come.

## THE LIBYAN STORY

The chronicle of early Libyan Christianity is not a story for a Christian audience only but also for Muslims, especially those who have an African heritage. Just as Spain has a rich history of Islam, Libya has a rich history of Christianity. In both cases the history has centuries of experience to offer to a broken and conflicted world. Libyans will benefit by more clearly realizing this fact: the soil on which they walk daily has embedded in it five hundred years of Christian roots and residues. This does not imply any claim to any form of territorial or political legitimacy. It only asks for the accurate recollection of a story long forgotten. Nor is it a story whose audience primarily resides in schools and churches and mosques. It is for all who seek the truth that is revealed through the honest study of history.

All three of the monotheistic faiths—Judaism, Christianity and Islam—hark back to Abraham. All three impinge on Libyan history. All three agree on one crucial premise: The majesty of God is revealed in history. The providence of God is being worked out in actual personal histories. This history can be examined by skeptics and secularists, as well as those already convinced. Whether recognized or not, the truth of God's presence is being revealed before our eyes daily through human history, according to Jews and Christians, with some analogies in Islam. This is a beginning point in the comparative exegesis of sacred texts of all three traditions.

The Christian narrative will be informative to open-minded Muslims willing to listen to the ancient African background and ancestry of their own classic Muslim intellectual history. The Muslim phase of the African story emerges in the last half of the common era's first millennium. The Muslim narrative will be illuminating to open-minded Christians without denying their faith. Christians will learn about how much of the spirit of Western intellectual achievement began in Africa, and in no small part in Libya. In doing so, they will learn of the ways in which Christians of Spain and Europe have been beneficiaries of Muslim philosophical, moral and scientific wisdom. Whether Christian or Muslim or secular or tradition-oriented, African youth have not had the opportunity to hear their own full story told. The texts and ideas and movements that Africa spawned before Europe discovered them must be more fully translated, disseminated and studied before this will happen.

Many Christians around the globe are intrigued by modern Africa. But most have not begun to ponder it in the light of its own stirring religious history. Similarly there are Muslim believers today who have a lively interest in contemporary Africa, yet many of them, especially those in modern Euro-American universities, have not had sufficient opportunity to glimpse the centuries that preceded modernity.

## WHY DID LIBYAN CHRISTIANITY ALMOST DISAPPEAR?

At a dinner at the British Embassy in Tripoli, a high-ranking and well-informed Muslim diplomat asked me: Why didn't the Christian efforts endure in Libya in the same way that they persisted among the Copts of Egypt? I was sitting at same table with the Anglican Primate of North Africa and the British Ambassador and several Orthodox and Catholic bishops, along with several distinguished Muslim scholars. I answered quickly with five reasons, off the top of my head:

First, the myth of disappearance. Christianity has never been completely absent since it arrived in Libya. The evidence was at hand at that table. Christian believers still inhabit a modest but real place in Libyan life. The vital survival today of Libyan Christianity through the many centuries of Islamic authority is evidenced by the continuing presence of Christians in Libya. Most of these are Orthodox or Catholic, but some are Anglicans or Protestants, along with growing numbers of evangelicals, charismatics and Pentecostals. But under contemporary conditions they must remain largely silent, lest their precarious status be shaken or further risked. If they proclaimed their faith publicly apart from certain allotted and approved spaces, they would be endangered.

Second, a history of weak indigenization. Christianity was never adequately indigenized and locally enculturated in Libya. But it was in the Nile Valley. Profoundly so. Why did Nile indigenization persist when Libyan did not? It was partly a matter of scale and the proportion of believers, but more so a matter of genuine holiness along with a combination of intrepid courage and conviction. Small numbers are easier to overwhelm. Convictions are unconquerable. The Copts of Egypt held steadfast even after they had been heavily taxed, deprived of civil posts and repeatedly marginalized. Libyan Christianity was more fragmented and less united.

Third, a divided Christianity. At that crucial century of the Arab conquest, Libyan Christianity was deeply divided by the internal conflict between Byzantine and Latin Christian forms of Christian practice, and by the conflict between Donatists and Catholics. There were often two or more bishops in a single Libyan city. The churches were also sharply divided between Chalcedonian and non-Chalcedonian views.

Fourth, facing the military fact of total conquest. This was largely a military reason: the fast-moving armed military victory was absolute. The Arab swordsmen were unusually thorough in conquest. The Byzantine armies and navies were at a point of historic weakness during the decade of the 640s. Constantinople had been repeatedly under threat. The once powerful but now weakened Byzantine navy was insolvent. It was incapable of providing the Libyan coast even with minimal protection against a small but determined Arab land-based onslaught. The Arab military forces were overwhelming in relationship to those of a divided Byzantine culture that had exhausted its economic resources, its military vitality and its capacity for self-defense. Libyan Christians had already suffered for two centuries under the coercive rule of the Vandal invasion, followed by Byzantine reconquest.

Fifth, all this yielded limited choices. The resulting choices given to Christians in the early years of the Arab conquest were very hard to make. For many it meant either conversion to Islam or flight to safety if they had the means. If they were determined to remain, they would remain under conditions of high taxes, second-class citizenship, dhimmi status and often under threat of life and limb. Believing Christians who remained in Libya faced severe limitations from governing authorities. These conditions were destined to become more severe as the decades wore on. The result was the gross depopulation of Christian Libya and the mass movement of the leadership of Christianity to safe havens to the north. It is easy for modern observers to criticize the leadership at that time. But few of these observers have grasped the enormity of the dilemma. The clerical leadership was expelled, killed, imprisoned or sent to the copper mines. The survivors landed in Sardinia, Sicily and Malta. They went to the coast of France to places like Lérins, or to the Vivarium, in the arch of the lower boot of Italy, where Cassiodorus had founded his international monastic community. Some went to Spain, where they again would soon be overtaken by the Moors.

At this point one of the bishops present at the table poignantly reminded me that the faithful bishop does not leave his diocese, though he may seek temporary refuge in order to continue to serve the church awaiting improved conditions, as did Cyprian and Athanasius. He is married for life to his diocese.

In my view these five points were among the compelling reasons the Coptic Orthodox and Catholic Christians of Libya found it increasingly less feasible to continue on the African continent, though they did persist in Italy, Sicily, Sardinia and France. The Egyptian Church through heroic persistence was able to continue by divine providence to this day.

## IN DEFENSE OF PRESERVING COMMUNITIES OF FAITH

After a century of Arab rule there were only a few Christians left in Libya. A few remained in remote monastic communities. They were valiant confessors whose lives were constantly in danger. Some were able to flee, never to return despite the five centuries of Christian presence before Islam. These displaced Christians of Africa had gone away from Africa to the north. There they began making their remarkable contributions to the formation of pre-Charlemagne Europe. They continued to be energized and inspired by the intense memory of African Christian wisdom and suffering. They had been martyred by the Romans, harassed by the Vandals and totally defeated by the Arab military victory in the 640s A.D. They brought this hard-won wisdom with them to the islands of the Mediterranean, where it continued to grow and produce the cherished fruits of endurance. The churches of Libya and the Nile Valley survived in the faithful flocks and monasteries of Europe and Ireland. The days of African Christianity were not over, but only being replanted. After ten centuries some of the intrepid descendents of these believers would return to Africa.

The transition of Christian leadership from Africa to the northern shores of the Mediterranean after the Arab conquest was not simply a loss of faith. It was a temporary harbor of faith to a place more congenial to its preservation and serenity, and further extension. It was in these communities that profound reflections on providence in universal history, temptation in individual life, and endurance amid conflict would be reborn.

If they had stayed in Libya they would have faced high taxation and dhimmitude at best, and at worst imprisonment and torture or slave labor camps or death. They cannot be condemned for fleeing to the safety of Christian havens in Sicily and Malta. After the Islamic conquest the immediate need for Diaspora Christians was evident: to redeem from imprisonment those who were working in the salt and iron mines of Africa and the Middle East. There were many recorded instances of attempts to buy these slaves back from ransom. Many in early Christianity had been slaves before they became Christians. New forms of involuntary servitude followed hard upon the heels of war and conquest.

## THE WANING DAYS OF LIBYAN CHRISTIANITY

The churches of Libya were divided by heresies and differences, such as fourth-century Donatism, and the fifth-century struggle between Chalcedonians and non-Chalcedonians, as well as ravages of Vandal Arianism. These schisms were strongly shaped by nationalisms and ethnocentrisms inimical to the international vision of classic ecumenical Christianity. Despite these schisms there remained many dioceses continuing until the end of the millennium. Most in Libya were utterly erased.

Continuing correspondence between Christian bishops of the Maghreb and Rome persisted fragmentarily into the ninth century. This indicated that Christianity had not died out entirely. As late as the tenth century there were forty episcopal residences listed in North Africa west of Egypt. Significantly, a Christian church in the great Muslim academic center of Kairouan in Byzacena would continue until at least 1046.

By the end of the millennium, Christians were compelled by law to use Arabic to communicate in all ways except in their own liturgy. In a letter from the pope of Rome dated December 17, 1053, we hear that there are only five bishops left in all the Maghreb. They were instructed to recognize Thomas, archbishop of Carthage, as their metropolitan. By A.D. 1073, Cyriacus was named the archbishop of Carthage, but with only two active dioceses left. By 1076 he was alone, and another bishop, Servandus of Tunis, had to travel to Rome to be consecrated. With the capture by Abd al-Mu'min of the beleaguered Christian remnant in the holdout center in Tunis in 1159, the earlier vital Christianity of the Maghreb was depleted. The Normans were driven out from what is now Tunisia. Regrettably, there were no great figures remaining in Libya—nothing to compare to the mind of St. John of Damascus, who served Palestinian and Syrian Christianity by arguing the Orthodox cause with an experienced understanding of early Islam, its culture and its language.

Even after A.D. 1000 isolated survivals are reported in the Maghreb, such as a Christian community in inland Qal'a, Algeria, in 1114. As late as the mid-twelfth century an Africanized Latin was still being spoken in Gafsa near the Libya-Tunisia border. In 1194 a church and community dedicated to the Mother of God is recorded in Nefta, in the south of Tunisia (LCM, 338-39). In about 1400, after seven hundred years of faithfulness, the lamp of Christian orthodoxy in the Maghreb was virtually extinguished, smoldering with only vestiges in folklore and cultural and linguistic remnants.

## SOUTH OF LIBYA

Sub-Saharan African believers are now learning more about what happened with Christians many centuries ago on the African continent in remote places like Libya, the Maghreb, Egypt and the Sudan. Southern Africans are beginning travel to the north of their own continent to grow businesses and to learn more about their own early African Christian roots.

If they go to Europe to discover those roots, they will find their own African story filtered through the adaptations of European Christianity. They will find later-planted roots that derived from Africa through an ecumenical consensus that was significantly formed by African councils many centuries earlier.

Of liturgy and architecture in ancient Christian Ethiopia we know quite a bit, but far less of Somalia and the Sudan. There are first-millennium ancient Christian archaeological sites in Upper Nile locations not far north of Uganda and the Congo. From Dongala to Meroe in the southernmost Nile, the Christian voices were heard. Christianity flourished in the Sudan in the decade before Islam. In the Merovian kingdom of the Sudan, Christians resisted Islam vigorously. These sites are finally being excavated and recovered. They bring sub-Saharan Africa in closer touch with the Christians of the north of the continent.

Those who elect to not take note of the African sources of early Judaism, Christianity and Islam may miss major pieces of the puzzle in the understanding of the long course of African cultural history. False stereotypes of Orthodox Copts, portraying them as superstitious and rigid, are being corrected by believers from the north who now have business and economic interests in the south, and southerners who pursue commerce in the north. Some evangelicals and Pentecostals who have portrayed Copts as lacking in emotive depth and experiential religion are changing their perceptions as personal knowledge increases.

North Africans of the Nile and Maghreb have much to benefit from better empathic understanding of the southern part of Africa. When Coptic Christians get acquainted with Pentecostals of central and southern Africa they come to recognize that they have a similar love for the work of the Holy Spirit. Protestants who do not think much of a linear view of apostolic succession may come to affirm the Spirit-led continuity and unity of the apostolic teaching held by the Orthodox. As Baptist Independents of the south of Africa get better acquainted with ancient Libyan church architecture, they quickly see that the building of baptisteries all over fifth-century North Africa hinged on their strong commitment to believers' baptism.

When I speak of early African Christianity, I am referring as a scholar

to the vast library of written texts that report the life of Christians in the
first millennium on the continent of Africa. These were harvests gar-
nered from thousands of communities of indigenous believers residing
for centuries in the areas now known as Egypt, Sudan, Ethiopia, Eri-
trea, Libya, Tunisia, Algeria and Morocco, and far south into the upper
Niger and Nile River valleys. The scope is far more southerly into the
continent than has often been assumed, possibly extending in the first
millennium to the reaches of the Nile in Kenya and Uganda.

We now know better than before that early African Christians spoke
many indigenous African languages—not just Greek and Latin. Since
the third century African Christians were increasingly speaking Am-
haric, Bohairic, Ge'ez, Meroitic, Nilo-Saharan, Luo, Dinka and Arabic.

Before air flight, the physical geography of the Sahara stood as a formidable, even impenetrable, obstacle to travel to the south. The fact that
African Christianity found its way first to the north of the Sahara in the
first millennium, but not to the south is not due to neglect but to impass-
able geography. Hazardous sea travel might have made it past Somalia to
the Kenyan coast. If the Christian witness went further, there are little or
no evidences of it before the sixteenth century. This gradual unfolding is
hardly cause for a harsh value judgment. In due time both north and
south will bless each other by crossfertilization out of an enduring heritage of centuries of religious wisdom long indigenized in Africa.

## MULTICULTURAL AFRICANEITY

African Christianity has arisen out of distinctly African experiences on
African terrain. Most of the cultures to which it came were already
intensely multicultural and ethnically diverse.

The vast majority of those who were the earliest to suffer and die as
witnesses to Christian truth were born as indigenous Africans from
families who had never lived on any other continent. One has to search
hard to find exceptions. Virtually all the martyrs of Africa had been
born and bred for generations on the continent of Africa. They lived
and struggled their whole lives in quintessential African settings.[3] They

---

[3]Marcel Bénabou, *La résistance africaine á la romanisation* (Paris: F. Maspero, 1975).

were nurtured within untold generations of home-grown African cultures. These believers were not imports from outside the continent of Africa. They have felt the heat of African deserts and known the dangers of African rivers.

When Christian scriptural interpretation, doctrinal formation, church law, ethics and polity were at their earliest postapostolic formative stage, Leptis and Cyrene were among the leading cities of the ancient world. At their zenith these Christian communities would be as thoroughly multicultural as anywhere in the world and as multilingual as anywhere in Africa.

While Christianity was growing to its earliest maturity, the greatest city on the Nile was Alexandria. "Most of us take it for granted that two cities, Athens and Rome, completely dominated the classical world," write Justin Pollard and Howard Reid in *The Rise and Fall of Alexandria: Birthplace of the Modern World*. "In fact, there was a third city that, at its height, dwarfed both of these in wealth and population as well as in scientific and artistic achievement."[4] Alexandria was equal in size to any city of its time, and of equal importance in the world of ideas, literature and learning.

This city was thriving not on European ideas and genius, but offering new ideas to Europe. It had a large population of native Egyptians. Its social reality was indigenously African and had been for three centuries. Its economic strength was the fruitful valley of the five-thousand-mile-long Nile River flowing from the heart of Uganda.

The numbers of early Christians living in the Nile delta, speaking Nilotic languages in African cadences, were far larger than those on the Danube or Volga or Thames or Seine. African Christianity arose in Libya and Egypt about the same time as it appeared in Carthage and Numidia. So it should not be surprising that the first Christian apostle to both Libya and Egypt (St. Mark) would come to symbolize apostolic teaching to all Christians all over the known African continent of the first millennium.

In early Christianity there were three predominant apostolic pa-

---

[4]Justin Pollard and Howard Reid, *The Rise and Fall of Alexandria: Birthplace of the Modern World* (New York: Viking, 2006), p. xv.

triarchates in the third century: all Asia's Antioch, all Europe's
Rome, and all Africa's Alexandria. These three eminent ecumenical
leaders were in regular correspondence and consultation. On most
occasions they agreed. The grassroots lay consensus they articulated
helped form classical ecumenical teaching. When they spoke together, their voices expressed the united voice of Christian believers
in the known world. Believers in Leptis, Damascus and Milan all
celebrated essentially the same apostolic doctrine of the world, as attested by Irenaeus.

The lighthouses of Apollonia and Leptis received ships from as far
as both India and Britain. They welcomed traders into the world's most
advanced seaports and trading centers. This greatest city of Africa was
to Africa what Antioch was to all of Asia—the known world stretching
east from the Mediterranean. It symbolized to Africa what Rome was
to the whole known world stretching north and west from the Mediterranean—Europe. In cities like Cyrene and Alexandria the resources
of Africa encountered all the known world's cultures, economies and
ideologies.

Only after Charlemagne in 800 would Europe emerge as a relatively
cohesive literary and political culture. Until then, an embryonic Europe
often sat at the feet of African minds to learn to think philosophically,
explore scientifically and, for Christians, interpret Scripture and settle
controverted questions of Christian teaching.

## THE APOSTOLIC DIMENSION OF THE ECUMENICAL
## CHARACTER OF CHRISTIANITY IN AFRICA

Early African Christianity is no less ecumenical by having grown up on
a particular continent. Today there are many other African cities that
have stepped up alongside the classic leadership position of Alexandria
and Cyrene and Carthage as emblematic of Africa—among them are
Nairobi, Cairo, Accra, Addis Ababa, Johannesburg and others.

For early Western or Latin Christianity, Carthage was the key African city. For Eastern Orthodox Christianity, Alexandria was the pre-
eminent African city. For early Christianity in Libya, Cyrene was the
key city in the Pentapolis. But even in Carthage, there was respectful

deference given to Cyrene and Alexandria, partly due to their apostolic origins in Mark. Carthage had no Mark.

The African tradition recalled that Mark was born in Cyrene and brought his Gospel to the whole of Africa through the greatest cosmopolitan populations of the first-century world: the African cities of Cyrene and Alexandria. This apostolic identity gave strength and authority to the unity of believers in all the varied early African paleo-Christian cultures. Carthage lacked a known figure from eyewitness New Testament times. This lack was supplied by Mark. The apostolic teaching of Mark in Africa was respected wherever African Christians dwelt.

In this way the whole of the vast continent of Africa became symbolized within the *oikoumenē* by the greatest cities in Africa and unified under Mark: Cyrene is the city where the earliest awakenings of Gentile Christianity likely arose. Alexandria is the city where the sacred Scriptures of the Hebrew Bible were first translated into Greek and understood typologically in the light of the history of Jesus. The cohesion of African Christianity is symbolized in the apostolic leadership of Mark in Libya and Alexandria.

## ASPECTS OF RECOVERY

In ancient pilgrimage sites of North African, Christianity honored the saints and martyrs that would be later celebrated in Europe. They had names like George and Barbara and Felicity. Many common names point to African-born saints, such as Eugene (Carthage/Tunisia), Victor of Africa, Anthony (Egypt), Augustine (Algeria), Catherine (Egypt), Dorothy (Egypt) and Theodore of Cyrene.

African Christianity produced holy men and women now silently honored by families the world over by the ways they name their children. Their holy lives are the reason why their names are still remembered. These include the righteous mother St. Monica of Numidia, her son St. Augustine bishop of Hippo, the martyr St. Julia of Carthage (fifth century), St. George, who having slayed the dragon died in Selena in Libya, and many other African saints. Other Libyan saints and martyrs appear in the ancient synaxaries of various traditions: the deacon James, Nemesianus and Maximillian, Crispin and Marcian, and innumerable others. Many flourished in North Africa in the third century. By the time of Cyprian's death in 258 there already may have been about seven hundred martyrs.

Many Christians are named after African saints but do not know it. If your name is Mark, George or Ted, your spiritual ancestor may have roots in Libya. There are many remains in the villages of North Africa of oratories dedicated to remembering the martyrdom and hence heavenly birthdays of these saints. These sites will someday be made more recognizable to believers all over the world. New travelers will be coming to places like Libya, as well as Algeria, Tunisia, Sudan and Ethiopia—to parts of Africa that have not been thought of as places where classical Christianity dwelt over many centuries!

Scratch the surface of Libya and you will find the patina of ruins of unheralded sites recalling African martyrs and saints. They are found in catacombs, oratories, cemeteries, churches and mosaics that date to the third, fourth and fifth centuries. Many sites of former Christian monasteries, bishoprics and cathedral churches are not yet properly identified by mapmakers. These faceless and signless sites await further excavation.

This is the part of the world where pilgrimages to honor martyrs began. Cyrene and Leptis may once again become abiding pilgrimage cities in Libya, not only for Christians but for all who are interested in the roots of human culture. Now they are not pilgrimage sites at all. There is a systematic abstention from saying anything at all about their religious importance. The presumption is that visitors come only to see Punic, Greco-Roman or Islamic ruins, not Christian. But at some future time believers will better understand their stories.

The difficulty: Many of these ancient church and monastic locations in the escarpments and oases of inland Libya remain hard even to find or identify, and some are virtually unknown even to highly experienced historians, archaeologists, cartographers and aficionados. The archaeological imagination is aroused by the sheer number and potential importance of unexcavated sites. Libya is rich in both. I hope a time will come when the definitive studies will be made not by Europeans or Westerners but by young African scholars on their own continent.

Those interested in reading more in African history of the first millennium will have to await these developments. Until then, well-meaning visitors will be unprepared to even see, much less interpret, the very historic treasure they are standing on. Belatedly, pilgrims in a dry place will bring an empty cup to a full spring.

## RESTRICTED TRAVEL IN LIBYA

Some believers, upon learning of the depth and influence of early African Christianity on world Christianity, may feel called to undertake service missions or educational efforts or offer medical services in these locations. They will find the task daunting. Learning Arabic and understanding Islamic law and culture are among the most basic assignments. If they appear in North Africa unsent and uncalled, they will soon find themselves lost, or worse, arrested. They do better first to explore solid academic programs in crosscultural studies, linguistics and missiology. Even then their chief path to gaining a hearing will be largely through commerce, education or health delivery.

Already there are Christian businessmen and women from sub-Saharan Africa who are founding international business operations and entrepreneurial enterprises that have reason to locate North African branches as viable businesses, but not primarily as having any religious identification. Those who do not grasp these realities will suffer premature disappointment. To gain admission to Libya the businessman must first show how an enterprise will actually be helpful to Libya. Economic and business interests in the southern two thirds of Africa are already beginning to awaken to common interests with cooperative enterprises in Egypt, Ethiopia, Tunisia and Morocco. Libya is already crossing this threshold of recognition. Muslim and Christian laity may be the most viable peacemakers in an era of belligerence. This commerce may provide a fit platform for respectful interaction between Muslims and Christians that could benefit both equally and increase the understanding required for durable peace.

It is understandable that archaeological projects that rightly require government approval and surveillance would tend to emphasize those monuments that reflect their own values and history. To take their rightful place among these efforts Christian need to remind the authorities that Christianity was for five centuries a vital part of Libyan history. No one will learn this history by examining only English sources. Many important sources still remain untranslated into French or English.

## BURIED BASILICAS, BURIED TEXTS

The preoccupation of Libyan archaeology on pre- and post-Christian monuments has diverted attention from the noteworthy Christian archaeological sites in the Pentapolis and Tripolitania. Many are in heedless disarray, still hard to find, unheralded, with limited logistical support or food or public services for convenience or even accessibility. They are not yet ready for the shiploads of voyagers who someday will be coming to Libya to admire its archaeological treasures.

The weeds growing around important Christian archaeological sites may be compared to untranslated manuscripts on the shelves of dusty archives. The manuscripts are scattered all around the world. These are texts that sub-Saharan Africans will some day be treasuring, but to which they now have minimal access. An international archive of African texts is desperately needed. It should be located in Africa.

Both stone and papyri have been buried, one by sand and the other by selective scholarship. They will someday be recovered, not just by scholars of the north of Africa but also by sub-Saharans. They belong to the whole of Africa and of the whole world. While the scholars will be pouring over the ancient texts, the laity will be visiting the ancient sites.

Scholars currently educated in leading Western universities may miss most of this action. They have learned their lessons all too narrowly. The evidence has already been totally discounted as mere hagiography. It is a dysfunctional form of historical study to assume that something is not really history because its subject is merely people who were willing to give their lives for their witness to the truth.

## AFRICAN TEXTS AND AFRICAN SELF-ESTEEM

In the Maghreb, African traditional religions were commonly conveyed by *both* oral and written means. But the written records and epigraphy, papyrus, and stone artifacts that have survived are vast. Regrettably those bearing Christian histories are neglected. This neglect has weighty bearing on vexing issues in modern African self-esteem. They bear on a reasonable assessment of the Africaneity of early Christian identity. They impinge indirectly on Muslim-Christian relations. The mending of the distance and alienation between the north of Africa and sub-Saharan Africa to some extent hinges on the recovery of these histories.

The study of the genre of "African traditional religions" has at times been defined so narrowly as to rule out the great written traditions of the continent of Africa. It is as if these indigenous African documents were not quite as "truly African" as the oral traditions. The distressing result is the false impression that African traditional religion largely lacks written texts. However mistaken, that premise has nonetheless been taken by some for fact.

Is Islam to be considered more profoundly an "African traditional religion" than the Christianity that preceded it in Africa? This can only occur among those who have somehow managed to blot out the memory of the distinguished pre-Arabic history of African Christianity. Let them see and touch the stones of the Christian basilicas in Leptis and Cyrene. Let them be exposed to the literary evidences stretching all the way from Numidia to Marmarica from the second through the seventh centuries. A broader perspective on African history requires a more fitting definition of African traditional religion that includes written texts. Anthropologists have not yet adequately assessed the artifacts of Christian history of the fourth to eighth centuries, nor of Islamic history after the seventh century, especially regarding the texts of the early African Islamic contributions to the history of exegesis.

It is a category mistake to exclude from "traditional African religion" the centuries of sacred texts produced in Africa by the three Abrahamic families. It is ostrichlike and self-defeating to cast them out of early African culture. All three have long histories of many centuries, even millennia, on the continent of Africa. The oral traditions of Africa are in no way diminished or undermined just because they have existed for centuries alongside the Septuagint of the third century B.C., the New Testament of the first century A.D. and the African commentaries on the Qur'an of the seventh century and following. The result is a needless feeling of vulnerability that characterizes much of the rhetorical defense of African traditional religious consciousness. This double bind squeezes tighter when the case for African traditional religion is juxtaposed to Western modernity with its intimidating technologies and pride.

When the value of the oral traditions of Africa are exalted so as to ignore the value of the written traditions of Africa, the crucial ground has been given up before the game begins. Delicate questions of identity must be dealt with. In any double bind, either way you move tightens the knot. This bind is doubled twice when the highly esteemed value of the southern African oral traditions appears to be diminished when placed side by side with the sacred written texts of the north of Africa. This may elicit an unnecessary adverse reaction: sometimes the written Pharaonic hieroglyphic and Jewish and Christian and Muslim sacred texts and their histories of interpretation are then oddly ruled out of the definition of authentic Africaneity and traditional African religion. However well intended, this puts African traditional religion in a more disadvantaged position than it needs to be.[5]

The heart of the double bind is this: Oral traditions are neglected because they do not have a written African history and centuries of texts of commentary. Meanwhile the early written traditions are neglected because they appear not to have a modern history of authentic Africaneity. Breaking out of the double bind is a task for young Africans who practice a more accurate and holistic form of historical inquiry.[6]

The cure is plain: This defensiveness can be overcome by more accurately conceiving African traditional religion to include some of its most stable and durable components: the sacred texts of the religions of the Abrahamitic covenant—Hebraic, Christian and Muslim.

---

[5]Roger Bastide, "L'expression de la prière chez les peuples sans écriture," *La Maison-Dieu* 109 (1972): 98-112.
[6]O. Bimwenyi, "Le Dieu de nos ancêtres," *Cahiers des religions africaines* 4 (1970): 137-51.

## WHETHER CHRISTIANITY WAS INDIGENOUS
## OR IMPORTED

Scholars of African culture narrowly trained in the most dubious of Western academic habits have regrettably acquired from the West a persistent habit of self-demeaning ego negation. They assume that Christianity began in Africa only a couple of centuries ago, an untrue stereotype. The myth is that Christianity was imported to an immature Africa from a mature Europe. The evidence is to the contrary: Europe (and later America) learned from Africa much of their earliest layers of religious wisdom. The myth is that African biblical teaching is only two centuries deep, not two millennia. That modern mythology is demeaning to the earliest African Christians and to modern Africans. The myth is most laughable in the Maghreb of North Africa.

So when avant-garde African scholars capitulate too quickly to what they perceive to be the textual strength and intellectual acumen of the West, they do well to recall that early African texts were neither intellectually weak nor morally underdeveloped. They were not. This fact is gradually being recognized. But to make this point convincingly, one must read the texts of early African Christianity.

Even the brightest of young African Christian theologians have been tempted at times to indulge in the defeatist stereotype that Christianity comes from Europe, when in fact Europe learned much of its wisdom from Africa. The first three centuries were the most fruitful time when African thought and imagination shaped and influenced virtually every village and city of worldwide Christianity. This is what we have been trying to show in the case of Libya. This modernist prejudice does not do justice either to Islam or to Christianity's bimillennial history in Africa.

The fertile literature of African theologians in the last half century has been preoccupied with fighting the dominance of the modern West. This fight has been conceived amid the struggle for political independence and national identity so crucial to African aspirations. Some recent popular African theology has tried to fight this battle by first asserting the legitimacy of African traditional oral religious motifs. It has been fought without its most powerful potential ally: the ancient texts of African Christianity and Islam. If twenty centuries of presence in Africa do not make a religion traditional, what is to be done with Islam, which is younger to Africa by six centuries?

What has happened to the classic Christianity that matured intellectually first under African skies? It has sometimes been prematurely excluded from the prevailing definitions of "African traditional religion." Accordingly, Christianity could not be traditionally African because it was supposedly imported from Europe. If it were not for the fact that the ecumenical consensus of early Christianity was largely hammered out and consensually defined on the continent of Africa, this would appear almost credible. This appears credible only by ignoring a basic fact: the maturity of the Christian intellectus in early Africa.

Modern Christianity has been thought to have brought only oppression to Africa. But this critique cannot apply to the valiant intellectual endeavors of early African Christian writers of over a thousand years ago who were indigenous Africans. If Christianity brought only oppression to Africa, then it becomes a temptation to imagine that to be truly African requires little more than a politics of resentment. Becoming sullenly embittered by Christianity is hardly a step ahead.

But what if the West itself is more deeply indebted to Africa than has been imagined? What if some of the greatest strengths of European philosophy, exegesis and religious formation, and ethics were pounded out in the cauldron of African history before Europe discovered and appropriated them?

To answer we must go back to the pre-Nicene African literary texts of the second, third and early fourth centuries (*Letter of Barnabas*, *Kerygma Petri* and the works of Tertullian, Clement, Origen and Cyprian). These sources were available and fully digested in the Nile and Maghreb. They were not from Europe.

A brilliant perennial and precolonial African Christianity awaiting rediscovery, but seldom noticed amid the political rhetoric.[7] It does not depend on either Western or European sources. It is richly and thoroughly African. It is a written intellectual tradition of the highest

---

[7]Kwame Bediako, "The Roots of African Theology," *International Bulletin of Missionary Research* 13, no. 2 (April 1989): 58-65.

order. It was viewed as a major source of Christian wisdom until the modern era.

The period of its greatest vitality in Africa was the first quarter of the first millennium. There the African intellect blossomed so profusely that it was sought out and prized and widely emulated by emerging cultures along the northern and eastern Mediterranean shores. Examples of this include the following: (1) Origen was actively sought out by the teachers of Caesarea Palestina. His African identity was no barrier to his brilliance. (2) Lactantius was invited by Diocletian to be an honored teacher of literature in his Asian palace in Bithynia. (3) Augustine was invited to teach in Milan. There are dozens of similar cases of intellectual movement from Africa to Europe—Plotinus, Valentinus, Tertullian, Marius Victorinus, Pope Victor and Barsanuphius among them. Pilgrims from the north Mediterranean like Jerome, Rufinus, Palladius, Egeria, Evagrius, John Cassian and Orosius came to Africa to sit at the feet of the masters of ascetic wisdom (LCM, 332).

## WHEN EUROPE SAT AT THE FEET OF AFRICA

Once the Christians of Africa were the teachers and spiritual mentors of the Christians of Europe and Asia. These ideas spread from Africa to Gaul and Rome and Spain to Anatolia and Syria. Africans were informing, instructing and educating the very best minds of the earliest Latin, Cappadocian and Greco-Roman Christian teachers. This flow of intellectual leadership in time would mature into the ecumenical consensus on how to interpret the relation of Old and New Testaments, and hence the core of Christian dogma.

It took years of working daily in the history of exegesis for those of us privileged to edit the Ancient Christian Commentary on Scripture to fully realize the implications. How profound has been the African stratum of influence on every subsequent phase of scriptural interpretation. As Western scholars, none of us were prepared for the breadth and power of this evidence. Nowhere in the standard literature could we find this influence explained. Everywhere in the secondary literature it seemed to be either ignored or resisted, or portrayed as European.

Our conviction emerged slowly only out of decades of hands-on experience with African texts and ideas. Finally, we learned to trace the
path backward from the Nile Valley to Rome, from Cyrene back to
Antioch, from Hippo back to Bobbio, from Wadi al-Natrun back to
Cappadocia, from the Thebaid back to Gaza. This is simply a report of
our hard-won experience. This intellectual leadership moved steadily
north by land and sea from the Maghreb and Nile Valley to the deserts
of the Negev, into the hills of Judea, and north through Syria and Cappadocia, and finally beyond the Bosphorus into Europe.

These brilliant centers of mind and spirit were constantly being fu-
eled by scriptural exegesis flowing from North Africa in the third and
early fourth centuries. The minds of African Christians were working
deftly to figure out how to read the sacred texts of Moses and the
prophets meaningfully in the light of the history of Jesus. They were
among the first Christians to learn to think philosophically. They were
among the first to grasp the ecumenical rule of triune faith cohesively
long before these patterns had clear articulations elsewhere. Core ideas
of prayer and the ordering of time in the monastic movements moved
from the Nitrian desert north to the lauras and monastic communities
of the Jordan and all the way to the Tigris and Halys Rivers during the
fourth and fifth centuries.

Inattention to this south to north transfer of intellectual wealth has
been unhelpful (even hurtful) to the contemporary African sense of
intellectual self-worth. It has seemed to leave Africa as if it lacked any
distinguished literary and intellectual history. But this is a history that
Africa actually already possesses, even if ignored. It has only temporarily been buried and ignored, and it is recoverable.

European intellectual history has gone on to live as if the great pre-
European Christian intellectual and literary textual traditions of the
Nile Valley and the Maghreb did not even exist. Africa's vast effects on
the West have not been studied or understood. Its history has been
dismissed as borrowed, heretical or deficient. It has been negatively
judged by criteria that came to prevail only centuries later in post-
Enlightenment Europe. Even today many African-born scholars
trained in the West seem all too ready to play the role of advocacy of

only modern Western ideas while remaining stubbornly inattentive to the exegesis of their own early African Christian writers.

Ancient African writers whose ideas were formed far inland on African soil (Pachomius, Didymus, Lactantius and Optatus) are still being stereotyped as if they were essentially European, even if they lived their entire lives in the deep interior of the African mountains, hills and valleys.[8]

This disregard is an inadvertent form of self-deprivation that African Christianity must now transcend. It is absurd for Africans to disown their own illustrious exegetical brilliance and theological roots that came out of African soil amid Africa-specific struggles. It is especially vexing to misconceive this denial as if it were a true defense of African identity. It is time for young African scholars to study these defensive dynamics diligently.

## RETELLING A FORGOTTEN STORY

Though the story of Libyan Christianity awaits fuller telling, there is some reticence to think that anyone from a Western university is suitably equipped to tell it. Yet it is so important to the history of North Africa and global Christianity that it needs to be told accurately and now.

Some Westerners will turn away from even hearing of remote Libya because of durable prejudices about the assumed unimportance of Africa to larger world intellectual history. The political barriers that have until recently prevailed in Libya, Algeria and Sudan have prevented this inquiry from being launched earlier.

The story begs not only to be told in rough sketches but to be much further developed by research into its primary texts and artifacts. It requires study by those who have expertise in the relevant languages of the historic texts. Though Coptic and Orthodox Christians in the north of Africa will already have heard some of the episodes of this story, most global Christians have only the sketchiest notion.

Non-Africans are as deeply moved by this story as Africans when it

---

[8]Yosef A. A. Ben-Jochannan, *African Origins of the Major Western Religions* (Baltimore: Black Classical Press, 1991), an interpretation commonly called Afrocentric.

is honestly told. How Africa shaped the Christian mind is a story that belongs first to Africa and then to all the world. Yet I have remained reticent until now to bear the responsibility for helping to tell this story, despite years of study of the religious texts of the first millennium written in Africa. This attempt should be understood only as an early embryonic effort inviting others to improve on it. Its purpose is to encourage future generations of indigenous African scholarship to tell the story more thoroughly. But these young voices are still in preparation.

# CONCLUSION

## THE LIBYAN CONTRIBUTION
## TO CHRISTIANITY

■■■

I t was in Libya that the triune teaching was first tested by Sabellian-ism and Arianism. It was out of Libya that issues of Christology would first be maturely advanced so as to allow ecumenical teaching to achieve a firm consensus. This consensus became normative for virtually all the rest of Christianity.

Much of the story of Libyan Christianity has not been told due to obstinate political barriers and intractable linguistic blocks. The story begs to be told now, but it must be accompanied by ongoing research into its exegetical as well as its economic, sociological, political and archaeological realities.

This is the tenacious story of the Christian people of Libya—of long ago and still today. Once they thrived in large numbers—for centuries—in Libya. Today there may be few, but the body of Christ has never been totally absent in the Jebel Akhdar over the last two thousand years.

## A CHALLENGE FOR CHRISTIANS AND MUSLIMS

Muslims and Christians need to know much more than is now known about their North African intellectual and religious histories and sacred texts in order to enter honestly into meaningful dialogue. Basic steps need to be taken toward the digital integration of a widening storehouse of information on early African religious texts. Hence, without discounting my own practical limitations, I have decided that there are justifiable reasons to recount this story with the resources available. Count the lines on my face and you will see why I do not have forever to contemplate this.

Especially to the Muslims of Libya I feel urgently called to say: You have an unexcelled opportunity to actually become the country where your laudable vision of African unity is brought toward actualization. The Libyan form of Islam is on the whole classic and moderate. It is based on the fair-minded study of the classic Qur'anic commentaries, many of which were written in North Africa only shortly after the Byzantine period. This interest in exegesis you share in a formal sense with Orthodox, evangelical and Catholic Christians. The methods of inquiry are very similar. The seeds of rapprochement could be planted in Libya.

## AFTERWORD

Suppose an attorney has an innocent client he is defending against false charges. Suppose this attorney works so actively on this case that at times he becomes restless about his own objectivity. In his effort to gain his client's release, he wonders if he may have unconsciously obscured something from his own objective judgment. He wonders whether he might have developed a case that is basically truthful and correct, but at its obscure edges he may have set forth the evidence in a tendentious way that appears to be a bit stronger rhetorically than he himself thinks it may be in reality. This elicits a struggle of conscience for him. He has two competing duties: honestly defending his client versus guarding his own integrity.

Suppose I am that attorney. Suppose my clients are the people of early African Christian communities. Like a class action suit, this involves thousands (and over history, millions) of neglected believers. Most are dead. It's a little like building an oratory for a martyr. Someone must speak for those who cannot. But no one asked me to speak up for this client. My own conscience has compelled me to speak plainly. From within the criteria of strict historiography some of my conclusions have had to remain tentative. I have felt something like this attorney's dilemma in the African phase of my research during the last decade. So badly has my client been treated that at times I feel that I may have contended too vigorously for the defense. After I had accepted the weight of evidence in favor of the African memory of Mark, and once the light broke through on its implications, I wondered if I might have prosecuted the evidence too boldly. I wondered if I have imagined scenarios that could explain my client's behavior and provide a remedy for a suffering friend. I suspect that this is a dilemma that has been faced by many who write passionately on history. Did I have sufficient evidence to argue the probable birth of Tertullian in Leptis? Was Victor the African really from Africa? These remain tender points at which my conscience will not let me go.

Hence I appeal to academic colleagues to please show me where I am wrong.

These questions present an enigma that has preoccupied my mind for more years than I want to concede. I have been privileged to study and travel often to Africa and the Middle East for over four decades. Like many American scholars I was not able to visit many archaeological sites in Algeria and the Maghreb until more recently. I have long wanted to visit Libya. Ever since I stood breathless at the stunning visuals of the 1999 book by Antonio Di Vita and associates on the lost cities of Libya (*Libya: The Lost Cities of the Roman Empire*), it has been my desire to understand what happened to them in their formation, deterioration and demise. Hence when I received an invitation to come to Libya to introduce this subject to Muslim university students there, I was overjoyed. This book records and extends the lectures I gave in Tripoli in 2008.

So about what do I remain unsatisfied? The country's resistance to being fully known by Westerners, the hiddenness of the literary sources and physical evidence, and the wide dispersal of literary sources. Worse: I knew intuitively of its riches in early Christianity but seemed blocked from fully examining how they emerged and in due course almost disappeared after five centuries. As a consequence I have, like any scholar, been pressed to cautiously hypothesize reasonable conjectures at points even when I could not demonstrate them as fully as I would have wished. There have been points along the way where my only option has been to qualify and express regret for my best conjectures. These impediments have made this the most difficult research task I've faced since I undertook the editing of the Ancient Christian Commentary on Scripture in 1993. Despite these impediments, the joys of hard-won discovery, like the labors of gem mining, have yielded unusual satisfactions and pleasures.

Why, then, have I continued to pursue this difficult task to the very end, when I had other urgent projects sitting on the shelf awaiting my attention at a late date in my life? Because so few know about this obscure arena; because its role in early Christianity was so significant; because it has been so neglected as a subject of historical inquiry by Western academic colleagues. These motives have been the engines of desire.

Now that I am at last ready to offer its results for scholarly and public examination, I am all the more aware that many of its conclusions may seem at first hard to defend and easy targets for academics who are working out of very different premises about reliable knowledge. I hope that someday someone will do more justice to this subject than I. But my time to do anything in this world is limited and growing more so. Hence I offer it for the reader's consideration, hoping for clemency.

# REGISTRY OF KNOWN LOCATIONS
## OF EARLY CHRISTIANITY IN LIBYA

Here are the Churches and Diocesan Episcopal Residences of Libya, beginning with Eastern Cyrenaica—Marmarica or Libya Inferior—and moving east to west (asterisks represent bishoprics).

What follows are known Christian sites in Libya in east to west order. Since there are many unexcavated sites, this is a preliminary list with no pretense that it is exhaustive. (The listings should be read column-by-column vertically.)

## Eastern Cyrenaica (Libya Secunda or Marmarica)

Zygris (Zygeis)*

Kalamion (Kallias)

Paraetonium* (Ammonia, Misrata)

Apis

Azy

Zagylis*

Tetrapyrgia (Catabathmus Major)

Petrus Megas

Geras* (El Gaa)

Gariatis*

Kyrthanion

Antipyrgos*

Siwa (inland; Jupiter Ammon, Wadi Marcos)

Derna (Darnis)*

Elatrun (L'atrun)

Hydrax* (inland)

## Western Cyrenaica (Libya Superior)

Palaebisca* (Palabiscus)

Erythra*

Apollonia* (Sozopolis, Marsa Susa)

Cyrene* (inland)

Barce* (inland; El Marj)

Ptolemais (Tolmeta)*

Gsar el Ebia (inland)

Arsinoe* (Tauchira, Tokra, Tauorga)

Berenike* (Benghazi)

Boreum* (Gsar bu Grada, Boreion, modern Bu Grada)

Aujila (inland)

## Tripolitania (Emporium)

Madinat Sultan—Aurae Philaeno-
rum (Fines Africae-Cyrenisium)

Sirte* (Syrte, Macomades,
Euphranta)

Ghirza

Tubactis (Thubactis)*

Sinipsa* (Kinypus)

Leptis Magna* (Neapolis, Al-Kums,
Homs)

Mesphi (inland)

Tarhuna (inland)

Thenadassa* (inland)

Breviglieri (inland)

Gasr Es Sug (inland)

Jebel Nefuca (inland)

Oea* (Tripoli)

Mizda (inland)

Tebedut

Asaaba (el-Asabaa, Djendouba)

Wadi Crema

Chafagi Aamer

Sabratha* (Zuara, Abrotonium)

Vax (Villa Repentina)

Pisidia*

Carcabia*

Villa Magna*

Gergis

Meninx* (Jerba, Girba Is.)

Gigthi (Gigthis)*

# BIBLIOGRAPHY

Abun-Nasr, Jamil M. *A History of the Maghrib.* Cambridge: Cambridge University Press, 1971.

"Acts of Mark." In *New Testament Apocrypha*, 2:461-64. Edited by Wilhelm Schneemelcher. Translated by R. McL. Wilson. 2 vols. Louisville, Ky.: Westminster/John Knox Press, 1991–1992.

Adeyemo, Tokunboh. "African Contribution to Christendom." *Scriptura* 39 (1991): 89-93.

Aguessy, H. "Religions africaines comme effet et source de valeurs de la civilisation de l'oralité." In *Les Religions africaines comme source de valeurs de civilisation*, pp. 25-49. Colloque de Cotonou. Paris: Présence africaine, 1972.

Aigrain, René. "La fin de l'Afrique chrétienne." In *Histoire de l'Église depuis les origines jusqu'à nos jours*, 5:211-30. Edited by Augustin Fliche and Victor Martin. 26 vols. Paris: Bloud & Gay, 1934–.

Akoi, Patrick. *Religion in African Social Heritage: A Handbook on African Mystical Sociology.* Rome[?]: 1970.

Alföldi-Rosenbaum, Elisabeth, and John Ward-Perkins. *Justinianic Mosaic Pavements in Cyrenaican Churches.* Monografie di archeologia libica 14. Rome: L'erma di Bretschneider, 1980.

Ameen, Hakim. "St. Mark in Africa." In *St. Mark and the Coptic Church.* Cairo: Coptic Orthodox Patriarchate, 1968.

Ammianus Marcellinus. *History.* Translated by J. C. Rolfe. 3 vols. Loeb Classical Library 300, 315, 331. Cambridge, Mass.: Harvard University Press, 1939–1950.

Appelbaum, Shimon. "The Jewish Revolt in Cyrene in 115–117 and the Subsequent Recolonization." *Journal of Jewish Studies* 2 (1951): 177-86.

Athanasius. *The Letters of Saint Athanasius Concerning the Holy Spirit.* Translated by C. R. B. Shapland. New York: Philosophical Library, 1951.

Atiya, Aziz S., ed. *The Coptic Encyclopedia.* 8 vols. New York: Maxwell Macmillan International, 1991.

Bagnall, Roger S., and Dominic W. Rathbone. *Egypt from Alexander to the Copts—An Archaeological and Historical Guide.* London: British Museum Press, 2004.

Bahoken, Jean-Calvin. *Clairiéres métaphysiques africaines: essai sur la philosophie et la religion chez les Bantu du Sud-Cameroun.* Paris: Présence africaine, 1967.

Barnard, L. W. "St. Mark and Alexandria." *Harvard Theological Review* 57 (1964): 145-50.

Barth, Heinrich. *Travels and Discoveries in North and Central Africa.* 5 vols. 1857. Reprint in 3 vols. London: F. Cass, 1965.

Basset, M. René. "Les sanctuaires du Djebel Nefousa." *Journal Asiatique* 13 (1899): 423-70 and 14 (1899): 88-120.

Bastide, Roger. "L'expression de la prière chez les peuples sans écriture." *La Maison-Dieu* 109 (1972): 98-112.

Baumeister, Theofried. *Martyr invictus, der Martyrer als Sinnbild der Erlösung in der Legende und im Kult der frühen koptischen Kirche: Zur Kontinuität des ägyptischen Denkens.* Forschungen zur Volkskunde 46. Münster: Regensberg, 1972.

Bediako, Kwame. *Christianity in Africa: The Renewal of a Non-Western Religion.* Edinburgh: Edinburgh University Press, 1995.

———. "The Roots of African Theology." *International Bulletin of Missionary Research* 13, no.2 (April 1989): 58-65.

———. "The Significance of Modern African Christianity—A Manifesto." *Studies in World Christianity* 1, no. 1 (1995): 51-67.

———. *Theology and Identity: The Impact of Culture upon Christian Thought in the Second Century and in Modern Africa.* Oxford: Regnum, 1992.

Bénabou, Marcel. *La résistance africaine á la romanisation.* Paris: F. Maspero, 1975.

Ben-Jochannan, Yosef A. A. *African Origins of the Major "Western Religions."* Reprint, Baltimore: Black Classical Press, 1991.

Bergna, Costanzo. *La missione Francescana in Libia.* Tripoli: Nuove Art Grafiche, 1924.

Berilengar, A. "L'initiation traditionnelle, un processus d'intégration sociale: L'expérience des Murum au Tchad." *Telema* 17 (1991): 65-70.

Bertarelli, L. V. *Libia*. Guida d'Italio del Touring Club Italiano. 2nd ed. Milan: Touring Club Italiano, 1937.

Bimwenyi, O. "Le Dieu de nos ancêtres." *Cahiers des religions africaines* 4 (1970): 137-51.

Birley, Anthony Richard. *Septimius Severus: The African Emperor*. London: B. T. Batsford, 1988.

Boardman, John, and John Hayes. *Excavations at Tocra, 1963–1965*. 2 vols. London: British School of Archaeology at Athens, 1966–1973.

Boer, Harry R. "Time as an Aspect of Traditional African Eschatology." *Reformed Review* 39 (1986): 199-205.

Bonacasa Carra, R. M. "Sabratha Cristiana." *Rivista di Archeologia Cristiana* 72 (1996): 383-91.

Booth, Newell S. "Time and Change in African Traditional Thought." *Journal of Religion in Africa* 7 (1975): 81-91.

Boulaga, F. Eboussi. *La crise du Muntu: authenticité africaine et philosophie: essai*. Paris: Présence africaine, 1977.

Boyd, Paul C. *The African Origin of Christianity*. Vol. 1, *A Biblical and Historical Account*. London: Karis Press, 1991.

Bregman, Jay. *Synesius of Cyrene: Philosopher-Bishop*. Berkeley: University of California Press, 1982.

Brown, Peter. "Christianity and Local Culture in Late Roman Africa." *Journal of Roman Studies* 58 (1968): 85-95.

———. *The Cult of the Saints*. Chicago: University of Chicago Press, 1981.

Bryant, M. D. "African wisdom and the recovery of the earth." *Orita* 27 (1995): 49-58.

Buck, D. J., and David Mattingly, eds. *Town and Country in Roman Tripolitania: Papers in Honour of Olwen Hackett*. BAR International Series 274. Oxford: BAR, 1985.

Budge, E. A. Wallis. *The Book of the Saints of the Ethiopian Church: A Translation of the Ethiopic Synaxarium*. 4 vols. Cambridge: Cambridge University Press, 1928.

Bujo, Bénézet. "Kultur und Christentum in Afrika; Bemerkungen zu einem Aufsatz." *Neue Zeitschrift für Missionswissenschaft* 32 (1976): 212-16.

———. "Nos ancêtres, ces saints inconnus." *Bulletin de Théologie Africaine* 1 (1979): 165-78.

Callahan, Allen Dwight. "The Acts of Mark: Tradition, Transmission, and Translation of the Arabic Version." In *The Apocryphal Acts of the Apostles:*

*Harvard Divinity School Studies*, pp. 62-85. Edited by François Bovon et al. Cambridge, Mass.: Harvard University Center for the Study of World Religions, 1999.

———. "The Acts of Saint Mark: An Introduction and Translation." *Coptic Church Review* 14 (1993): 2-10.

Cameron, Alan, Jacqueline Long, and Lee Sherry. *Barbarians and Politics at the Court of Arcadius*. Berkeley: University of California Press, 1993.

Cameron, Averil. *The Mediterranean World in Late Antiquity, A.D. 395–600*. London: Routledge, 1993.

Caputo, Giacomo. *Il teatro augusteo di Leptis Magna: scavo e restauro (1937–1951)*. Monografie di archeologia libica 3. Rome: L'erma di Bretschneider, 1987.

———. *Schema di Fonti e Monumenti del primo Cristianesimo in Tripoltania*. Tripoli: Zard, 1947.

Chadwick, Henry. *Early Christian Thought and the Classical Tradition: Studies in Justin, Clement, and Origen*. New York: Oxford University Press, 1966.

Chinchen, Delbert. "The Art of Hospitality African Style: An Indigenous Method of Discipleship." *Evangelical Missions Quarterly* 36 (2000): 472-81.

Chitando, Ezra. "African Christian Scholars and the Study of African Traditional Religions: A Re-evaluation." *Religion* 30 (2000): 391-97.

Courtois, Christian. *Les Vandales et l'Afrique*. Paris: Arts et métiers graphiques, 1955.

Cox, James L., and Gerrie ter Haar, eds. *Uniquely African? African Christian Identity from Cultural and Historical Perspectives*. Trenton, N.J.: Africa World Press, 2003.

Coxe, Arthur Clevland, trans. *Fathers of the Second Century: Hermas, Tatian, Athenagoras, Theophilus, and Clement of Alexandria*. ANF 2. Reprint, Peabody, Mass.: Hendrickson, 1999.

Crum, W. E., ed. "Martyrdom of Mark the Evangelist." In *Theological Texts from Coptic Papyri*. Anecdota Oxoniensia. Semitic series 12. Oxford: Clarendon Press, 1913.

Daly, J. "Notes on Penance and Reconciliation in an African Culture." In *Evangelizzazione e Culture*, 3:69-75. Atti del congresso internazionale scientifico di missiologia, Roma, 5-12 Ottobre 1975. Rome: Pontifical Urbanian University, 1976.

Davidson, Basil. *The Africans: An Entry to Cultural History*. London: Longmans, 1969.

Davis, Stephen J. *The Early Coptic Papacy: The Egyptian Church and Its Leadership in Late Antiquity.* New York and Cairo: American University in Cairo Press, 2004.

Delehaye, Hippolyte. "Les martyrs d'Egypte." *Analecta Bollandiana* 40 (1922): 5-154, 299-364.

Deschamps, Hubert. *Les religions de l'Afrique noire.* Paris: Presses universitaires de France, 1954.

Devreesse, Robert. "L'église d'Afrique durant l'occupation Byzantine." *Mélanges d'archéologie et d'histoire* 57 (1940): 143-66.

Dickson, Kwesi A., and Paul Ellingworth, eds. *Biblical Revelation and African Beliefs.* London: Lutterworth, 1969.

Dieterlen, Germaine. *Textes sacrés d'Afrique noire.* Paris: Gallimard, 1965.

Dionysius of Alexandria. *Letters and Treatises.* Translated by Charles Lett Feltoe. Translations of Christian Literature, series 1. New York: Macmillan, 1918.

Di Vita, Antonino. "Gli *Emporia* di Tripolitania dall'età di Massinissa a Diocleziano: un profilo storico-istituzionale." In *Aufstieg und Niedergang der römischen Welt* 2.10.2, pp. 515-95. New York: Walter de Gruyter, 1982.

———. "La diffusione del Cristianesimo nell'interno della Tripolitania attraverso i monumenti e sue sopravvivenze nella Tripolitania araba." *Quaderni di archeologia della Libia* 5 (1967): 121-42.

———. "Leptis Magna: Die Heimatstadt des Septimius Severus in Nordafrika." *Antike Welt* 27, no. 3 (1996): 173-90.

———, Ginette Di Vita-Evrard, Lidiano Bacchielli, and Robert Polidori. *Libya: The Lost Cities of the Roman Empire.* Cologne, Germany: Könemann, 1999.

Dopamu, P. Adelumo. "Traditional Values: A Means to Self-Reliance." *Orita* 25 (1993): 12-21.

Driberg, J. H. "The Secular Aspect of Ancestor-Worship in Africa." Supplement to the *Journal of Royal African Society* 35, no. 138 (1936): 1-21.

Dzielska, Maria. *Hypatia of Alexandria.* Translated by F. Lyra. Cambridge, Mass.: Harvard University Press, 1995.

Dzobo, Noah K. "African Ancestor Cult: A Theological Appraisal." *Reformed World* 38, no. 6 (1985): 333-40.

Ejizu, Christopher I. "Human rights in African indigenous religion." *Bulletin of Ecumenical Theology* 4 (1991): 31-45.

———. "Oral Sources in the Study of African Indigenous Religion." *Cahiers des religions africaines* 23 (1989): 37-47.

Ela, Jean-Marc. *L'Afrique des villages.* Paris: Editions Karthala, 1982.

Ferdinando, Keith. *The Triumph of Christ in African Perspective: A Study of Demonology and Redemption in the African Context.* Carlisle: Paternoster Press, 1999.

Fitzgerald, Augustine, trans. *The Essays and Hymns of Synesius of Cyrene,* 2 vols. London: Oxford. 1930.

————, trans. *The Letters of Synesius of Cyrene.* London: Oxford University Press, 1926.

Forde, Daryll, ed. *African Worlds: Studies in the Cosmological Ideas and Social Values of African Peoples.* New York: Oxford, 1954.

Forget, Jacobus. *Synaxarium Alexandrinum.* 2 vols. in 6. Corpus Scriptorum Christianorum Orientalium, vols. 47-49, 67, 78, 90. Louvain: Peeters, 1905–1932.

Fortes, Meyer. *Oedipus and Job in West African Religion.* Cambridge: Cambridge University Press, 1983.

Frankfurter, David, ed. *Pilgrimage and Holy Space in Late Antique Egypt.* Leiden: Brill, 1998.

Frend, W. H. C. *Martyrdom and Persecution in the Early Church.* London: Blackwell, 1965.

Gachiri, Ephigenia W. "Myth on Origins and Other Truths." *AFER* 31, no. 2 (1989): 108-20.

Gadallah, Fawzi F., ed. *Libya in History: Historical Conference 16-23 March 1968.* Benghazi: Faculty of Arts, University of Libya, 1969.

Gehman, Richard J. *African Traditional Religion in Biblical Perspective.* Kijabe, Kenya: Kesho Publications, 1989.

Gennep, Arnold van. *The Rites of Passage.* Chicago: University of Chicago Press, 1960.

Girgis, Samir Fawzy. *A Chronology of Saint Mark.* Cairo: St. John the Beloved Publishing House, 2002.

Githige, R. M. "African Traditional Religion Today. Its Prospects for the Future: A Review of Scholarly Opinions." *A Journal of African Studies in Religion* 1 (1980): 1-7.

Glenday, D. K. "God Spoke to Our Wise Men—Dialogue with African Traditional Religions." *Worldmission* 27 (1976): 8-14.

Goehring, James E. *Ascetics, Society, and the Desert: Studies in Early Egyptian Monasticism.* Studies in Antiquity and Christianity. Harrisburg, Penn.: Trinity Press International, 1999.

Goodchild, R. G. *Cyrene and Apollonia: An Historical Guide*. 4th ed. Libya: Department of Antiquities, 1981.

———. "Mapping Roman Libya." *Geographical Journal* 118 (1952): 142-52.

Grant, Robert M. *Eusebius as Church Historian*. Oxford: Clarendon Press, 1980.

Gravrand, Henri. "Les religions africaines traditionnelles comme source de civilisation spirituelle." *Cahiers des religions africaines* 4, no. 8 (1970): 153-74.

———. "Towards a dialogue with the African Religions." *Bulletin of the Pontifical Council for Interreligious Dialogue* 3 (1966): 137-47.

———. *Visage africain de l'Église: une expérience au Sénégal*. Paris: Éditions de l'Orante, 1961.

Gregg, Robert C., and Dennis E. Groh. *Early Arianism: A View of Salvation*. Philadelphia: Fortress, 1981.

Greschat, Hans-Jürgen. "Understanding African Religion." *Orita* 2 (1968): 59-70.

Groves, C. P. *The Planting of Christianity in Africa*. 4 vols. London: Lutterworth, 1948–1958.

Gsell, Stéphane. *Histoire ancienne de l'Afrique du nord*. 8 vols. Paris: Hachette, 1913–1928.

Gualandi, Giorgio. "La presenza Cristiana nell'Ifriqiya l'area cimiterialedi En-ngila (Tripoli)." *Felix Ravenna* 105-106 (1973): 257-59.

Haile, Getatchew. "A New Ethiopic Version of the Acts of St. Mark." *Analecta Bollandiana* 99 (1981): 117-34.

Hama, Boubou. *Enquête sur les fondements et la genèse de l'unité africaine*. Paris: Présence africaine, 1966.

Hardy, E. R. *Christian Egypt, Church and People*. New York: Oxford University Press, 1952.

Harmless, William. *Desert Christians: An Introduction to the Literature of Early Monasticism*. New York: Oxford University Press, 2004.

Harnack, Adolf. *The Mission and Expansion of Christianity in the First Three Centuries*. 2 vols. New York: G. P. Putnam, 1908.

Hass, Christopher. *Alexandria in Late Antiquity*. Baltimore: Johns Hopkins University Press, 1997.

Hastings, Adrian. *African Christianity: An Essay in Interpretation*. London: Geoffrey Chapman, 1976.

Haynes, Denys Eyre Lankester. *An Archaeological and Historical Guide to the*

*Pre-Islamic Antiquities of Tripolitania.* Tripoli: Antiquities Department of Tripolitania, Libya, 1956.

Hebga, Meinrad. *Afrique de la raison, Afrique de la foi.* Paris: Editions Karthala, 1995.

———. "Penance and Reconciliation in African Culture." *AFER* 25, no. 6 (1983): 347-55.

Heijer, Johannes den. "History of the Patriarchs of Alexandria." In *Coptic Encyclopedia,* 4:1238-41. Edited by Aziz S. Atiya. 8 vols. New York: Maxwell Macmillan International, 1991.

———. "Sawirus Ibn al-Muqaffa', Mawhub ibn Mansur ibn Mufarrig et la genèse de l'Histoire des Patriarches d'Alexandrie." *Bibliotheca Orientalis* 41 (1984): 336-47.

Heusch, Luc de. "Myth as Reality." *Journal of Religion in Africa* 18, no. 3 (1988): 200-215.

Hochegger, Hermann. "Les 'âmes' de l'homme et la conception de l'esprit de mort dans la pensé occidentale et africaine." *Publications CEEBA* 1, no. 3 (1969): 118-24.

Hoek, Annewies van den. "The 'Catachetical' School of Early Christian Alexandria and Its Philonic Heritage." *Harvard Theological Review* 90, no. 1 (1997): 59-87.

Hubai, Péter. "The Legend of St. Mark: Some Coptic Fragments." *Studia Aegyptiaca* 12 (1989): 165-234.

Ibn 'Abd Al-Ḥakam. *Conquête de l'Afrique du Nord et de l'Espagne* (= Futûh' Ifrîqiya wa'l-Andalus). French and Arabic. Translated into French by Albert Gateau. Algiers: Éditions Carbonel, 1947.

Idris, H. R. *Contribution à l'histoire de l'Ifrikiya (d'après le Riyād En Nufūs d'Abū Bakr El Māliki).* Paris: P. Geuthner, 1936.

Ifesieh, Emmanuel I. "Vatican II and Traditional Religion." *AFER* 25 (1983): 230-36.

Iloanusi, Obiakoizu A. *Myths of the Creation of Man and the Origin of Death in Africa.* New York: Peter Lang, 1984.

Ishola, A. A. "Ancestors or Saints: African Understanding of Ancestors in Relation to Christian Saints, with Particular Reference to the Yoruba of Nigeria." *Euntes docete* 36 (1983): 257-81.

Isizoh, Chidi Denis, ed. *Christianity in Dialogue with African Traditional Religion and Culture.* Vatican City: Pontifical Council for Interreligious Dialogue, 2002.

Jackson, John Glover. *The African Origin of Christianity.* Chicago: L. & P., 1981.

Jahn, Janheinz. *Muntu: An Outline of Neo-African Culture.* Translated by Marjorie Grene. London: Faber and Faber, 1961.

Johnson, David W. *Coptic Sources of the History of the Patriarchs of Alexandria.* Ph.D. diss. Catholic University of America. Washington, D.C., 1973.

Johnson, John L. *The Black Biblical Heritage: Four Thousand Years of Black Biblical History.* Chicago: Lushena Books, 1999.

Jones, A. H. M. *The Later Roman Empire 284–602: A Social, Economic and Administrative Survey.* 3 vols. Oxford: Blackwell, 1964.

Kalilombe, Patrick A. "The Salvific Value of African Religions." *AFER* 21 (1979): 143-57. Also in *Faith Meets Faith,* edited by Gerald H. Anderson and Thomas F. Stransky. Mission Trends 5. Grand Rapids: Eerdmans, 1981.

Kannengiesser, Charles. *Handbook of Patristic Exegesis: The Bible in Ancient Christianity.* 2 vols. Boston: Brill, 2004.

Kato, Byang H. *Biblical Christianity in Africa.* Achimota, Ghana: Africa Christian Press, 1985.

Kenrick, Philip M. *Excavations at Sabratha: 1948–1951.* Journal of Roman Studies Monographs 2. London: Society for the Promotion of Roman Studies, 1986.

Kibicho, S. G. "Revelation in African Religion." *Africa Theological Journal* 12 (1983): 166-77.

Kitewo, N., and M. Nzensili. "Être Africaine et religieuse." *Telema* 6 (1980): 47-53.

Kraeling, Carl H. *Ptolemais, City of the Libyan Pentapolis.* Chicago: University of Chicago Press, 1962

Kraft, Charles H., and Tom N. Wisley, eds. *Readings in Dynamic Indigeneity,* esp. pp. 493-515. Pasadena, Calif.: William Carey Library, 1979.

Laronde, André. *Cyrène et la Libye hellénistique = Libykai historikai: de l'époque républicaine au principat d'Auguste.* Paris: Editions du Centre de la Recherche Scientifique, 1987.

————. "Le port de Lepcis Magna." *Comptes-rendus des séances de l'Académie des Inscriptions et Belles-Lettres* 132, no. 2 (1988): 337-53.

Layton, Bentley. *The Gnostic Scriptures.* Garden City, N.Y.: Doubleday, 1987.

Layton, Richard A. *Didymus the Blind and His Circle in Late-Antique Alexandria: Virtue and Narrative in Biblical Scholarship.* Urbana: University of Illinois Press, 2004.

Lee, G. M. "Eusebius on St. Mark." In *Studia Patristica* 12:425-27. Texte und
    Untersuchungen zur Geschichte der altchristlichen Literatur 115. Berlin:
    Akademie-Verlag, 1973.

Lepelley, Claude. *Les Cités de l'Afrique romaine au Bas-Empire.* 2 vols. Paris:
    Études augustiniennes, 1979–1981.

Liebeschuetz, J. H. W. G. "Why Did Synesius Become Bishop of Ptolemais?
    *Byzantion* 56 (1986): 180-95.

Lilla, Salvatore Romano Clemente. *Clement of Alexandria: A Study in Chris-
    tian Platonism and Gnosticism.* London: Oxford University Press, 1971.

*The Lives of the Holy Apostles* [based on Russian Orthodox and Greek Synax-
    aries], Buena Vista, Colo.: Holy Apostles Convent, 1988.

Madu, Raphael Okechukwu. *African Symbols, Proverbs and Myths: The Herme-
    neutics of Destiny.* New York: Peter Lang, 1996.

Malaty, Tadros Y. *The Gospel According to St. Mark.* Translated by George
    Botros. Revised by Samy Anis and Nora El-Agamy. Orange, Calif.: Cop-
    tic Orthodox Christian Center, 2003.

———. *The School of Alexandria.* 2 vols. Jersey City, N.J.: St. Mark's Coptic
    Orthodox Church, 1995.

Maluleke, Tinyiko Sam. "In Search of 'The True Character of African Chris-
    tian Identity': A Review Article of the Theology of Kwame Bediako." *Mis-
    sionalia* 25, no. 2 (August 1997): 210-19.

Marrou, H.-I. "La 'conversion' de Synésios." *Revue des études grecques* 65
    (1952): 474-84.

———. "Synesius of Cyrene and Alexandrian Neoplatonism." In *The Conflict
    Between Paganism and Christianity in the Fourth Century*, pp. 126-50. Ed-
    ited by Arnaldo Momigliano. Oxford: Clarendon, 1963.

*Martyrium Marci.* In *New Testament Apocrypha*, 2:461-64. Edited by W. Sch-
    neemelcher. Translated by R. McL. Wilson. 2 vols. Louisville, Ky.: West-
    minster/John Knox Press, 1992.

Mattingly, David J. *Tripolitania.* Ann Arbor: University of Michigan Press,
    1994.

Maurier, Henri. "Chronique bibliographique sur la religion africaine tradi-
    tionnelle." *Bulletin of the Pontifical Council for Interreligious Dialogue* 69
    (1988): 222-38.

Mbiti, John S. *African Religions and Philosophy.* 2nd ed. Oxford: Heinemann,
    1990.

———. *New Testament Eschatology in an African Background: A Study of the*

*Encounter Between New Testament Theology and African Traditional Concepts.* London: Oxford University Press, 1971.

McCray, Walter Arthur. *The Black Presence in the Bible: Discovering the Black and African Identity of Biblical Persons and Nations.* Chicago: Black Light Fellowship, 1990.

McKenzie, Judith. "Glimpsing Alexandria from Archaeological Evidence." *Journal of Roman Archaeology* 106 (2003): 35-61.

Merriam, Alan P. *An African World: The Basongye Village of Lupupa.* Bloomington: Indiana University Press, 1974.

Metuh, E. I. *African Religions in Western Conceptual Schemes: The Problem of Interpretation: Studies in Igbo Religion.* Ibadan, Nigeria: Pastoral Institute, 1985.

Momigliano, Arnaldo, ed. *The Conflict Between Paganism and Christianity in the Fourth Century.* Oxford: Clarendon Press, 1963.

Mudimbé, V. Y. *The Idea of Africa.* Bloomington: Indiana University Press, 1994.

Muga, Erasto. *African Response to Western Christian Religion: A Sociological Analysis of African Separatist Religious and Political Movements in East Africa.* Kampala: East African Literature Bureau, 1975.

Mugambi, J. N. Kanyua. *The African Heritage and Contemporary Christianity.* Nairobi: Longman Kenya, 1989.

Mugambi, J. N. Kanyua, and Nicodemus Kirima. *The African Religious Heritage.* Nairobi: Oxford, 1976.

Muzungu, Bernardin. *Le Dieu de nos pères.* 3 vols. Bujumbura, Burundi: Presses Lavigerie, 1974–1981.

Nicoliello, Dominic A. *Our Ancestors in the Faith: African Saints.* Nairobi, Kenya: Paulines Publications Africa, 1995.

Norris, H. T. *The Berbers in Arabic Literature.* New York: Longman, 1982.

Nyamiti, Charles. *Christ as Our Ancestor: Christology from an African Perspective.* Mambo Occasional Papers, Missio-Pastoral 11. Gweru, Zimbabwe: Mambo, 1984.

Nyeme Tese, J. "Continuité et discontinuité entre l'ancien Testament et les religions africaines." In *Christianisme et identité africaine*, pp. 83-112. Edited by D. Atal sa Angang et al. Kinshasa, Democratic Republic of the Congo: Faculté de théologie catholique de Kinshasa, 1980.

Oden, Thomas C. *The African Memory of Mark.* Downers Grove, Ill.: InterVarsity Press, 2011.

————. *How Africa Shaped the Christian Mind.* Downers Grove, Ill.: Inter-Varsity Press, 2008.

————, and Christopher H. Hall, eds. *Ancient Christian Commentary on Scripture.* 29 volumes. Downers Grove, Ill.: InterVarsity Press, 1998–2010.

Oduyoye, M. A. "In the Image of God. A Theological Reflection from an African Perspective." *Bulletin of African Theology* 7 (1982): 41-54.

Okeke, D. C. "African Concept of Time." *Cahiers des religions africaines* 7, no. 14 (1973): 297-302.

Orlandi, Tito. "Hagiography." In *Coptic Encyclopedia*, 4:1191-97. Edited by Aziz S. Atiya. 8 vols. New York: Maxwell Macmillan International, 1991.

Oshitelu, G. A. *The African Fathers of the Early Church.* Ibadan, Nigeria: Sefer, 2002.

Pacho, Jean-Raimond. *Relation d'un voyage dans la Marmarique, la Cyrénique et les oasis d'Audjelah et de Maradeh.* Paris, 1827-1829. Reprint, Marseille: J. Laffitte, 1979.

Parrinder, Edward Geoffrey. *Africa's Three Religions.* 2nd ed. London: Sheldon, 1976.

p'Bitek, Okot. *African Religions in Western Scholarship.* Nairobi: Kenya Literature Bureau, 1970.

Pearson, Birger A. *Gnosticism and Christianity in Roman and Coptic Egypt.* Studies in Antiquity and Christianity. New York: T & T Clark, 2004.

————. *Gnosticism, Judaism, and Egyptian Christianity.* Minneapolis: Fortress, 1990.

————, and James E. Goehring, eds. *The Roots of Egyptian Christianity.* Studies in Antiquity & Christianity. Philadelphia: Fortress, 1986.

Pringle, Denys. *The Defence of Byzantine Africa from Justinian to the Arab Conquest: An Account of the Military History and Archaeology of the African Provinces in the Sixth and Seventh Centuries.* British Archaeological Reports, International Series 99; 2 vols. Oxford: British Archaeological Reports, 1981.

Procopius. *On Buildings.* Translated by H. B. Dewing and Glanville Downey. Loeb 343. Cambridge, Mass.: Harvard University Press, 1940.

Procopius. "The Vandalic War." In *History of the Wars*, vol. 2. Translated by H. B. Dewing. Loeb 81. Cambridge, Mass.: Harvard University Press, 1916.

Purcaro, Valeria. "Le rotte antiche tra la Grecia e la Cirenaica e gli itinerari marittimi e terresti lungo le coste cirenaiche e della Grande Sirte." *Quaderni di archeologia della Libia* 8 (1976): 285-352.

Ranger, T. O., and I. N. Kimambo, eds. *The Historical Study of African Religion*. Berkeley: University of California Press, 1972.

Rebuffat, R. "Routes d'Egypte de la Libye Intérieure." *Studi Magrebini* 3 (1970): 1-20.

Reynolds, J. M. "Inscriptions from the Cyrenaican *Limes*." *Africa Romana* 5 (1988): 167-72.

———. "Twenty Years of Inscriptions." *Libyan Studies* 20 (1989): 117-26.

———. "Zawiet Msus." *Libya Antiqua* 8 (1971): 39-42.

———, and J. B. Ward-Perkins et al. *The Inscriptions of Roman Tripolitania*. Rome: British School at Rome, 1952.

Romanelli, Pietro. "Il confine orientale della provincia romana di Cirene." *Atti della Pontificia Accademia romana di archeologia* 16 (1940): 215-23.

———. *Leptis Magna*. Africa Italiana 1. Rome: Società editrice d'arte illustrata, 1925.

———. "Monumenti cristiani del museo di Tripoli." *Nuovo bulletino di archeologia cristiana* 24-25 (1918–1919): 27-49.

———. "Una piccolo catacomba giudaica di Tripoli." *Quaderni di archeologia della Libia* 9 (1977): 111-18.

Roques, Denis. *Synésios de Cyrène et la Cyrénaïque du Bas-Empire*. Paris: Éditions du Centre national de la recherche scientifique, 1987.

Russell, Dorthea Moore. *Medieval Cairo and the Monasteries of the Wādi Natrūn, a Historical Guide*. New York: Thomas Nelson, 1963.

Russell, Norman, trans. *The Lives of the Desert Fathers: The Historia Monachorum in Aegypto*. Kalamazoo, Mich.: Cistercian Publications, 1981.

Saakana, Amon Saba, ed. *The African Origins of the Major World Religions*. London: Karnak House, 1988.

Sanneh, Lamin. *Translating the Message: The Missionary Impact on Culture*. 2nd ed. Maryknoll, N.Y.: Orbis, 2009.

———. *Whose Religion Is Christianity? The Gospel Beyond the West*. Grand Rapids: Eerdmans, 2003.

———, and Joel A. Carpenter, eds. *The Changing Face of Christianity: Africa, the West, and the World*. New York: Oxford University Press, 2005.

Sarpong, Peter. "Media of Revelation in African Traditional Religion." *The Ghana Bulletin of Theology* 4 (1975): 40-47.

Sawirus (= Severus of Ashmunein [Sawirus ibn al-Muqaffa']). *History of the Patriarchs of the Coptic Church of Alexandria*. Patrologia Orientalis 1:101-24 and 381-518. Arabic text edited and translated by B. T. Evetts. Paris:

Firmin-Didot, 1906, 1948; Cairo: Society of Coptic Archeology, 1943–1959.

Schenkel, Wolfgang. *Kultmythos und Märtyrerlegende: Zur Kontinuität des ägyptischen Denkens*. Göttinger Orientforschungen 4.5. Wiesbaden: Harrassowitz, 1977.

Schneemelcher, Wilhelm, ed. *New Testament Apocrypha*. Translated by R. McL. Wilson. 2 vols. Louisville, Ky.: Westminster/John Knox Press, 1991–1992. See esp. "Acts of Mark," 2:461-64.

Scobie, Edward. "African Popes." In *African Presence in Early Europe*, pp. 96-107. Edited by Ivan Van Sertima. New Brunswick, N.J.: Transaction Books, 1985.

Senghor, Léopold Sédar. *Liberté*, Vol. 3, *Négritude et civilisation de l'universel*. Paris: Éditions du Seuil 1977. Cf. Senghor. "Negritude and the Civilization of the Universal." In *African Presence in the Americas*, pp. 21-32. Edited by Carlos Moore. Trenton, N.J.: Africa World Press, 1995.

Smith, Morton. *The Secret Gospel: The Discovery and Interpretation of the Secret Gospel According to Mark*. London: Victor Gollancz, 1974.

Stucchi, Sandro. *Architettura cirenaica*. Monographie di archeologia libica 9. Rome: L'erma di Bretschneider, 1975.

———. "L'architettura funeraria suburbana cirenaica." *Quaderni di archeologia della Libia* 12 (1987): 249-377.

Suter, Robert, and Lilly Suter. *Das Synaxarium: das koptische Heiligenbuch mit den Heiligen zu jedem Tag des Jahres*. Waldsoms-Kröffelbach: St.-Antonius Kloster, 1994.

Sylvanus, Nina. "The Fabric of Africanity: Tracing the Global Threads of Authenticity." *Anthropological Theory* 7, no. 2 (2007): 201-16.

Telfer, W. "Episcopal Succession in Egypt." *Journal of Ecclesiastical History* 3 (1952): 1-13.

Thompson, Peter. "Negritude and a New Africa: An Update." *Research in African Literatures* 3, no. 4 (Winter 2002): 143-53.

Tiénou, Tite. "Recapturing the Initiative in Theology in Africa." *Evangelical Review of Theology* 11, no. 2 (1987): 152-56.

———. *The Theological Task of the Church in Africa*. Achimota, Ghana: Africa Christian Press, 1990.

———. "Which Way for African Christianity? Westernization or Indigenous Authenticity?" *Africa Journal of Evangelical Theology* 10, no. 2 (1991): 3-12.

Tkaczow, Barbara. "Archaeological Sources for the Earliest Churches in Alexandria." In *Coptic Studies*, ed. W. Godlewski, pp. 431-36. Acts of the Third International Congress of Coptic Studies, Warsaw, 20-25 August 1984. Warsaw: PWN 1990.

————. *Topography of Ancient Alexandria (An Archaeological Map)*. Travaux du Centre d'archéologie méditerranéenne de l'Académie polonaise de sciences 32. Warsaw: Zakład Archeologii Śródziemnomorskiej, Polskiej Akadmii Nauk, 1993.

Trevijano, R. "The Early Christian Church of Alexandria." In *Studia Patristica* 12:471-77. Texte und Untersuchungen zur Geschichte der altchristlichen Literatur 115. Berlin: Akademie-Verlag, 1973.

Uzoho, Vincent N. "The Sacred and the Profane in the Traditional Religion of Africa." *West African Religion* 15 (1974): 30-43.

Verstraelen, Frans J. *History of Christianity in Africa in the Context of African History: A Comparative Assessment of Four Recent Historiographical Contributions*. Gweru, Zimbabwe: Mambo Press, 2002.

Vickers, M., and A. Bazama. "A Fifth Century B.C. Tomb in Cyrenaica." *Libya Antiqua* 8 (1971): 69-84.

Vickers, M., D. W. J. Gill and M. Economou. "Euesperides: The Rescue of an Excavation." *Libyan Studies* 25 (1994): 125-36.

Vickers, M. J., and J. M. Reynolds. "Cyrenaica, 1962–72." *Archaeololgical Reports* 18 (1971–1972): 27-47.

Vivian, Tim. *St. Peter of Alexandria, Bishop and Martyr*. Philadelphia: Fortress, 1988. Includes translation of "Life and Martyrdom of Peter of Alexandria."

Ward, Benedicta. *The Sayings of the Desert Fathers*. London: Mowbrays, 1975.

Ward, P. "Place Names in Cyrenaica." In *Geology and Archeology of Northern Cyrenaica, Libya*, pp. 3-12. Edited by F. T. Barr. Amsterdam: Holland-Breumelhof, 1968.

Ward-Perkins, John B. "The Christian Antiquities of Libia Since 1938." In *Actes du Ve Congrès Internationl d'Archéologie Chrétienne*, pp. 159-62. Studi di antichità cristiana 22. Vatican City: Pontificio Istituto di archeologia Cristiana, 1954.

————. "A New Group of Sixth-Century Mosaics from Cyrenaica." *Rivista di archeologia cristiana* 34 (1958): 183-92.

————, and R. G. Goodchild. "The Christian Antiquities of Tripolitania." *Archaeologia* 95 (1953): 1-84.

Welsby, Derek A. "A Late Roman and Byzantine Church at Souk el Awty in the Tripolitanian Pre-desert." UNESCO Libyan Valley Surveys 24. *Libyan Studies* 22 (1991): 61-80.

Westerlund, David. *African Religion in African Scholarship: A Preliminary Study of the Religious and Political Background.* Stockholm: Almqvist & Wiksell International, 1985.

White, Donald. "Before the Greeks Came: A survey of the Current Archaeological Evidence for the Pre-Greek Libyans." *Libyan Studies* 25 (1994): 31-44.

White, L. Michael. *Building God's House in the Roman World: Architectural Adaptations Among Pagans, Jews, and Christians.* Baltimore: Johns Hopkins University Press, 1990.

Wilhite, David E. *Tertullian the African: An Anthropological Reading of Tertullian's Context and Identities.* New York: Walter de Gruyter, 2007.

Williams, Ethel L., and Clifton F. Brown. *The Howard University Bibliography of African and Afro-American Religious Studies: With Locations in American Libraries.* Wilmington, Del.: Scholarly Resources, 1977.

Williams, Rowan. *Arius: Heresy and Tradition.* 2nd ed. London: SCM, 2001.

Young, Frances M. *Biblical Exegesis and the Formation of Christian Culture.* Cambridge: Cambridge University Press, 1997.

Young, Josiah Ulysses, III. *A Pan-African Theology: Providence and the Legacies of the Ancestors.* Trenton, N.J.: Africa World Press, 1992.

Zahan, Dominique. *The Religion, Spirituality and Thought of Traditional Africa.* Translated by Kate Ezra Martin and Lawrence M. Martin. Chicago: University of Chicago Press.

# Subject Index

# Ancient Texts Index

# Scripture Index

# Image Credits

Tertullian (p. 107): Wikimedia Commons/http://en.wikipedia.org/wiki/File:Tertullian.jpg

African Pope Saint Victor I (p. 119): Used by permission. Hulton Archive/Getty Images

Mosaic of an angel in the Church of Ptolemais in the era of Synesius [Museum of Ptolemais] (p. 238): Used courtesy of Jona Lendering. Jona Lendering/www.livius.org/

Historic map of Tripoli by Piri Reis (p. 264): Wikimedia Commons /<http://en.wikipedia.org/wiki/File:Tripoli_by_Piri_Reis.jpg>

Map of Tripolitania and the Fezzan (p. 269): Probert Encyclopaedia/www.probertencyclopaedia.com/photolib/maps/Map of Fezzan 1906.htm